DATE DUE

DEMCO 38-296

Sobering Tales

Edmund B. O'Reilly

SOBERING TALES

Narratives of

Alcoholism

and Recovery

University of Massachusetts Press
Amherst

Copyright © 1997 by
The University of Massachusetts Press
All rights reserved
Printed in the United States of America

LC 96-20323
ISBN 1-55849-064-7 (cloth); 065-5 (pbk.)

Designed by Dennis Anderson
Set in Galliard and Gill Sans
Printed and bound by Braun-Brumfield, Inc

Library of Congress Cataloging-in-Publication Data

O'Reilly, Edmund B., 1943–
    Sobering tales : narratives of alcoholism and recovery / Edmund B. O'Reilly.
        p.   cm.
    Includes bibliographical references and index.
    ISBN 1-55849-064-7 (cloth : alk. paper).—ISBN 1-55849-065-5
(pbk. : alk. paper)
      1. Alcoholism—United States.   2. Alcoholics Anonymous.
3. Alcoholics—Rehabilitation—United States.   I. Title.
HV5279.O76   1997
362.29'28'0973—dc20   96-20323
                                                            CIP

British Library Cataloguing in Publication data are available.

Lines from Euripides, *The Bacchae,* translated by William Arrowsmith in *The Complete Greek Tragedies,* general editors David Grene and Richard Lattimore, © 1959 by the University of Chicago, are used by permission of the publisher, the University of Chicago Press.

For concord or consonance really is the root of the matter, even in a world which thinks it can only be a fiction. The theologians revive typology, and are followed by the literary critics. We seek to repeat the performance of the New Testament, a book which rewrites and requites another book and achieves harmony with it rather than questioning its truth. One of the seminal remarks of modern literary thought was Eliot's observation that in the timeless order of literature this process is continued. Thus we secularize the principle which recurs from the New Testament through Alexandrian allegory and Renaissance Neo-Platonism to our own time. We achieve our secular concords of past and present and future, modifying the past and allowing for the future without falsifying our own moment of crisis. We need, and provide, fictions of concord.

Frank Kermode, *The Sense of an Ending*

Contents

Preface

      In the Introduction to *Sobering Tales* I have said something about the origins of the book, the circumstances that led to its inception and development. But I'm not sure that a different kind of account of the origins wouldn't have been more compelling and more truthful.

A collage of images from the late sixties and early seventies were before me as I worked, from the time I was a grad student in the English department of the State University of New York at Buffalo. I actually witnessed one of those poetry readings where John Berryman showed up drunk. I suspect now that most of the audience knew he would, or in some sense hoped he would, relishing the keen tension before the poet's arrival. Led to the podium by a folklore professor assigned to look after him who left him propped up there, unable to work the microphone properly, mumbling, incoherent, Berryman came through; we were rewarded with a fine repast, this discomfiting modernist transformation of pity and terror.

I spent a couple of boozy nights trying to get Frederick Exley on the phone, pestering the information operator in Watertown, New York. It must have seemed important. *A Fan's Notes* had hit a nerve. Its overall impact aside, there was an odd personal note: Exley had spent a short time during his long drinker's odyssey in White Plains, New York, where I had gone to high school. In the novel he evoked a restaurant there, Sam's, an old-fashioned steak house and emblem of the classic 1950s. Exley conjured the rich density of the atmosphere: tobacco smoke and whiskey, and the smell of charred meat; the thick-sliced rare roast beef sandwiches; and a comforting past-midnight murkiness that held sway even on sunny afternoons.

Another poet, John Logan, occupied the top floor of an apartment building where I lived for a while in Buffalo. He was a regular

in the North Main Street hangouts, notorious for his frequent par-
ties and for displays of unpredictably weird behavior when he was
swacked. Logan's "problem" was well known by his colleagues and
friends, and variously tolerated, ignored, laughed at, encouraged,
or explained away. He was a talented poet and a good all-round
man of letters when his head was clear; when he'd sometimes attend
Murray Schwartz's Shakespeare seminar, his contributions were lu-
minous.

Donald Barthelme also stayed in Buffalo for a few months. He
was often observed in a paralytic state from the large amounts of
scotch he consumed daily. One night on his way home to the room
he rented at the University Manor Motel, he tripped and fell over
the low iron railing that surrounded the parking lot and had to
spend the rest of the semester with a cast on his wrist. Some people
might have taken that as a sign, a kind of metonymic condensation
asking us to consider long-range consequences.

Jim Ringer was an estimable traditional country singer and
guitarist from Bakersfield, California, who would come through
Buffalo every now and again with his partner Mary McCaslin.
Ringer was quite open about his drinking and could apparently
run through most of a quart of Jack Daniels by the end of a performance. Once in a while he'd fall off the stage.

There was a piece in *Rolling Stone* about the rock musician War-
ren Zevon, who had a drink problem but was set on the road
to sobriety by crime novelist Ross Macdonald in a hair's-breadth
only-on-the-West-Coast intervention. I used the article in my
course in detective fiction; I believed there was some hermetic connection between alcoholism and the mystery and detection genre.
Fortunately, Zevon is still with us. Berryman and Logan, Barthelme
and Exley are not; nor is Ringer.

One night my friend Dwight came over, pounding on the door
at two in the morning with an order of chicken wings he'd bought
to take away when the bar where he'd been all night was closing.
He stumbled as he was climbing the steps, and scattered the wings
up and down the filthy staircase. But he picked them up, one by
one, brought them inside, and sat at my kitchen table eating them,
unperturbed by the cat hair and dust balls and mud from the steps
clinging to them as if they'd been deliberately coated in the stuff.
As he ate, blood from a huge gash on his forehead that he'd mysteri-

ously acquired on the way over was running down his face and dripping into the foil take-out container.

It is possible that as we beat on ever closer to the millennium, Alcoholics Anonymous will undergo qualitative changes that will turn it into a new and different form of life. Perhaps worldwide interactive fiberoptic channels will obviate the need for meetings in smoke-filled church basements, and grateful recovering alcoholics will tap in their messages of hope on keyboards from all over the globe.

John Crowley has firmly established that alcoholism goes hand in hand with literary modernism; it may be that as modernity continues to break up and recede, so too will a modernist-populist enterprise like AA. There are already signs of dispersion and recombination, call it fragmentation or fluidity, depending on your temperament. It may be that *Sobering Tales* will swiftly become a historical curiosity, providing a fleeting synchronic glimpse of AA's storytelling process as it was practiced in the late twentieth century just before the last days of face-to-face interaction.

I regret that the many contributors to this undertaking cannot be credited by name, but that's part of the deal with AA. My gratitude to them is nevertheless unending. I should make known on their behalf—and my own as well—an underlying, scarcely whispered hope that something in this volume might one day help someone along in the difficult process of getting out from under an addiction.

Thanks are due to many people who are not addicted—to anything I know about, at least. Robert Cantwell—*il miglior fabbro* and all that—made this publication possible by his intervention on my behalf with Clark Dougan of the University of Massachusetts Press. John Crowley and an anonymous second reader for the press provided valuable suggestions for improvement of the manuscript, some of which I followed. Mickey Rathbun's scrupulous copyediting brought clarity to dark places. Ernest Kurtz and Thomas Gilmore responded considerately when I sent them uninvited copies of my dissertation some years ago. Roger Abrahams supervised the writing of the dissertation at the University of Pennsylvania; Henry Glassie and the late Kenneth S. Goldstein provided encouragement in various forms and sat on my committee. Kenny Goldstein's contribution to American culture has yet to be properly appreciated; I am sorry he couldn't have seen this book. Donald Newlove gave gracious permission to use the long quotation from *Those Drinking Days,* and sent me a warm letter and a copy of his novel *Curranne Trueheart* as well. Donald Newlove is, as we used to say, a trip.

Thanks to Vance Aandahl, Jeanie Elliott, Vicki Faoro, Jane Kelton, Lisa Null, Tommy Peterson, and Andy Woolf, who, knowingly or not, contributed to this project. Thanks to friends who kept faith during tough times. And blessings, of course, on Jane Grant and Chloe Grant.

Introduction

Sobering Tales

Listening to stories about alcoholism may be the best means we have of comprehending and delineating the disorder, because stories alone can begin to contain its bewildering, protean, contradictory nature. Stories, unlike statistical representations, diagnostic criteria, symptomatologies, and so on, can lay hold of the lived experience of alcoholism, and sometimes transform seemingly ineffable states of mind into patterns of enacted response that are available to interpretation. By means of their poetic and pragmatic strategies as well as their overt content, the narratives discussed here may represent for a sympathetic reader something of the actual quality of alcohol addiction, and suggest what conditions must be in place for recovery to become possible.[1]

The chapters that follow develop an approach to the personal accounts of addiction and recovery that are told by nonprofessional speakers at Alcoholics Anonymous meetings. This work is not an ethnography of Alcoholics Anonymous or an ethnographic record of any particular AA group, but is rather an exploration of one of the key processes by which AA functions and, I hope, a contribution to an understanding of the overall dynamic of that organization.

Literary fiction is used in Part 1 to establish a provisional framework within which the oral narratives addressed in Part 2 may be measured and construed; perhaps the spoken narratives can illumine the written ones reciprocally. The literary works are charged in various ways with setting the stage: they provide preliminary thematic cues, sketch in some admittedly scanty historical background, and establish certain recurring expressive tonalities. Concerned readers may find traces of willful misreading in my use of literature from other times and places; but it seems important to bring alco-

holism's past into view, even if somewhat unscrupulously. I hope
some compensatory utility accrues from my overfamiliar treatment
of distant texts.

I make use in Part 2 of spoken narratives that were tape recorded
at AA open meetings and of directed personal interviews with members of AA.[2] My interviews elicited thoughtful accounts of the making of spoken stories, along with ancillary ruminations on the special
dynamics of ex-drunks trying to help each other and on fundamental issues in human communication: story, situation, intention, exemplification, and interpretation. Storytelling is the idea that unifies
all of the material under consideration rather than the contingencies
of specific times and places or the idiosyncracies of particular disor-
dered and reconstituted personalities.

This is not to suggest an ahistorical or radically anti-relativist
stance. Historians' and anthropologists' interpretations of alcohol-
related behaviors and attitudes—often supplementary, alternative,
or even antithetical to the narrow conceptual repertory of our own
time and place—have only just begun to challenge thinking about
alcoholism and treatment that for many years has been complicit
with a dominant therapeutic orthodoxy. Their project is to be applauded, but whether measurable advantage will be gained in terms
of interdisciplinary collaboration remains to be seen. Prospects are
uncertain in large measure because of the inertias of comfort, habit,
material success, and professional "fit," all of which are inhospitable
to innovation, regardless of its promise. To take an example: the
notion that "alcoholism" is an equivocal culture-specific construction—a notion to which many anthropologists are committed—is
abhorrent to those in the therapeutic community who depend upon
the stability of a professional discourse (in fund-raising and public
relations, at least, if not always in everyday practice).[3]

The anthropologist Dwight Heath usefully summa-
rizes some of the "most significant generalizations that derive from
cross-cultural study" of alcohol use:

1. In most societies, drinking is essentially a social act . . . embedded in
   a context of values, attitudes, and other norms.
2. These values, attitudes, and other norms . . . influence the effects of
   drinking, regardless of how important biochemical, physiological,
   and pharmacokinetic factors may also be. . . .

3. The drinking of alcoholic beverages tends to be hedged about with rules. . . . Often such rules are the focus of exceptionally strong emotions and sanctions.
4. The value of alcohol for promoting relaxation and sociability is emphasized in many populations.
5. The association of drinking with any kind of specifically associated problems . . . is rare among cultures throughout both history and the contemporary world.
6. When alcohol-related problems do occur, they are clearly linked with modalities of drinking, and usually also with values, attitudes, and norms about drinking.
7. Attempts at Prohibition have never been successful except when couched in terms of sacred or supernatural rules. (Heath, 1987, p. 46)

The radical relativization of motives and consequences of drinking and an insistence upon the importance of situational social dynamics are both inconsistent with an absolutist version of the disease model of alcoholism and a range of therapeutic and socially prescriptive strategies derived from it.[4]

But cross-cultural issues are really tangential to the present inquiry. Whether Aran Islanders or the residents of Truk experience mood-changing substances, the rigors of addiction, and the disquieting contradictions of sobering up in the same way "we" do is of little consequence here—although my approach is generally consistent with a constructivist position. Nor is it my purpose to enter debate over the comparative efficacy of Alcoholics Anonymous vis-à-vis behavioral modification, psychoanalysis, genetic interference, Christian fundamentalism, or any other competitive therapy.

The disease concept continues to be debated, and perhaps some skepticism should be brought to bear whenever the rhetoric becomes inflamed on either side. George Vaillant retains the disease concept but makes room for social and behavioral dimensions as well in his effort to circumscribe the disorder. "The fact that alcoholism is intricately woven into the individual's social fabric does not mean that alcoholism cannot also be regarded as a disease" (Vaillant, 1983, p. 44).

"Alcoholism," Vaillant explains, "becomes a disease when loss of voluntary control over alcohol consumption becomes a necessary and sufficient cause for much of an individual's social and physical morbidity" (p. 44). Aiming for a viable taxonomic synthesis—an integration of functions and signs that, regardless of nebulous causation issues, qualifies alcoholism to be accorded a "unitary medical diagnosis"—Vaillant asserts that alcoholism must be regarded as "both disease and behavior disorder" (p. 44). To merit inclusion within the medical framework, a behavior disorder must meet at least four criteria:

> First, the diagnosis should imply causative factors that are independent of the presence or absence of social deviance. Alcohol addiction is often a necessary and sufficient cause for such social deviance as is observed, and alcohol dependence is significantly more likely when biologic relatives have also been alcoholic. . . . Second, the diagnosis should convey shorthand information about symptoms and course. . . . The diagnosis of alcoholism predicts that a whole constellation of symptoms are present . . . [and] implies a disorder that lasts for several years. Third, the diagnosis should be valid cross-culturally and not dependent on mores or fashion. Certainly, alcoholism is no respecter of class, ethnicity, or historical epoch. Finally, the diagnosis should suggest appropriate medical response for treatment. Alcoholism . . . often requires detoxification in a medical setting, and . . . specific treatment is often required in order to maintain sustained abstinence from alcohol. (P. 44)

Heath's summary of the anthropological findings might seem to conflict here and there with Vaillant's reasoning in support of the primacy of the medical model. But for our purposes, the possibility of contradiction is deferred if not dissolved in the recognition that it arises out of the contingencies of question-framing and not as a result of misrepresentations or duplicity. The language of Heath's global descriptive phenomenology will necessarily differ from that of Vaillant's domestic interventionist pragmatics; the real problem is to find an interface or conduit by which each can enrich the other in productive synthesis.

But the kind of validity capable of withstanding the microanalytic scrutiny of a medical practitioner or even a social scientist is finally not much to the point here. Vaillant's notion of the disease concept of alcoholism probably has little in common with what most AA speakers would mean by the phrase. To a podium storyteller at an AA meeting, "the disease of alcoholism" is probably more a matter of symbols than symptoms, a complexly mediated imaginative field rather than a testable medical hypothesis.

However, *regardless of the ultimate assessment of its validity,* the disease model of alcoholism is of signal importance here as a cornerstone of AA philosophy and therefore as a building block of AA narrative.

Our principal consideration here is simply that people tell stories and that, in Alcoholics Anonymous as in other human clusters, these stories seem to enable them to feel better and to live in ways that help preclude self-destructive states of mind, equivocal behaviors, or severe social dislocations. The governing questions in this inquiry, then, are these: how does storytelling in AA help to enable speakers to achieve and maintain sobriety? Does the curative property of storytelling lie in its function as representation of lived experience, as exhortation, or as gesture of commitment? I hope the interpretations offered will contribute to our understanding of the nature of narrative, especially in its consoling, exemplifying, and utopian aspects.

Background and Methods; Confessions and Claims

I am not a wholly disinterested spectator. A full account of the circumstances which led to my interest in AA in the first instance is for another time and place; but a few remarks may be helpful to the reader in situating my attitudes and evaluating my commentary.

Until about fifteen years ago, when I was in my late thirties, heavy drinkers and users of mood-changing chemicals seemed to make up the majority of my circle of acquaintances, including my family and closest friends. The era of the so-called sixties—less an exact decade than a complex of attitudes and transitions whose significance in the shaping of the late twentieth century can scarcely be overstated—was characterized by an enthusiastic acceptance of alcohol and other drugs among what seemed garrulous multitudes, an openness that veered from trivializing casualness to ludicrous overvaluation. When that era drew to a close a sizable casualty count was taken. Many of the sixties generation, camouflaged within its libertarian flamboyance, found, when the smoke cleared, that they were unable or unwilling to get on with their lives without the aid and comfort of their drugs of choice.

Growing up amid the suburban drink culture of lower Westchester County, New York—mercilessly anatomized by such attentive ethnographers as John Cheever, Peter De Vries, and Richard Yates —I had left unquestioned since early childhood an assumption that heavy drinking was a natural part of routine social behavior. With adolescence and the discovery of the belletristic drug chronicles of De Quincey and Baudelaire, Huxley and Cocteau, Burroughs and Mailer, Ken Kesey and Hunter Thompson, I adopted for my own the tenet—common enough among the would-be antithetical— that "experimentation" in controlled substance use was philosophi- cally and artistically obligatory. It seemed to offer a staving off of the desolating monotony of everyday life and to provide, if not a guarantee, at least the possibility, of transcendence.

But the lurid social consequences of these attitudes became ines- capable. During the past quarter century I have witnessed a dis- turbing number of otherwise seemingly productive and satisfying careers derailed in addiction, and lives of considerable promise, both public and private, disintegrated in alcohol. For some, no measure of intelligence, talent, or determination could warrant exemption once the processes of craving, habituation, resistance, denial, capitu- lation, and repetition had been set in motion. Some acquaintances have returned to addiction–free lives—recovered—and others have not; they are "still out there," as the saying has it in AA; in some cases, all options have been forfeited.

It was with this later knowledge that I began, desultorily at first, to take an interest in self-help programs, to examine their tutorials and manifestos, and to look at a different kind of addiction literature —cautionary and rueful, diagnostic, remedial. I have attended hun- dreds of AA meetings, first as a participant and then, a few years later, as an observer and analyst; I have had the opportunity to witness the dynamics of one particular AA group over a two-year period and to make some comparative observations of different groups scattered throughout the urban northeastern United States.

In the mid-1980s, comfortably abstinent for a number of years and well into the course of graduate work in the Department of Folklore and Folklife at the University of Pennsylvania—where I had gone to pursue interests in American folk music and "nonca- nonical" literary culture—I recognized that Alcoholics Anonymous was a community to which the concerns of contemporary folklore studies were optimally fitted: AA was interwoven historically with popular American religious and social textures; it relied on extemporaneous but patterned spoken narratives and other modes of formulaic discourse; its organizational and philosophical principles, although printed in numerous publications, were propagated primarily by means of oral transmission and exemplary praxis. But AA did not seem to me simply a laboratory for the testing of conceptions in theoretical folklore; it was, rather, a living body in which the communicative processes in which folklorists interest themselves had very real life-and-death consequences. AA, that is, seemed to me a locus in which my academic work and pertinent social questions might be wedded with at least a possibility of viable issue.

I remain respectful of the idea that scholarly efforts can have consequences beyond the final exam, the dissertation defense, or the tenure committee hearing. It is unarguable that much academic work that makes its way past the bounds of university libraries is linked to institutional self-congratulations and pressed into the service of public relations and the reinforcement of existing social arrangements. Nowhere is this more evident than in certain types of books and public events for which folklorists, in the past, have been responsible. Though often tireless in congratulating themselves for "giving voice" to those without access to strategic channels of communication, for "representing" the marginalized and powerless, folklorists nevertheless have remained marginal themselves, widely regarded by scholarly colleagues as brokers of triviality, without discipline or vision, and by the greater public—if the greater public thinks of them at all—as eccentrics, antiquarians, potterers, opportunists, or worse. There is a measure of justice in these views; but the negative truths should be outweighed, I think, and *can* be, as folklorists bridle under such perceptions and turn to the task of translating personalized meliorist visions into real social commitments, critically grapple with their discipline's history, labor to contravene its unwanted restrictions, and insert themselves into the dialogues that help make rather than simply serve public policy.

This is not a one-way street. During the summer of 1985 I attended a session of the Summer School of Drug and Alcohol Studies at Rutgers University, and was alarmed at the negligible representation there of students from the humanities and the social sciences. Admittedly the summer session is in business largely to produce updated credentials for state-certified drug and alcohol counselors, but such programs could still go far to enhance interdisciplinary sensitivities. At one point I expressed surprise to a counselor-instructor that Gregory Bateson's "The Cybernetics of 'Self': A Theory of Alcoholism"—on which, below, I place much emphasis—was apparently unknown to the counseling community and seemed to go unnoticed in the therapeutic and social policy literature with which I was becoming acquainted. The instructor told me, with no further interest expressed, that the article was probably "too difficult."

Now, there is certainly no reason why a person uncomfortable with, say, the vocabulary of contemporary literary theory cannot be a good and effective counselor of alcoholics. But the idea that "difficulty"—particularly "difficulty" that may be produced by habituated and probably class-bound mystifications concerning "abstract" or "theoretical" or "academic" writing rather than by any quality inherent in the text or any presumptive deficiency in the mind of the reader—should stand between an important hypothesis and its potentially life-giving applications is appalling. My point here is not to attack the therapeutic establishment of New Jersey, but rather to suggest a precise point of entry for those who are trained in the interpretation of texts. And the texts need not be specialized or hermetic in vocabulary, tone, or theme. Profane texts, too, are often laden with secrets, and special tools may be required to pry those secrets out and make them accessible. I am arguing in favor of literary critics in the teaching hospitals and folklorists patrolling the halls of rehabilitation units.

My own informants, I should note, interviewees and speakers alike, were curious about the processes of interpretation that I was undertaking and were avid for new perspectives, new ways of thinking and speaking about the experiences that they had undergone as drinkers and that were refigured continually in their lives as active members of AA. Most AA affiliates that I have met take a lively interest in their condition; they are challenged by inconsistency or contradiction, and bemused by logic insufficient to accommodate the rich complexity of their experience.

The original fieldwork for this book was conducted in the northeastern United States, in or near several cities where I found myself during a two-year period in the middle 1980s. I tape recorded about twenty-five stories, of which the five included here are representative—not only of my own collection, but of the hundreds of other AA narratives I have read and listened to over two decades. The recordings were always made with the permission of the speaker. There was occasional controversy—usually settled in my favor—among AA members about whether tape recording was in accord with the spirit of AA's Eleventh Tradition: "We need always maintain personal anonymity at the level of press, radio, and films." The serious, sympathetic character of the project together with my own AA "credentials" seemed to provide sufficient reassurance in most instances.[5]

I recorded, or attempted to record, only in open meetings—meetings which members of the public are free to attend—and only when I was sure that I could remain inconspicuous and would cause no disruption. It was important that no one, especially no one making an exploratory first visit to AA in search of a path to sobriety, should be disconcerted by a researcher who might appear to be flouting AA's promise of confidentiality. I was, in fact, violating no confidences; but a suspicion of surveillance would be a terrible thing to lodge in the mind of a first-time AA candidate, half-drunk, shaking, paranoid, and resistant. At many meetings my cassette recorder stayed untouched in its container and I did not even pose the question of taping, so inhibiting were the aggregated impressions: perhaps there were lines of tension on the faces in the room, or subliminal sounds of grief or despair; perhaps the anxieties of a new arrival focused the energies of the group so that I thought I should not intrude; sometimes I experienced feelings of estrangement that were difficult to interpret.

I conducted interviews on the subject of narrative construction among a smaller and more restricted group of people with whom I had developed some personal compatibility and who seemed comfortable enough with me to speak freely. I used a typewritten set of questions to structure the interviews, though the questions acted as reminders or suggestions—talking points—rather than a rigid agenda.[6] Interviews were conducted in familiar settings—restaurants or the subjects' homes. The people I talked to shared their experiences freely, glad to be helpful, interested in the issues raised, thoughtful in their responses, and encouraging about the project. Without further evidence, the views expressed cannot be claimed as universal, but in my judgment they would find general acceptance across at least the liberal segment of the AA spectrum. (There is a strain of literalist or fundamentalist rigidity in AA which is not well represented here.)[7]

The transcriptions of the interviews, like those of the stories, are exact. Proper names, place names, businesses, and other possible indicators of personal identity have been fictionalized in all cases. Still, my gratitude to "Scott," "Hank," "Margaret," "Hugh," "Patrick," "Elliot," "Mark," and "Terry and Selena" is immense. Their collaboration is evident as the bulk of Chapters 4 and 5, but their contributions—their gifts—to this work and to me personally extend well beyond the boundaries of the printed page.

Sobering Tales may be seen, from a certain vantage, as a compendium of suggestions for further research. Several scholarly or journalistic lifetimes might be spent in pursuit of issues raised here.

Numerous self-help programs based on the Twelve Steps of Alcoholics Anonymous are not specifically treated here; these include Alanon (for spouses and concerned relatives and friends of alcoholics), Narcotics Anonymous (NA—for users of controlled substances other than alcohol), Adult Children of Alcoholics (ACOA), and programs for—among others—smokers, gamblers, compulsive overeaters, and people with a variety of psychiatric diagnoses. Most of these programs have at least one "authoritative" central text and a handful of peripheral pamphlets, but an enormous body of commercially produced secondary literature has come into existence as well, marketed to these interests.

In *I'm Dysfunctional, You're Dysfunctional*, Wendy Kaminer (1993) sardonically considers the proliferation of the self-help industry, noting the symbiosis of corporate greed with a bored, self-pitying, and culturally enervated population. Kaminer, however, fails to discriminate between legitimate needs and spurious ones; and like other social critics, she seems insensitive to the idea that an "inauthentic" need is probably experienced very much like a real one by its host. The ludicrous dimensions of the twelve-step explosion can of course claim no exemption from criticism and even derision, but we should be wary of obscuring deeper and more ominous issues by the overlay of self-satisfied laughter.

All stories, alas, do not compel our attention equally, and limits must be set on the expansion of our already overloaded and under-used archives. Still, there is more to be gained from systematic collection, classification, and analysis. Regional variants in AA prac-tice should be examined, and so should divergences of custom and practice along lines of ethnicity, age, sex and gender, and economic status. Close cooperation with particular AA speakers should be arranged, and their stories evaluated in contexts that are at most only hinted at below. The metamorphoses of individuals' stories over time must be studied, perhaps with willing and articulate sub-jects acting as their own ethnographers or collaborating with re-searchers in self-scrutiny and analysis, carefully monitoring the interconnectedness of story form and meaning, intellectual develop-ment, emotional well-being, social circumstances, and so on. Care-fully designed projects might elicit important insights into the determinants of story production that are at present only conjec-tural. Complementary or cooperative studies with therapeutic and medical interests should be pursued.

In recent years pertinent criticisms of AA methods have been aired in public forums—no doubt in part because AA and its coun-terparts have attracted considerable media attention. Some of this criticism targets practices of exclusion and restriction that are in sharp conflict with program principles. Users primarily of drugs other than alcohol, for example, although encouraged by rehabilita-tion personnel to make use of AA, have often found themselves marginalized or unwelcome at meetings even in the face of their own willingness to adapt to AA practice and adopt AA jargon. Internal debate has resolved some of these difficulties; in other instances schism has resulted.

Perhaps the most urgent criticism has been advanced by women and by people of color who have argued that, in essence, their drink and recovery experiences are not congruent with models and assumptions implicit in AA policy.

For poet and essayist Judith McDaniel, the AA program is domi-nated throughout—in the Twelve Steps, major texts, and meeting protocols—by a middle-class heterosexual white male outlook. The AA emphasis on spiritual submission to a "Higher Power" is exactly the wrong medicine for women whose lives have been damaged by excessive submissiveness already. For the most part, McDaniel claims, men in AA "have experienced their right to choose for themselves, to exercise self-will very differently from nondominant members of this society" (McDaniel, 1989, p. 21). In the course of conversations during an AA retreat, McDaniel was able to locate and confront the problem. "For myself . . . I needed to talk about self-esteem, not humility. I needed to believe that my life, that *I*, was important enough, mattered enough, to struggle for. As women . . . we have all spent a great deal of time struggling for others' survival needs. One of the first lessons feminism taught us was that we need to struggle for ourselves in order to have anything authentic to offer others" (p. 21). She found that by scrutinizing the notion of humility she could reappropriate it not as a stipulation of defeat and self-abnegation, but as "an accurate and honest assessment of who we are [that] will include knowing our strengths and our weaknesses." For many men in AA, humility becomes an outward sign of their recognition at depth of powerlessness and attains therapeutic utility as an attitude or embodiment of philosophical and behavioral realignment; for women, the emphasis must shift to "acknowledging and acting on our strengths, since many of us have felt ourselves to be victims of our lives and have experienced our weaknesses over and over" (p. 22).

In England, journalist Brigid McConville developed a similar perspective in the course of conversations with women drinkers. Each of the women with whom McConville worked connected her drinking "to the feeling that there is something 'wrong' with herself as a woman, a woman who is unable to fit comfortably into the expected role of wife/mother/worker/lover" (McConville, 1994, p. 30). "Women's drinking," McConville asserts, "can only be understood in this wider social and political context" (p. 32). Although she does not analyze AA in any detail—perhaps a reflection of the organization's comparatively lower profile in the United Kingdom—she has observed an uneasy fit between program principles and women's needs. "There is a certain repressive strain in AA practice, and the women who have been through the AA programme tend to denigrate their desires and aspirations as unhealthy egotism" (p. 31). McDaniel strikingly echoes McConville's findings: "Women do need to talk about self-esteem. We need to understand the power we *do* have, and to discuss in safe places ways in which we can exercise that power in the world. It is an essential precondition to going out in the world and being self-empowered" (McDaniel, 1989, pp. 21–22).

Addressing the problems of addictions among black Americans, and especially black women with addictions or codependency difficulties, the radical cultural critic bell hooks affirms the priority of the social and political influences. "A culture of domination undermines individuals' capacity to assert meaningful agency in their lives. It is necessarily a culture of addiction, since it socializes as many people as it can to believe that they cannot rely on themselves to meet even their basic human needs." Though not necessarily in conflict with a disease hypothesis, hooks's emphasis points away from individualized therapeutic solutions and toward collaborative radical social action. For hooks, the repossession of means to assert agency in everyday life will inevitably accomplish its own secondary "therapeutic" benefits; it is perhaps only after the establishment of universal social equity that debate over disease theory may usefully begin.

> Considering the way black people have been socialized, from slavery to the present day, to believe that we can survive only with the paternalistic support of a white power structure, is it surprising that addiction has become so all-pervasive in our communities? It is no mere accident of fate that the institutionalized structures of white-supremacist capitalist patriarchy have created a modern society where the vast majority of black people live in poverty and extreme deprivation—most often with no hope of ever changing their economic status. Living without the ability to exercise meaningful agency over one's material life is a situation that invites addiction. Concurrently, addiction among black people who have high incomes, who are professionals, is often directly related to the stress and low self-esteem engendered by working in settings with white people who have not unlearned racism, and by the feeling that we cannot effectively confront life's difficulties. (hooks, 1993, p. 68)

Literary critic and novelist Carolyn Heilbrun has suggested that all the available paradigms for the life story in Euro-American society are ordered by and for a white male culture of dominance, and that the full realities of women's lives have historically been suppressed or distorted in the available channels of narrative representation. Heilbrun believes that female textual models must be newly invented by the concerted actions of women in groups: "Women must turn to one another for stories; they must share the stories of their lives and their hopes and their unacceptable fantasies.

. . . We must stop reinscribing male words, and rewrite our ideas about what Nancy Miller calls a female impulse to power, as opposed to the erotic impulse which alone is supposed to impel women. We know we are without a text, and must discover one" (Heilbrun, 1988, p. 44). Her prescription is straightforward: "To put it simply, we must begin to tell the truth, in groups, to one another. Modern feminism began that way, and we have lost, through shame or fear of ridicule, that important collective phenomenon" (p. 45).

Heilbrun advocates a return to some of the collective practices, emblematized by consciousness raising, of the women's movement of the seventies. Only through the widespread exchange of stories will recurrent patterns become recognizable; in the patterns of recurrence, bonds of identification will develop; in the evolution of new forms, a utopian prospect can be nurtured.

Heilbrun speaks here of the recent past of the late-twentieth-century women's movement:

> What became essential was for women to see themselves collectively, not individually, not caught in some individual erotic and familial plot and, inevitably, found wanting. Individual stories from biographies and autobiographies have always been conceived of as individual, eccentric lives. I suspect that female narratives will be found where women exchange stories, where they read and talk collectively of ambitions, and possibilities, and accomplishments.
>
> I do not believe that new stories will find their way into texts if they do not begin in oral exchanges among women in groups, hearing and talking to one another. As long as women are isolated one from another, not allowed to offer other women the most personal accounts of their lives, they will not be part of any narrative of their own. (Pp. 46–47)

Though Heilbrun displays no interest in addiction or twelve-step groups in *Writing a Woman's Life,* her account of the power-engendering force inherent in feminist collectivity bears compelling similarities to the "official" narrative version of the early days of AA. Overcoming their isolation and becoming a part of a "narrative of their own" are precisely what enabled the founding members of AA to achieve their initial momentum and to develop the confidence to confront the obstacles that lay ahead.

The precept expressed by each of these writers is the same: usable new patterns of female narrative—narratives that embody and respond to the actual conditions of women's lives—must be brought into existence through autonomous collaborative practice. In the framework of twelve-step programs, this might mean the formation of women's groups committed to critical inquiry; in a spirit of imaginative receptivity, such meetings might usefully suspend the rigid narrative structures and meeting protocols that are conventionally followed.

       Narratives are elaborated out of the raw materials and unmediated data of lived experience. But they are also informed and conditioned by other narratives, and are subject to rules of genre and the impositions of archaic and contemporary contexts. The examination of literary narratives from the past has two major functions in this inquiry. First, they provide a means of comprehending certain definitional and conceptual issues with more of the complexity that the issues warrant and less of the leveling positivist "clarity" esteemed by behaviorists; second, they represent moments in the history of alcohol abuse in ways that should assist us in refining our conceptions of the contemporary responses offered by AA.

At the start of Part 1, I review Gregory Bateson's theory of alcoholism and then suggest a use of *The Bacchae* as a kind of narrativized schematic representation—almost an allegory—of the theory. Euripides helps to focus attention on addiction as a systemic disorder and reveals the dynamic of self-destruction in the name of a self-deceptive yearning for transcendence. My reading of *The Bacchae* in terms of Bateson's theory is a departure from conventions inspired by Nietzsche; whether or not one assents to my method, the chapter should usefully amplify my brief presentation of Bateson's arguments and prepare the ground for a generic approach to narratives of alcoholism.

Walt Whitman, arguing for temperance in his long-unappreciated novel *Franklin Evans,* celebrates the idea, vigorous in contemporary AA, that it is sobriety and not intoxication that has true liberating potential. In addition, Whitman provides a brief course in conventional American imagery about alcohol—an imagery of duplicity and darkness that seems often to have been its own worst enemy with respect to the pragmatics of both institutional and individual reform. In *John Barleycorn,* Jack London exposes the lived inner experience of that pathological pride that controls drinking behavior even as he argues in support of national prohibition—a poignantly ineffectual remedy for alcohol's disorders.

Three contemporary writers with strong personal credentials in alcohol consumption represent some of the possible outcomes of chronic dependency: Frederick Exley, locating the disorder outside of himself, falls into seemingly bottomless despair; John Berryman, canny but terrorized by guilt and foreboding, is unable to make his way out through the labyrinthine structure of denial within which he has concealed his own best interests; and Donald Newlove, rhapsodically reborn in the Fellowship of the Sun (his epithet for AA), lives to write his rebirth twice—as both fiction and memoir—in a curious visionary inversion with Dionysian connotations.[8]

In Part 2, I discuss the form, intentions, and meanings of oral narratives of recovery in AA in some detail. These stories are understood to be complex events dominated by the symbolic participation of speaker and listeners in the ratification of a kind of master story. The master story superimposes an autobiographical reconstruction upon a patterned field of propositions and possibilities among which the speaker may navigate according to personal designs. Audience unity in the storytelling event is facilitated by a shared respect for injunctions to draw purpose from past disorder, to provide help to other alcoholics who still suffer, and to contribute to the continuing integrity of the AA fellowship.

Part One

Alcoholism:
A Literary Framework

One

The Ecology of *The Bacchae*

Bateson's Theory of Alcoholism: A Starting Point

In 1971 Gregory Bateson published an article called "The Cybernetics of 'Self': A Theory of Alcoholism" (in *Psychiatry*, 34, pp. 1–18; reprinted in *Steps to an Ecology of Mind*, 1972), based on primary data obtained two decades earlier when he worked with alcoholic patients at the Veterans Administration Hospital in Palo Alto, California. "These men," Bateson noted, "carried other diagnoses—mostly of 'schizophrenia'—in addition to the pains of alcoholism. Several were members of AA. I fear," he poignantly added, "that I helped them not at all" (Bateson, 1972, p. 310).

During the twenty years it had taken for his observations to ripen, Bateson had studied psychiatric patients intensively and put forth the influential "double bind" theory of schizophrenia; he had spent time with dolphins and otters; he had worked his way through substantial bodies of literature in communications theory, cybernetics, and the philosophies of logic and learning; and he had prepared an amplified revision of his 1936 ethnography of the Iatmul people of New Guinea. Bateson made substantial contributions within and across several discrete disciplines; the breadth of his interests led him to a unitary systems-based comprehension of the human world —to be characterized in his collected essays as an "ecology of mind." His vision of the unity of mind and nature, together with his intense curiosities, rigor, and an angry compassion, generated the commitment of his later years to redefine the role of science in addressing the stupefying moral, social, and political problems of the twentieth century.[1]

"The Cybernetics of 'Self' " is an act of intellectual revisitation that brings subsequent learning to bear on problems which in the first instance must have seemed intractable or simply bewildering.

These hypotheses and speculations seem to me indispensable to comprehending certain key processes in alcohol addiction and to making headway in grasping the successes achieved by Alcoholics Anonymous.[2]

According to Bateson, the basic fault in the alcoholic personality system is an erroneous self-concept that is experienced as a hierarchical, compartmental structure in which interests are pitted against one another—almost like class interests in a nineteenth-century factory. Some elements or components of this incorrectly delimited self-system are experienced as controllable by others, and particular positions are prized. A complex internal dynamic develops from shifting patterns of dominance and subordination among the competing values of reified "parts" of the system. Some demarcated sectors of the self are felt to be at war with others (as in "part of me knows this is wrong"; "I can beat this thing"; or even, "I didn't know what I was doing"). We are in the somewhat shopworn domain of the schizoid sensibility, of course—for which the blame for incalculable damage done to Western cognitive processes is customarily laid to Descartes and subsequently the Enlightenment. *Body* and *mind* are incorrectly perceived as discrete and in some sense adversarial, just as *self* and *environment* may be felt to exist in opposition to one another rather than as complementary aspects of a functional integrated ensemble.

This self-division, a product of socioculturally facilitated epistemological error, motivates and confirms alcoholic drinking, but may be "healed" by the quietist precepts of AA if the alcoholic's acceptance of them is thorough. From this perspective, drinking and AA may both be seen at a certain depth as remedies for the same underlying disorder, and not one for the other. Alcoholism itself is a subspecies of the more general affliction.

In Anthony Wilden's words: "Bateson traces alcoholism to its source in the counter-adaptive, dualistic epistemology of western society. . . . This 'splitting of the subject' is symptomatic of the mind-body split endemic to our form of socioeconomic organization. It is the pre-programmed splitting which allows the alcoholic to personalize his battle with the bottle by depersonalizing himself. He becomes the mind ('I'), and the bottle becomes the body ('it'): '*I* can resist *it*'. What he has done, of course, is to consciously make himself the equivalent of an 'it' " (Wilden, 1980, p. 71).

Bateson's propositions are not an absolute beginning, not truly an etiological account of alcoholism; the schizoid process that concerns Bateson is postulated only as the *mechanism* of alcoholism. Bateson does not address the question of why alcoholism may be lodged in one individual and not another. Perhaps one day brain chemists and geneticists will divine a particular organic disjunction for which the relief afforded by alcohol is specific: a particular kind of biochemical irritability that, from the start, senses itself swabbed and cleansed by alcohol. From the point then of the first drink, a decisive formation of exchange would be forged between the drunk self and the sober self, with the drunk self—now "healed" by drink—construed as the "real" self and the sober self —prickly, barely controlled, suspicious, on guard, resentful of regulation—construed as "false" or impaired, wounded and in need of healing.

Developing from within the adversities of the segmented self is a defining and potentially lethal influence in the life of an active alcoholic: pride. As defined by Bateson, alcoholic pride is based not on past achievement, but on the mastery of one component of the self by another—a controlling, rational element against an impulsive, insurgent affect, for example. Hence, it is a point of pride, a challenge, to be able to drink well, to hold one's liquor; or, when that fails, to seem to be able to *stop* drinking in the face of powerful physical cravings (for short periods, at least: "going on the wagon," "cleaning up [one's] act"). But then, having achieved the short-term goal of a provisional renunciation, the situation reverses itself and the relocated challenge is provided by the risks of returning to drink—usually to "controlled" drinking. Playground metaphors —seesaw and merry-go-round—abound in the language of AA, suggestive at once of "meaningless" compulsive repetition and of inadequately repudiated childhood egocentrism.

Implicated in the alcoholic's pride is a "real or fictitious 'other' " (Bateson, 1972, p. 323), a performer created out of materials from the alcoholic's own private psychic playpen, or a real person, pathologically mediated, with whom the alcoholic can coexist only competitively or symmetrically. The *other* challenges the alcoholic to seemingly ever more destructive behavior.

> As things get worse the alcoholic is likely to become a solitary drinker and to exhibit the whole spectrum of response to challenge. His wife and friends begin to suggest that his drinking is a *weakness* and he may respond, with symmetry, both by resenting them and by asserting his

strength to resist the bottle. But, as is characteristic of the symmetrical responses, a brief period of successful struggle weakens his motivation and he falls off the wagon. Symmetrical effort requires continual opposition from the opponent.

Gradually the focus of the battle changes, and the alcoholic finds himself committed to a new and more deadly type of symmetrical conflict. He must now prove that the bottle cannot kill him. (Bateson, 1972, p. 326)

Bateson believes that symmetrical escalation is inescapable until the alcoholic is utterly degraded. (AA speakers often use escalators, elevators, and moving trains as metaphors for the progress of their drinking careers.) The condition of radical defeat—if it does not kill —breaks the cycle and forces an epistemological restructuring that is more "correct." This is AA's "hitting bottom" and compels recognition that "the 'self' as ordinarily understood is only a small part of a much larger trial and error system which does the thinking, acting, and deciding. This system includes all the informational pathways which are relevant at any given moment to any given decision. The 'self' is a false reification of an improperly delimited part of this much larger field of interlocking processes" (p. 331).

This recognition merges with the First Step of the AA program: "We admitted we were powerless over alcohol and that our lives had become unmanageable." Simultaneously, a point of access is gained to the beginnings of the remedial process implied in Steps Two and Three ("Came to believe that a Power greater than ourselves could restore us to sanity" and "Made a decision to turn our will and our lives over to the care of God *as we understood Him*"). In acknowledging a greater power and deferring to it, the alcoholic situates himself as a system within a nested structure of larger pertinent systems—within, and not outside or against that structure. The pathology is identified and located not as a discrete and antithetical other with which the alcoholic is engaged in interminable contest (the Bottle, John Barleycorn, the Bright Lights, the Boss, the Wife, "Society"), but as an inherent and pervasive aspect of the entire perceptual, cognitive, affective system. Ideally, smaller and larger systems become reoriented, achieving congruence and harmonious relationship with one another; complementarity becomes an ordering principle in the subject's mental life. In its social dimension, the principle of complementarity engenders a sense of implication and involvement in the human community and fosters an aspiration to participate usefully. The humility attained in the experience of absolute surrender gives rise to a service orientation which is codified in AA as Step Twelve, Tradition Five, and the Preamble, all of which affirm a commitment to help other alcoholics.[3]

The anthropologist Edward Sapir—in another context—describes religion as "the haunting realization of ultimate powerlessness in an inscrutable world, and the unquestioning and thoroughly irrational conviction of the possibility of gaining mystic security by somehow identifying oneself with what can never be known." Sapir's language carries us into the heart of what Bateson identifies as complementarity. This is "religion" not in the sense of an ideological orthodoxy, but rather a deeply felt, unmediated recognition of limits.

> Religion is omnipresent fear and a vast humility paradoxically turned into bedrock security, for once the fear is imaginatively taken to one's heart and the humility confessed . . . the triumph of human consciousness is assured. There can be neither fear nor humiliation for deeply religious natures, for they have intuitively experienced both of these emotions in advance of the declared hostility of an overwhelming world, coldly indifferent to human desire.
>   . . . It is the pursuit, conscious or unconscious, of ultimate serenity following total and necessary defeat that constitutes the core of religion. (Sapir, 1956, pp. 122–123)

Bateson's complementarity, religion in Sapir's sense, and the crucial first three of AA's Twelve Steps—none of these implies a tearful groveling before an anthropomorphized oversoul or the uncritical acceptance of any particular narrative of origins. Rather, they denote recognition that there are objects and processes outside of and unresponsive to an individual's control, and signal a renunciation of the toxified, corrupted, and false perceptual order that had gradually moved the individual will to a mistaken conviction of its own omnipotence.

The Steps signify less a relinquishment of "power" than a clarification of personal power's finiteness. From this standpoint a more realistic ground is prepared from which to appraise one's true capabilities, and the Steps may be seen therefore as a marshaling of what is available rather than a wholesale abnegation of control or initiative. There is considerable bemused talk in AA about the paradoxically "empowering" nature of "surrender." In less metaphysical terms, the Steps are a stress-management tool (glossed by the Serenity Prayer, as pervasive a text as any in AA), a method for learning to discriminate between real personal power and false promises, whatever their source (from unregulated promptings of the limbic system to the appetite-inducing misteachings of our popular culture and advertising) and to cultivate a quietist acceptance of what cannot be altered in any event.[4]

AA teaches ways of speaking that work toward reinforcing the new comprehension learned in surrender, and habits of thought marked by a positive reorientation toward that surrender, all in the name of healing the split(s) remarked by Bateson. One such healing strategy is the use of the three-part narrative—a performed, oral description of the speaker's own gradual degradation, transformation, and recovery. Telling the story—it may be said that, in a sense, there is really only *one* story in AA—enables the speaker to reconstrue a chaotic, absurd, or violent past as a meaningful, indeed a *necessary,* prelude to the structured, purposeful, and comparatively serene present. Sober alcoholics share the story and rights to its telling with absolute equality; it is a democratization that celebrates a certainty of having attained a special knowledge, a privileged intimacy with those things whereof, in the absence of symbols adequate to the task, we may not speak. Alcoholics become metonymic signifiers to each other; a whole range of unspeakable, nondiscursive modalities are hinted at, but never precisely captured, by such terms as "serenity" and "spiritual awakening."

Comprehension, the historian Louis Mink reminds us, is an act of grasping as a whole, of making sense—whether provisional and temporary or institutional and fixed—through selection and seriation of the chaotic profusion of data before us. Comprehension is not science—it does not preside at the determination of truth—but it is surely an epistemological precondition for survival in the cultural world.

> It is by reference to standards other than comprehension that we must decide what is true and what is false. Knowledge is essentially public and may even be distributed through a community; we know collectively what no one individual could possess. But comprehension is an individ-

ual act of seeing-things-together, and only that. It can be neither an input nor an output of data-retrieval systems, nor can it be symbolically transformed for convenient reference. As the human activity by which elements of knowledge are converted into *understanding,* it is the synoptic vision without which (even though partially and transiently attained) we might forever pass in review our shards of knowledge as in some nightmare quiz show where nothing relates "fact" to "fact" except the fragmented identities of the participants and the mounting of the total of the score. (Mink, 1987, p. 55)

It is through history and fiction, the narrative modes, that comprehension is attained, and it is comprehension that is sought in AA narrative. Symbolic exchange and transformation of course enter into this process, and are carried on outside of it as well; but the primary, personal, exploratory aspects of comprehension should be held in mind as the AA narrative in its fullness is interpreted.

Epistemological reorientation and comprehension by narrative means lend support to one another as the principle of complementarity is integrated into the mental structure of the newly sober alcoholic. Complementarity, it should be noted, does not supplant symmetry, but dwells with it in a complementary relationship, and should provide a necessary corrective when symmetry in normal, nonalcoholic competitive or oppositional situations threatens to overgrow or override the totality of the system.

A set of associated qualities might seem to belong on either side of a division between symmetry and complementarity, thus:

symmetry	*complementarity*
division	unity
individual	community
bounded	boundless
locked grid	open field
demarcation	interaction
competition	cooperation
intensification	homeostasis
pride	humility
exclusion	inclusion
positivist	relativist

and so on

The binary may seem capable of indefinite exfoliation, but a kind of saturation point will be reached and states of paradox will set in: the symmetry column will take the entry "binary," and the complementarity side "nonbinary." The difficulty is clear in these opposed propositions: under symmetry, "this column *excludes* all things in column B," and under complementarity, "this column *includes* all things in column A." There is either interminable conceptual tail-chasing (escalation)—or a declaration of the priority of complementarity.

These are not unfamiliar themes. Complementarity may call to mind the "more regenerate sorts of happiness" associated by William James with the "religion of healthy-mindedness"; and those strains of popularized contemporary mysticism that aspire toward a kind of quietist perspectivism may also be evoked. Readers of twentieth-century poetry may recollect Eliot's "undissociated sensibility" or Yeats's "unity of being" as aspirations (or longings) put forth in response to the perpetual crisis of endemic modernist self-division. Contemporary publishers of self-help literature know by annual sales figures that a large reading public craves balm if not remedy for the cloven psyche, whether the wound's cause is identified as chemical, sexual, genetic, or sociopolitical.

The experience of subjectivity transformed by the "more correct epistemology"—complementarity—was characterized in the 1930s by AA's founder in terms of a set of "promises" that are often read aloud at AA meetings today, particularly as a propagandistic incentive for new or wavering members. Bill Wilson described the advantages of "the spiritual life" in sobriety this way:

> We are going to know a new freedom and a new happiness. We will not regret the past nor wish to shut the door on it. We will comprehend the word serenity and we will know peace. No matter how far down the scale we have gone, we will see how our experience can benefit others. That feeling of uselessness and self-pity will disappear. We will lose interest in selfish things and gain interest in our fellows. Self-seeking will slip away. Our whole attitude and outlook upon life will change. Fear of people and of economic insecurity will leave us. We will intuitively know how to handle situations which used to baffle us. We will suddenly realize that God is doing for us what we could not do for ourselves. (Alcoholics Anonymous, 1976, pp. 83–84)

In *The Gift: Imagination and the Erotic Life of Property,* the poet and cultural critic Lewis Hyde provides another perspective which may help to further clarify Bateson's ideas—and also to shed light on the AA practice of story exchange.[5] Much of Hyde's book explores the inexhaustible "healthy-minded" enthusiasms of Walt Whitman contrasted with the discords and fragmentation displayed in the work of Ezra Pound. Hyde appraises the relationship, the deep affinities and sharp disjunctions, between these writers against a theory of the circulation of poetry as a form of gift relationship— distorted in Pound's case—that forges a communicative bond among poets and their sympathetic readers. The poetic gift over- flows the consciousness to which it is mysteriously granted and spreads out into the human community where it bears fruit as wis- dom, consolation, encouragement, or rapture.

First, though, as an introduction to the discussion of Whitman and Pound, Hyde develops a general theory of gift behavior grounded in folktales, fragments of traditional wisdom, the pioneer- ing hypotheses of Marcel Mauss, and the classic ethnographic work of Malinowski among the Trobriand Islanders and Boas among the Indians of the Pacific Northwest.

Gifts, given freely, ungoverned by expectations or rules of equiva- lent exchange, have certain mysterious properties. An ideal gift is a substance that gives increase in use, either materially—grain, for example, that may be turned into bread but also sown and harvested to become still more bread—or spiritually, enriching the inner life of the recipient. This increase, the accrued surplus, then obliges the recipient to become a donor, not in direct reciprocation for the first gift, but turning in another direction where the gift impulse will work to diminish privation elsewhere. "A circulation of gifts nour- ishes those parts of our spirit that are not entirely personal, parts that derive from nature, the group, the race, or the gods. Further- more, although these wider spirits are a part of us, they are not 'ours'; they are endowments bestowed upon us. To feed them by giving away the increase they have brought us is to accept that our participation in them brings with it an obligation to preserve their vitality" (Hyde, 1983, p. 38).

Gift exchange is contrasted to market exchange—an externally regulated economy bereft of spiritual values—and "two groups of associated ideas" then fall into place for Hyde. "We have, on the one hand, imagination, synthetic thought, gift exchange, use value, and gift-increase, all of which are linked by a common element of *eros*, or relationship, bonding, 'shaping into one.' And we have, on the other hand, analytic or dialectical thought, self-reflection, logic, market exchange, exchange value, and interest on loans, all of which share a touch of *logos*, of differentiating into parts" (p. 155).

The analogy here to the principles of symmetry and complementarity is plain. Hyde, like Bateson, notes that neither cluster of ideas is "better" than the other; rather, it is balance and propriety that should be sought in the practical work of navigating among these oppositions. "Neither of these poles, the joining or the splitting, is more important or more powerful than its opposite. Each has its sphere and time of ascendancy, and it is not impossible to strike a balance between the two. But that harmony is easily lost" (p. 155).

It seems to me that the harmonizing precept itself must derive from the notions or experiences associated with the synthesizing principle of eros, the gift/imagination side of things; and that is, of course, the side of complementarity. But there is no issue raised, nothing which needs to be harmonized, if there is no oppositional construct to begin with; so primacy itself is elusive here. In any event the traditional wisdom of gift exchange circumscribes a state of mind where unfettered self-interest will be put aside—if there is conflict—in the name of a greater good.

AA is an example of the gift of teaching—where knowledge (experience, strength, and hope) and the history of its acquisition are imparted in the hope that they will be used, increased, and transmitted again. In AA, as in other circumstances where what Hyde calls "transformative gifts" are tendered, the teaching needs to ripen, to mature and diversify beyond the range and control of the giver. Then,

> if the teaching begins to "take," the recipient feels gratitude. I would like to speak of gratitude as a labor undertaken by the soul to effect the transformation after a gift has been received. Between the time a gift comes to us and the time we pass it along, we suffer gratitude. Moreover, with gifts that are agents of change, it is only when the gift has worked in us, only when we have come up to its level, as it were, that we can give it away again. Passing the gift along is the act of gratitude that finishes the labor. The transformation is not accomplished until we have the power to give the gift on our own terms. (P. 47)

Hyde, like Bateson, tacks between the global and the local, the cosmic and the mundane, in his examples: "In the present century the opposition between negative and positive reciprocity has taken the form of a debate between 'capitalist' and 'communist,' 'individualist' and 'socialist'; but the conflict is much older than that, because it is an essential polarity between the whole and the part, the one and the many. Every age must find its balance between the two, and in every age the domination of either one will bring with it the call for its opposite" (p. 38).

"The Cybernetics of 'Self' " pointed far beyond the exigencies of addiction, according to Bateson's biographer David Lipset. "The logic of alcoholic pathology" for Bateson "was an extended metaphor—reviling the somatically defined Occidental self," while the AA "theology of submitting to systemic power greater than self espoused the . . . ecological moralisms Bateson was advocating. Symmetrical competition was not in itself pathological, but to construe certain basic relationships (e.g., man-nature, man-society) in symmetrical terms must end in disaster" (Lipset, 1980, p. 269).[6] Bill Wilson found sustenance in limiting his theoretical ambitions and resisting grandiose or messianic impulses. Bateson forced no such restrictions upon his thought. "The dilemma of Western man, fighting to control and destroy nature, appeared in the opposition 'self vs. bottle.' It also appeared in the evolution of theological man-nature relations. The shift in belief from totemic, to animistic, to transcendent gods reflected the rise of modern egoism toward the environment. . . . The contemporary Occident . . . divided man from nature and separated him from his deity" (pp. 269–270).

The discussion has taken us well beyond the relatively modest goals of Alcoholics Anonymous, but perhaps something of the depth and complexity of the principles involved has been glimpsed.

Hitting Bottom in Thebes

A reading of *The Bacchae* against coordinates provided by Bateson in "The Cybernetics of 'Self' " generates insights that are surprisingly pertinent to contemporary chemical dependency issues. Euripides' ideas and images resonate in modernist literary works, in formulations of the nature of addictive disorders, and in stories told by alcoholics. John Berryman's elaborate rhetorical evasions in *Recovery* recall the pathos of the ineffectual Pentheus's strategies of self-deception; the black hole of Jack London's nihilistic White Logic conjures Euripides' powerful exposition of the irrelevance of ill-considered human desires for transcendence in the face of unforgiving necessity.

The Bacchae displays the pathological responses of a regulated system to the introduction of a powerful disordering principle. The system in question is the unitary mental landscape of the play—call it "Thebes"—an imaginative field in which the ideally complementary elements of governance and propriety, principles esteemed equally in psychology and civics, are set on paths of mutually destructive interplay. The agency of the disorder is a powerful complex of desires, evasions, and dissimulative techniques enunciated through the figure of Dionysus and symbolically condensed in his name; that complex is most clearly and simply understood as addictive intoxication.

The characters in *The Bacchae* may then be fruitfully understood as components—ideas, units of force, transformations—of a single mental system thrown into dissonance by the introduction of the extrinsic principle of intoxication and its entails. The play is perhaps best thought of as paradigmatic or modal rather than an attempt to correspond allegorically with a generalized "inner life" or social moment.

The principle of intoxication—Dionysus—which, at its extremity, produces a mental state typified by the irresoluble conflict of equal-valued oppositions, intrudes upon the regulated hierarchical dominion under the apparent governance of a "mental component," a "self"—Pentheus—that has heretofore succeeded in regarding itself as exempt from certain principles of control. Intoxication, once introduced into the regulated dominion, produces desired effects in some sectors, since it seems to erase distinctions which produce pain or frustration. (The promise of dedifferentiation implies the elimination of physical, mental, and social distinctions, the erasure of boundaries between people, the prospect of a kind of spiritual fusion, and, somehow, a consequent experience of bliss that lies well beyond mere tension reduction.)

The self-component which holds itself aloof from interactive systemic responsibility complains that the principle of intoxication has destabilized the domain and must, therefore, be expelled. This injunction is based on a failure to recognize the dependency of any one element in the system upon all the others, as a general truth and principle of harmonious organization. An impasse is quickly reached: the intoxicated sectors, their oppositional thinking intensified by the intoxicant, soon come to regard the aloof component as an absolute enemy, and the aloof component's isolation is deepened by the growing enmity from "below." An appeal to conservative principles comes too late—moderation is no longer an option, but neither is foreclosure of the inherent interests of either side. The situation is a tragic one, and severe damage to the system would seem to be inevitable before even the possibility of a restoration of regulated process may be considered.

I am suggesting here only family resemblance—not a comprehensive account of addictive mental processes or a master key to the literature of maladaptation. But *The Bacchae* may be usefully engaged at analytical and informational registers—supplementing its religious/philosophical dimension—without turning it to a temperance tract, a self-help treatise, or a fable. To begin to reappraise the play along these lines, however, we must first try to clear away some influential detritus left strewn along the interpretive pathway by the mischievous Friedrich Nietzsche.

The repossession of Dionysus by Nietzsche in *The Birth of Tragedy* is accomplished at the expense of a weakening of Euripides' incarnated god of intoxication. Nietzsche's abstraction of Dionysus may have seemed to mark a step forward in the history of thought, a movement toward refinement and maturation; but the movement, in fact, dilutes a concept that is most radically itself when specified and embodied. Euripides' subject in *The Bacchae* is intoxication as a disorder that afflicts whole systems, a notion the playwright imposes on a cluster of differentiated characters who engage with one another to reveal the nature and degree of their own subordination. This analytic strategy serves precision in the realization of nuance; particular characters experience systemic dysfunction in particular ways. Nietzsche's abstraction discards incarnation and particularities of affliction, moves away from human facts. Detached from narrative specificity, the Dionysian dilates and sublimates, effaces its own origins, and loses itself in the intricacies of Nietzsche's agenda.

Toxin turns to remedy; remedy becomes a form of therapy; and therapy is idealized as liberation.

For Nietzsche, "Dionysus" comes to designate a nostalgic yearning, an imaginative reassurance summoned from the margins and interstices of a continuum of past societies declining toward our insipid modernity—tedious, lackluster, bereft of classical civilizations' energetic notions of degree, rigor, and aspiration. In Nietzsche's account, an ignoble process of domesticating the god was inaugurated by Euripides, and *The Bacchae* is to be seen as an engine contrived for that purpose. By virtue of Euripides' intervention, according to Nietzsche, the influence of Dionysian mystery was to have been suppressed or, at least, inhibited and contained—in slavish adherence to the despicable maxim of Socratism and later the Enlightenment: "Everything must be intelligible."

But dismissed or unacknowledged by Nietzsche, powerful, dark urgencies inform *The Bacchae;* Euripides' Dionysus is by no means brought to heel, either by design or in effect. The unflinching disclosure of immitigable uncertainties, an unsettling alternation between doom and nervous caprice, and a formal control that is meticulous but hardly conciliatory, all seem to confute Nietzsche's milksop Euripides.

Nietzsche's Dionysus, less incarnation than disembodiment, more "the Dionysian" than Dionysus, represents a condition derived specifically from the "collapse of the *principium individuationis*" and from the "blissful ecstasy" that accompanies that collapse. This state of dedifferentiation, resistant to conventional representation, unshaped, inchoate, antithetical to the waking conventions of socialized, civilized, obedient man, is "brought home to us most intimately by the analogy of intoxication. Either under the influence of the narcotic draught, of which the songs of all primitive men and peoples speak, or with the potent coming of spring that penetrates all nature with joy, these Dionysian emotions awake, and as they grow in intensity everything subjective vanishes into complete self-forgetfulness" (Nietzsche, 1967, p. 36).

The analogy of intoxication—purveyed by Nietzsche in Edenic terms—is incomplete, of course, despite the concreteness of that "narcotic draught." Dedifferentiation is indeed at the heart of the subjective experience of intoxication, but its evocation here in exclusively pastoral imagery is misleading; the demonic or pathological complement of that state is suppressed. The word-picture conjured by Nietzsche to exemplify the Dionysian modality in this phase is suggestive of the "peaceable kingdom" motif once dear to the hearts of naive American folk artists in their coy and overstated representations of the promises of an unexamined Christian literalism.

> Under the charm of the Dionysian not only is the union between man and man reaffirmed, but nature which has become alienated, hostile, or subjugated, celebrates once more her reconciliation with her lost son, man. Freely, earth proffers her gifts, and peacefully the beasts of prey of the rocks and desert approach. The chariot of Dionysus is covered with flowers and garlands; panthers and tigers walk under its yoke. . . . Now the slave is a free man; now all the rigid, hostile barriers that necessity, caprice, or 'impudent convention' have fixed between man and man are broken. Now, with the gospel of universal harmony, each one feels himself not only united, reconciled, and fused with his neighbor, but as one with him, as if the veil of *maya* had been torn aside and were now merely fluttering in tatters before the mysterious primal unity. (P. 37)

It is probable that the pursuit of intoxication is preceded and accompanied by a feeling of privation or nostalgia for that earliest term of infancy, characterized by psychoanalysts as the state of dual-unity prior to the development of a sense of bodily integrity and isolation. But it is inexpedient for Nietzsche to endorse infantilism or something as commonplace as what might be called a kind of homesickness; the malaise that begets radical aesthetics must not be degraded to a regressive longing. Nietzsche, therefore, cautiously steps away from intoxication itself to the *analogy* of intoxication. Intoxication is transformed to a metaphor—for inspiration, trance, beatitude, epiphany—and his argument is saved from reduction (although the channel of access to visions of primal unity is no longer as near at hand as the nearest *Gasthaus*). The analogy, as we have noted, is only partial, articulated from a set of carefully chosen qualities and equally important exclusions. The Dionysian projection becomes a precarious kind of fiction—a collage of images that coalesce only by virtue of the force of Nietzsche's self-assured, exorbitant prose.

It is not that Nietzsche's intoxication-like Dionysian modality is free from tension; its essence, in fact, is the irresoluble contradiction between the dream of reunification and the solitary confinement of the dreamer's waking life. And a price must be paid by whoever would pursue the primal unity. The first intimation of hidden costs occurs with the eruption of unmediated artistic energies, nature celebrating itself in human consciousness, beginning "in the image world of dreams, whose completeness is not dependent upon the intellectual attitude or the artistic culture of any single being; and then as intoxicated reality, which likewise does not heed the single unit, but even seeks to destroy the individual and redeem him by a mystic feeling of oneness" (1967, p. 38). The sacrifice of intellect, culture, and individuation will be more than compensated in the utopian aftermath of access to the Dionysian fusion, or so we must believe if we have assented to the story thus far. But Nietzsche's language is increasingly laden with images of distressed flesh and physiological upheaval; we move from universal harmony to horrified dissonance; from the restoration of children and the liberation of slaves to the pastimes of the torture chamber: there is a heart of darkness in the peaceable kingdom. In search of the Dionysian one must pay tribute to "the phenomenon that pain begets joy, that ecstasy may wring sounds of agony from us. At the very climax of joy there sounds a cry of horror or a yearning lamentation for an irretrievable loss" (p. 40). And here at last, in "the pain and contradiction" of "the primal unity," is the originating impulse, the birth, of tragic drama.

One does not turn to Nietzsche for disinterested classical scholarship; indeed, it is precisely the unscrupulousness of his conception of the Dionysian that is of interest. By transforming the god to metaphor in the service of modernist polemics, Nietzsche has produced a specialized variant of the proposition—common in Western aesthetics at least since the inception of Romanticism—that the poet, already somehow selected out of the herd, can get access to transcendental knowledge through mental derangement. Exotic psychic states are accorded respect because of their putative susceptibility to a veiled but presumably desirable "higher" truth.

Intoxication—actual intoxication, and not a denatured, analogical cousin—may appear to be a short-cut to this alluring, revelatory, poetic derangement. Intoxication has the eerie capacity to insinuate itself disguised as a *complex issue* at the expense and in the place of actual intricacies, effacing political, philosophical, religious, sexual, and expressive considerations in a subject's mental life in order to give shrill voice to its own priority. "The shortest way out of Manchester is, notoriously, a bottle of Gordon's gin."[7] The invention of the Dionysian is a nineteenth-century change rung in the name of art on precisely that theme. We may begin to recognize the hazards of Nietzsche's refiguration.

Compressed within the facetious confines of the Manchester quip are intimations of a world of unremitting hopelessness. Drunkenness, addiction, penury, disease, brutish violence, contumely, and disgrace—and consignment to these things in endless recirculation —have little to do with the wrenching of artistic shape from inchoate spirit. The Dionysian in Nietzsche concedes not the smallest synchronism with the incoherent, the convulsive, the nauseated, the cirrhotic, the palsied, or the suppurating. The darkest aspect of the Dionysian for Nietzsche is regret, a kind of heightened but nonspecific nostalgia.

Nietzsche has misappropriated the idea of intoxication, lifting it without warrant from the world of everyday reality and deforming it irresponsibly in the service of his manifesto. Euripides' Dionysus, while conceived like Nietzsche's upon the premise of dedifferentiation, is not only more complex than Nietzsche's but has a good deal more to tell us outside the zone of prescriptive aesthetics.

The classicist H. D. F. Kitto observes that what is *religious* about Greek tragedy is its grasp of human position against a horizon of necessity.

> Divine activity . . . is a controlling element in Religious Tragedy precisely because it represents "the framework of inexorable law", or . . . of inherent natural forces. Our business is to see that the divine activity neither controls human activity and suffering nor renders them merely pathetic, but is rather a generalised statement about them. The divine background holds up to us . . . the system of co-ordinates against which we are to read the significance of what the human actors do and suffer. The gods are a controlling element in the plays, but not in what the actors do and suffer: that is entirely their own affair. The reason for saying that the divine element controls the play is this: the dramatist does not allow the human actors to do or suffer anything which does not have significance when it is read against the co-ordinates. (Kitto, 1956, pp. 243–244)

The immanence of divine necessity is perhaps complicated in *The Bacchae* because of the vigorous participation of Dionysus in the earthly action; but this unconventional figuration surely enriches the conception of the god's presence, layering and darkening it, rather than confuting it. Dionysus, in prologue and epilogue, brackets the action in his true form, undisguised, declaring his intentions and accomplishments explicitly. During the progress of the story he is disguised as his own avatar, blurring distinctions between man and god and objectifying the inscrutability of divinity's power. "Throughout the play," a stage direction reads, "he wears a smiling mask."

Dionysus is a masked deity in cult even before his annexation to tragedy. The classical scholar Walter F. Otto writes that "the mask tells us that the theophany of Dionysus, which is different from that of the other gods because of its stunning assault on the senses and its urgency, is linked with the eternal enigmas of duality and paradox" (Otto, 1965, p. 91). The figure of the masked actor—already a double dissimulation—glosses the idea of the "god incognito,/ disguised as a man" (Grene, 1959, p. 155). An incessantly smiling visage overseeing the devastation to come is certainly compatible with the conventional view of Euripides as "modern," "cynical," "skeptical," and "cruel." More radically still, the smiling mask may be taken as a challenge to complacency in the reading of any signs whatever in a problematic human world where the congruence of circumstance and desire cannot be guaranteed.

It is not until the final moments of the play that Dionysus is explicit about the inevitability of the action of *The Bacchae:* "Long ago my father Zeus ordained these things" (p. 218). But we may trust, from the outset, that we are inside a rigid frame of necessity; that Dionysus, unblinded by diseased interests, will speak truthfully to the audience; that "inherent natural force" will prevail. But, as Kitto cautions, "prophecy is not a special and arbitrary decree . . .; it is a prediction made by a god who, unlike men, knows all the facts and can therefore see in advance how the situation must necessarily work out. If life were random . . . then not even a god could prophesy" (Kitto, 1956, p. 76). It is not that the human agents are unfairly deprived of choice, but that the suppositious supernatural characters simply have more data.

Dionysus has a variety of names and epithets to choose among, along with his enigmatic embodiments and masquerades. In *The*

Bacchae he answers to Bromius, Evius, and Bacchus. Classical anthropologist Jane Harrison gives, in addition, Iacchos, Bassareus, Thyoneus, Lenaios, and Eleuthereus, "and the list by no means exhausts his titles" (Slater, 1968, p. 211). Translating a smirking Aristophanes, Dudley Fitts offers "son of Juice" (Fitts, 1962, p. 80). The Loud One, the Deliverer from Sorrow, Son of the Thunder, the Twice-Born, the Indian, the Offspring of Two Mothers, God of the Wine-Press, the Night-hallooed—these are among the names of Bacchus/Dionysus that Ovid supplies (Ovid, 1955, pp. 81–82).

Dionysus is associated with Sabazius, an older beer god, and Zagreus, the offspring of Zeus and Persephone, rent and devoured by malicious Titans at the instigation of a jealous Hera. At his birth he may appear as a horned serpent, or a horned child crowned with serpents (Graves, 1955, p. 103; Grene, 1959, p. 159); his animal associates or transformations include goats, bulls, lions, serpents, and panthers. Any rendition of the god's characteristics and guises, from the most naive to the most portentous, immediately signals an awareness of fundamental issues in human ontology: identity, mortality, transcendence, and transgression. The main kernels and anecdotal supplements of the Dionysus story are all concerned with radical mutability; they depict the metamorphoses of men and beasts, possession, mania and rage, cannibalism and infanticide, and the actual or implied or symbolic instability of sexual identity.

Classicist E. R. Dodds tries to get to the heart of the Dionysian phenomenon. Whether providing simple pleasures for a "country bumpkin" or presiding over the "ecstatic bacchanal," Dionysus had a wide appeal.

> He is . . . the god who . . . enables you for a short time to *stop being yourself,* and thereby sets you free. That was, I think, the main secret of his appeal to the Archaic Age: not only because life in that age was often a thing to escape from, but more specifically because the individual . . . began in that age to emerge . . . from the old solidarity of the family, and found the unfamiliar burden of individual responsibility hard to bear. Dionysus could lift it from him. . . . The aim of his cult was *ecstasis*— which again could mean anything from "taking you out of yourself" to a profound alteration of personality. And its psychological function was to satisfy and relieve the impulse to reject responsibility . . . [which] can

become under certain social conditions an irresistible craving. (Dodds, 1951, pp. 76–77)

This is a commonsensical sort of assessment, and probably a good corrective to the excesses of overwrought and rhapsodic argument. Dodds, it should be noted, is addressing the appearance of Dionysian cult observance in everyday life, and not its manipulation as symbolic action by a tragedian. Nevertheless, we might wonder if "the impulse to reject responsibility" is not a moralistic formulation that trivializes the powerful emotions that impel *The Bacchae*. There is a feeling of disdainful toleration that is inconsistent with the urgency that invests the play.

In order to represent the experience of *katharsis,* mythologist Joseph Campbell offers us a glimpse into the mind of the festivalgoer who is enjoying a mystery play under the auspices of "the dismembered bull-god, Dionysus."

> The meditating mind is united, in the mystery play, not with the body that is shown to die, but with the principle of continuous life that for a time inhabited it, and for that time was the reality clothed in the apparition (at once the sufferer and the secret cause), the substratum into which our selves dissolve when the "tragedy that breaks man's face" has split, shattered and dissolved our mortal frame. (Campbell, 1949, p. 26)

Campbell's playgoer is, of course, suffering Aristotelian pity and terror during this immersion in the terrible contradiction between life as continuity in abstraction and life as painfully self-conscious brevity in individuation. We are perilously close to territory staked out by Nietzsche, and the affinity should be noted.

> This death to the logic and the emotional commitments of our chance moment in the world of space and time, this recognition of, and shift of our emphasis to, the universal life that throbs and celebrates its victory in the very kiss of our own annihilation, this *amor fati*, "love of fate," love of the fate that is inevitably death, constitutes the experience of tragic art: therein the joy of it, the redeeming ecstasy. (Pp. 26–27)

Campbell tends here to exclude the cognitive dimension from his analysis. Aristotle's definitions of the experience of pity and terror —quoted in Campbell only a few lines earlier—seem rather coldly to suppose that the intellect would be at work in achieving the fullness of the tragic emotion. For Aristotle, the mind of the playgoer is united with the sufferer and the cause of the suffering in a manner that could not be achieved outside the analytic space of the theatrical demonstration. Kitto writes that catharsis, the tragic emotion, results because "when we have seen terrible things happening in the play, we understand, as we cannot always do in life, *why* they have happened; or, if not so much as that, at least we see that they have not happened by chance, without any significance. We are given the feeling that the Universe is coherent, even though we may not understand it completely" (Kitto, 1956, p. 235).

The Bacchae, however, seems not to project a feeling of coherence to its readers, at least not in any predictable way. Unresolved scholarly conflicts persist, particularly over the playwright's "point of view": does Euripides endorse the *sparagmos* and the comeuppance of Pentheus, or is he scornfully aloof, or contemptuous, or conciliatory, struggling to mediate the distressing but inevitable advent of unprecedented social behaviors? These seem to me the wrong kinds of questions to ask of such a play; and sociologist Philip Slater makes a pertinent observation:

> One can scarcely pick up a volume on Greek mythology and religion without encountering an expression of puzzlement when the topic of Dionysus is first broached. There is a quality of dissonance about the god, some incompleteness which resists interpretation. Although perhaps all gods in all religions are fusions of opposites, here the fusion has not altogether been achieved. No other religious figure so often arouses the fantasy that some important bit of evidence has been lost to us, which, if discovered, would illuminate him completely. (Slater, 1968, p. 211)

There is, indeed, an "important bit of evidence" that, while by no means lost, has certainly been attributed insufficient explanatory power; restored to its correct priority, this "bit" will go far toward rectifying the interpretive deficiencies Slater has detected. The "quality of dissonance," however, must remain affixed and intact, for dissonance is essential to this aspect of the god, and should be emphasized rather than bypassed or subordinated. I am referring to the complex of elements implied in the epithet by which any schoolchild—any nineteenth-century schoolchild, at least—might identify Dionysus: the god of wine.

We are, again, close to the problem that beset Nietzsche. To omit the mention of this function altogether would be unthinkable, but commentators seem unable to accommodate the range of its ramifications and, like the philosopher, sidestep the issue. Instead of focusing on alcohol use, attention is swiftly shifted to the spread of viniculture in Europe, or celebrations of seasonal recrudescence, or divine sacrifice and the collective expulsion of the scapegoat, or the ambivalences governing Greek mother-son relationships, or the institution of the dramatic festivals and the flowering of tragedy. These and a dozen other historiographic factors are, to be sure, indispensable to comprehending the Dionysian phenomenon—but so is alcohol ingestion and its effects. Intoxication is not merely a chip in a mosaic here—it is a *sine qua non* for a credible interpretation of Dionysus, and other key components of his characterization must be understood *in relation* to it. Walter F. Otto puts the matter thus: "Wine, which, as Aeschylus says, 'the wild mother' brought into existence, 'the fiery drink of the black mother,' as Euripides calls it, is a metaphor for the god himself. Like him, it, too, is complete only through the miracle of a second birth" (Otto, 1965, p. 146). Wine is a metaphor for the god, and the vine operates synecdochically for them both, in anecdote and graphic representation as well.

> Thus, of all that earth produces, the vine mirrors best the god's two faces and reveals most clearly his miraculous nature—both his endearing and his terrible wildness. It was doubtless always recognized as such, ever since one knew of him and of wine. We, on the other hand, are accustomed to use the gifts of nature to suit ourselves without being amazed by its secrets, and whenever there is talk of wine, we think of geniality, high spirits, and, perhaps, also of the dangers to health and morals. But the Greek of antiquity was caught up by the total seriousness of the truth that here pleasure and pain, enlightenment and destruction, the lovable and the horrible lived in close intimacy. It is this unity of the paradoxical which appeared in Dionysiac ecstasy with staggering force. (P. 151)

Otto's arguments are correct. Participating in the imagery of the vine and the twice-born grape is "the god who is mad," "a god, part of whose nature it is to be insane" (p. 136), and who embodies in a word the complex of extraordinary mental states, ranging from heightened clarity to fulgurating mania, that alcohol intoxication may bring.

In his exordium in *The Bacchae,* Dionysus reminds us of special qualities that link him to the intoxicating beverage. We have noted his extreme mutability and his resistance to definition. Alcohol, too, challenges the dominion of nomenclature, the rule of *logos,* to the extent of paralyzing the enabling faculties, forcing unexpected performances from the organs of speech. Dionysus has appeared at the site of his conception and first birth (a primal scene abreaction!) and activates the imagery of light and dark that follows him:

> My mother was Cadmus' daughter, Semele by name,
> midwived by fire, delivered by the lightning's blast.
>
> . . . .
>   There before the palace
> I see my lightning-married mother's grave,
> and there upon the ruins of her shattered house
> the living fire of Zeus still smolders on
> in deathless witness of Hera's violence and rage
> against my mother. But Cadmus wins my praise:
> he has made this tomb a shrine, sacred to my mother.
> It was I who screened her grave with the green
> of the clustering vine. (Grene, 1959, p. 155)

"Of light the son was born," the chorus says in the course of praising Dionysus a few lines later (p. 158). Although Otto ascribes a set of specifics to the imagery of light and dark (including a notion of the superiority of volcanic soil and the need for strong sunlight in grape growing), it seems likely that those specifics are subsumed here in an affirmation of the idea of opposition itself.

The god in wine connects the user to extremes, polarities, pairings in perhaps shocking contrastive relevance, and, finally, absolute contradiction. This is the territory of Batesonian symmetry, of course, of relationship that understands itself only in terms of what it is not. There is no need to draw up lists of particular binaries: opposition itself is the essence of the Dionysian vocabulary. Wine illuminates extremities; the confrontation may endanger, courting the user toward the darkness of dementia and self-destruction, or it may nurture fictive resolutions in the symbolic vocabularies of art, music, or the performance of self-mortifying spirituality. The emblematic vine that screens the grave of the mother, light-violated in an act that is both terrifying and necessary, may suggest the cooling occultation of shade provided by wine in confrontation with untenable internal paradox. This can be seen as a psychoanalytic aporia, an impasse where imperiously absolute infantile desire collides with absolute frustration, or its ontological cousin, the unbearable knowledge of life built on death's inexorability and the chaos of unending destruction.

The eastern origins of Dionysus and his cult suggest an "otherness" that holds power and danger and is consistent with positive and negative potentialities in alcohol use. Similarly, music and dance may impel the conflict-ridden subject toward momentary wordless resolutions in harmony and control, or may devolve into frenzied dissonances that may seem to abrogate contradiction but are in fact only a temporary suppression or a painful peeling-back that reveals deeper, snarled layers of the same. Here, too, is at least one aspect of the women of Thebes, the bacchantes, "driven from shuttle and loom" by Dionysus in his rage at the city's refusal to acknowledge his godhead:

> Because of that offense
> I have stung them with frenzy, hounded them from home
> up to the mountains where they wander, crazed of mind,
> and compelled to wear my orgies' livery. (P. 156)

What is attacked here is a principle of domestic felicity, the restrained virtues of the family circle with its hierarchy and division of labor and, by extension, the predictability of everyday life, the hegemony of an ideal of civility, of civic obligation, of social contract itself. Maenadism, participation in the Dionysian orgies, is the diseased travesty of celebratory inversion—it is inversion gone rotten in an uncomprehending neglect of inversion's rigid constraints. To turn a structure upside down is not to alter its shape in the slightest; maenadism bends the armatures and violently agitates the structure until its shape is irrecoverable—or, at least, that is the threat. Celebration, like wine, must be approached with respect, discretion, and a profound conservatism if it is not to become intractable.

But wine and celebration *must be* approached—approached and controlled, that is, through rules of mediation—and not repressed, ignored, or otherwise denied. The spirit of erroneous denial is embodied in Pentheus, the grandson of Cadmus. Dionysus is likewise the grandson of Cadmus, and the genetic affinity here underscores the importance of the thematic one: in their radical—symmetrical—opposition Dionysus and Pentheus participate in a subsuming unity that may be marked as *extremity* itself.

There are other qualities that attain significance only as members of oppositional pairs: Dionysus is the son of Cadmus's daughter Semele by Zeus, and is thus affiliated with the sky; Pentheus is descended from Cadmus's daughter Agave by Echion, one of the "sown men," a son of Earth. Dionysus is a god, but one who will die repeatedly in the course of his immortality—and, in the form of Zagreus, having been physically incorporated by the Titans from whom mankind will arise, now permeates all human substance; Pentheus is a mortal grotesquely fated to be consumed as the sacramental surrogate of an immortal. Dionysus is androgynous whereas Pentheus is male—although, to be sure, a male who will suffer transvestite degradation; and Dionysus represents necessity whereas Pentheus represents pride. These last two examples are not precisely oppositions, but they do point up deficiencies in Pentheus's makeup that might best be characterized as the absence of a "female" principle, subsuming the elements adduced above as "domestic felicity" together with such qualities as receptivity, modesty, concord, and sense of proportion. Pride in Pentheus should be understood as an epistemological error: the force of necessity is imaginatively arrogated to the self, displaced from its external or systemic position and recast in fantasy as servant to the subject's desire. Much significant world literature has concerned itself with the unpleasant consequences of mistakes of this kind.

Dionysus personalizes the issue, emphasizing Pentheus's impertinence—which, under the circumstances, is less insult than defective judgment:

> Cadmus the king has abdicated,
> leaving his throne and power to his grandson Pentheus;
> who now revolts against divinity, in *me;*
> thrusts *me* from his offerings; forgets *my* name
> in his prayers. Therefore I shall *prove* to him
> and every man in Thebes that I am god
> indeed. And when my worship is established here,
> and all is well, then I shall go my way
> and be revealed to other men in other lands. (Pp. 156–57)

Pentheus intemperately deprecates the rite in sexually charged language:

> I am also told a foreigner has come to Thebes
> from Lydia, one of those charlatan magicians,
> with long yellow curls smelling of perfumes,
> with flushed cheeks and the spells of Aphrodite
> in his eyes. His days and nights he spends
> with women and girls, dangling before them the joys
> of initiation in his mysteries.
> But let me bring him underneath that roof
> and I'll stop his pounding with his wand and tossing
> his head. By god, I'll have his head cut off! (P. 164)

Moments later Pentheus speaks of the rites as "filthy mysteries. When once you see/the glint of wine shining at the feasts of women,/then you may be sure the festival is rotten" (p. 165). The collapse of predictable sexual behavior—the disintegration of regulatory patterns sanctioned by authority and tradition—appears to be the most profoundly, *viscerally,* experienced dimension of the prospect of dedifferentiation, for better or worse. Pentheus's speech expresses a churning ambivalence, with elements of envy and revulsion, attraction and terror. His confusion circulates about the "lineaments of gratified desire" projected onto his own mother, intolerably but inescapably sexualized in imaginative visualization; the spectacle of androgyny joined with self-assurance channels that confusion into rage. Psychosexual and socio-political upheavals reinforce one another; Pentheus, soi-disant repository of authority and convention, reacts with threats of beheading and imprisonment, the projection of his own terrors of mutilation and encroaching darkness.

Latent dysfunction is intensified and brought to light by wine: it is wine that dredges up this unwelcome psychic clabber and compels the materialization of the spirit of extremity. Intoxication generates opposition and contradiction; but denial is only a subspecies of opposition and, hence, an unhelpful response. Rather than containing or invalidating the pathological process, further opposition augments it, fuels escalation, and obstructs transcendent synthesis or bilateral accommodation, both of which are functions of complementarity.

Teiresias who, along with Cadmus, is among the only men "who will dance for Bacchus"—who, that is, accept the advent of the new god—deplores Pentheus's recalcitrance. To Teiresias, Pentheus is controlled by a love of power, the glories of recognition, to a degree of excess that Teiresias calls "drugged with madness" (p. 167). The identity of Dionysus and Pentheus is reaffirmed in this assessment, but Teiresias also sees contrast:

> Give a wise man an honest brief to plead
> and his eloquence is no remarkable achievement.
> But you are glib; your phrases come rolling out
> smoothly on the tongue, as though your words were wise
> instead of foolish. The man whose glibness flows
> from his conceit of speech declares the thing he is:
> a worthless and a stupid citizen. (P. 165)

Repository of authority or not, Pentheus is committed to the ageless error of insubstantial eloquence. Participation in the Dionysian communion is not a matter for mediation by rhetoric; the situation lies outside the domain of language and its limited applications. Teiresias, who here as elsewhere "sees" in conjunction with his blindness, is conscious of disjunctions not only between word and deed, but between sign and referent as well. Language, severed from responsibility to facts, is as transient and powerless as vapor.

Teiresias is privileged to present what might be called the orthodox position on the new cult. He first invokes Demeter, or Earth, "who gave to man his nourishment of grain," and then extols Dionysus:

> But after her there came the son of Semele,
> who matched her present by inventing liquid wine
> as his gift to man. For filled with that good gift,
> suffering mankind forgets its grief; from it
> comes sleep; with it oblivion of the troubles
> of the day. There is no other medicine
> for misery. And when we pour libations
> to the gods, we pour the god of wine himself
> that through his intercession man may win
> the favor of heaven. (P. 166)

The gift of wine, placed in significant parallel to the gift of grain and conservatively represented, provides only comparatively benevolent forms of erasure; not even the innocuously penalizing trace of hangover is named, far less the sorts of consequence epitomized in the play as bacchantic frenzy.

The figure of Cadmus, shifting functions along a sublime-to-ridiculous axis, puts the immediate crisis in touch with the entire distressing Theban adventure, from its beginning when he slew the serpent and sowed its teeth to generate the Spartoi, through the disintegration of the Oedipus family—subsequent to the action of *The Bacchae*—to the fall of the city in the war of the Seven. Cadmus's presence, in fact, keys a set of mirroring structures surrounding and within *The Bacchae*. His killing of a serpent sacred to Ares before the start of the play is reflected by the metamorphosis of Cadmus into a serpent under Ares's auspices, prophesied at the end of the play. The death by lightning of Semele in bearing Dionysus, described in the opening scene, is inversely replicated by the electrifying illumination of Agave's dismemberment of Pentheus at the end. The arrival of Dionysus in Thebes, unrecognized and "effeminate," is paralleled by Pentheus's departure for Cithaeron, "blind" and cross-dressed.

At the center of these symmetries, conceivably at the center of the entire Theban cycle, is the destruction by supernaturally mandated lightning of the palace in which Dionysus has been detained. Pentheus's own demolition is anticipated, the inadequacy of his moral and political posture is underscored, and a miniaturized reminder is given of the chain of edifying disasters that is Theban political history. *The Bacchae,* like most Greek plays, is vitally concerned with the historical and political implications of its subject, and the presence of Cadmus draws attention to these implications. The symmetries and reversals in their own turn replicate formally the conceptual content of the play. The very structures of extremity and opposition favored by the god of wine are at play in the structure of this most intensive dramatization of his agency. Morphology recapitulates motif in a decisive and explicit manner.

Despite his comic aspect, Teiresias—that first pitiable exemplar of blindness and insight—speaks considerable truth, "good sense," during his brief term on the stage. He recognizes necessity and refuses to compete with it, urging the same for Pentheus. To Cadmus he articulates his simple understanding of the situation before them:

> Cadmus, let us go and pray
> for this raving fool and for this city too,
> pray to the god that no awful vengeance strike
> from heaven.

. . . .
                    And yet take care
        lest someday your house repent of Pentheus
        in its sufferings. I speak not prophecy
        but fact. The words of fools finish in folly. (P. 169)

Teiresias sees himself as implicated by necessity in a delicate net-
work of obligations that Pentheus, in his reckless insistence upon an
undeserved and illusory autonomy, is about to demolish. But, in
addition to his function as spokesman for tradition and circumspection, Teiresias, too, is an emblem. It will be recalled that Teiresias
has experienced the oppositions of sexuality from both sides, having
been transformed to a woman for a period of time in his younger
days; his blindness and his prophetic powers are both direct and
largely unwelcome consequences of this privileged sensibility. In the
present context, he provides a further link between the distempers
of intoxication and sexual exorbitancy. This is no casual cautionary
interpolation, but a substantial assertion about the immense and
categorically deforming power of immoderation, whatever the
arena. The idea examined throughout the play of a causal link between intoxication and sexual license is quite different from the
suggestion, embodied in Teiresias, of analogy. Varying forms of
dedifferentiation ultimately exhibit the same unhappy symptoms;
the question of priority becomes ambiguous, perhaps beside the
point. Skillful incisions, made at the correct locations, will reveal
instructive correspondences.

As if to dispel the possibility that the sensible utterances of Teiresias may, because of his comic aspect, be interpreted ironically, these
same ideas are elaborated by non-tendentious speakers. The
achievement of *sophia*, "the acceptance of necessity and doom
which teaches compassion" (p. 153), is the objective in its plainest
reduction; a key Chorus speech, occurring just after Pentheus has
ordered the imprisonment of Dionysus, contrasts the ideal with
misconceptions and counterfeits that control the king:

            —A tongue without reins
            defiance, unwisdom—
            their end is disaster.
            But the life of quiet good,
            the wisdom that accepts—
            these abide unshaken,

> preserving, sustaining
> the houses of men.
>
> . . . .
>
> Briefly, we live. Briefly,
> then die. Wherefore, I say,
> he who hunts a glory, he who tracks
> some boundless, superhuman dream,
> may lose his harvest here and now
> and garner death. Such men are mad,
> their counsels evil. (P. 170)

Later, echoing a principle laid down first by Teiresias—"we are the heirs of customs and traditions/hallowed by age and handed down to us/by our fathers" (p. 163)—the chorus associates wisdom with convention in an espousal of conservatism that leaves no space for amendment.

> Whatever is god is strong;
> whatever long time has sanctioned,
> that is a law forever;
> the law tradition makes
> is the law of nature. (P. 194)

Irrespective, that is to say, of the apparent novelty of the Dionysian epiphany in Thebes, the principle for which the god stands is outside of the mere human time that governs Pentheus and determines his impotency, his disadvantage. Tradition—an accumulation over time of safe bets—honors or at least accommodates the gods by counseling against the desire to surpass human range. "But he who garners day by day the good of life,/he is happiest. Blessed is he" (p. 195). Personal satisfactions and successes are not precluded; it is, rather, that certain imaginable but presumptuous aspirations are enjoined. Death is a grand synecdoche for limitation as well as punctuation for the short human sentences the gods may be pleased to utter:

> For death the gods exact, curbing by that bit
> the mouths of men. They humble us with death
> that we remember what we are who are not god,
> but men. We run to death. Wherefore, I say,
> accept, accept:
> humility is wise; humility is blest.
>
> . . . .

Let these things be the quarry of my chase:
purity; humility; an unrebellious soul,
accepting all. Let me go the customary way,
the timeless, honored, beaten path of those who walk
with reverence and awe beneath the sons of heaven. (P. 200)

In the confrontation between Pentheus and Dionysus we are witness to enactment of some of the complex interrelationships that inform *The Bacchae* among speaking, seeing, and knowing; sanity, darkness, and light; intoxication, sexuality, and death. The verbal duel between the two gives access to all the Dionysian issues with a compression that fosters a feeling of confluence; again, that is, themes are transmuted into formal properties, entrained by the very shape of the play.

"Your blasphemies have made you blind," Dionysus tells Pentheus, as Pentheus tries to humiliate the god by cropping his sacred curls and depriving him of the staff, or *thyrsus* (p. 176). Moments later Pentheus consigns the god to prison: "Since he desires the darkness, give him what he wants./Let him dance down there in the dark" (p. 177). Dionysus tells the king, "You do not know/the limits of your strength. You do not know/what you do. You do not know who you are" (p. 177). Indeed, nothing is what it appears, and no acts seem to produce the anticipated results. The visual symbols of his cult are unconnected to the real power of the god; but when transferred, subsequently, to Pentheus they invite lethal consequences, marking the meagerness of his control. The "blindness" of Pentheus is a refiguration of the prison darkness in which the god thrives, out of which he will be born yet again in the cataclysm that capsizes public order. The dark in which Dionysus dances is the lightless mind of the king, his rebirth the self-perpetuation of folly. Dionysus's resurrection from the shattered palace is the return of the repressed, the pathological eruption of unacknowledged disorder, the inevitable resistance of natural process against the human illusion of management.

The humiliation of Pentheus is accomplished as Dionysus wheedles and cozens him into accepting the *thyrsus,* donning a wig of blond curls and a woman's dress, and setting out for Cithaeron to "observe" the bacchantes. It is only the king's defective epistemological footing that enables the entrance of the god's punitive power; were Pentheus not so unyielding none of this would be

necessary. The requisite minimal accommodation of the god is neither enthusiasm, nor even advocacy; recognition is the only real
requirement.

Pentheus emerges from the palace, emblematically adorned as
everything he has stood against, "exactly like one of the daughters
of Cadmus."

> I seem to see two suns blazing in the heavens.
> And now two Thebes, two cities, and each
> With seven gates. And you—you are a bull
> who walks before me there. Horns have sprouted
> from your head. Have you always been a beast?
> But now I see a bull. (Pp. 195–196)

The hallucinatory world is more correct than that which Pentheus has left behind. This is not the state of transcendence to
which the poetic consciousness lays privileged claim, but a world of
symbolic retribution for inexpiable sins of cognitive omission. "You
see what you could not when you were blind," Dionysus tells him
(p. 196), and, indeed, Pentheus is now forced to an awareness of
mutability, of duality and opposition, of the inhuman foundations
of rationality, of the savagery central to the human experience of
intoxication. The two suns are duality, extremity itself, as well as the
intensified light of the god's violent birth, the sign of the father
and the hegemony of pain; a double illumination aggravates the
foregoing absence of insight. The doubled city is the riven city and,
too, the king's mind turned against itself in the impending surfeit
of truth. "Do I look like anyone?/Like Ino or my mother Agave?"
Pentheus asks, "coyly primping" (p. 196). The king now travesties
himself: the inflexible, rational, masculine monarch is effeminate,
silly, and compliant. The god of wine has turned him inside out,
ordained passivity, submissiveness, a profound identification with
the mother that malignantly presages the imminent act of incorporation. "You will be carried home," Dionysus says, ". . . cradled in
your mother's arms." "O luxury!" Pentheus cries, "you will spoil
me." With pitiless wit, Dionysus replies, "I *mean* to spoil you" (p.
198). Dionysus's repartee rings with black comedy, recalling the
empty rhetoric charged earlier to Pentheus. Condensations and
multivalences enhance the strength and utility of the god's words,

moving them toward a primitive, magical domain where symbol and entity are fused.

Dionysus leads Pentheus to Cithaeron, "to see but not be seen" (p. 202), to witness the revels. Ostensibly in order to better view the "shameless orgies," Pentheus finds himself, with the supernatural assistance of Dionysus, at the tip of a magically erectile tree. Unwilling objects of scrutiny, the frenzied bacchantes led by Agave uproot the tree and tumble Pentheus to the ground where they fall upon him and, deaf to his pathetic entreaties, tear him to pieces, playing ball with scraps of his bloody carcass. Agave impales her son's head on her *thyrsus,* condensing in a single image a whole range of psychosexual horrors fermented out of infantile misconstructions: the menace of retributive emasculation; chaotic, violent, destructive adult sexuality; maternal voracity intensified by superimposed phallic threat. This image-cluster renders discursively the absolute extremity of dedifferentiation in intoxication. Volatile primitive psychic material amplifies the already devastating narrative moment, and the lesson is vividly underscored by strategic consistency between ideas and emotions. The moral is drawn; the punishment of Pentheus and the social entity he embodies is completed; and the identification between Pentheus and the god is forced to a perfection of irony—for Dionysus is a master of irony. The sacramental rending of man and god is the same except in one noteworthy particular: the man will not come again. Death, for Pentheus, is terminal, no substation on the cyclic path of divine epiphany; transfiguration is not indicated. Pentheus has hit bottom—with a vengeance.

This scenario describes a possible generalized natural history of alcohol addiction based on "The Cybernetics of 'Self' " and the plot of *The Bacchae.* The advent of intoxication on the Theban scene is a "problem" that is larger, more pervasive, more fluid, than Pentheus, in the limitations of his spurious autonomy, can comprehend. That the "problem" involves him even though—perhaps especially because—he does not choose to participate is a conception that is particularly elusive to him. He will not understand that he *is* a participant irrespective of choice, and his resistance only intensifies and darkens his predicament.

Pentheus may not experience anything like a "spiritual awakening" on stage, but an attentive viewer should learn something about the dynamics of symmetrical escalation within a misconstrued self-system, and discover in Pentheus's stead some of the consequences of obstinacy and denial. We are overcome by an accelerating sense of *panic* as the king's undoing proceeds, not unlike "the panic of the man who thought he had control over a vehicle but suddenly finds that the vehicle can run away from him. Suddenly, pressure on what he knows is the brake seems to make the vehicle go faster. It is the panic of discovering that *it* (the system self *plus* vehicle) is bigger than he is" (Bateson, 1972, p. 330). This of course is precisely "the panic of the alcoholic who has hit bottom" (p. 330).

Dionysus is an extravagantly elaborated emblem of dedifferentiation by means of alcohol intoxication. Against this embodiment is mapped the particularized and restrictive outline of Pentheus. Pentheus can only be understood in terms of his deficiencies and of what he fails to comprehend; he is negatively specified, a pocket of absences, merely once-born, earth-born, and improvident. In the end, Pentheus is not the twin of Dionysus at all, but a depthless counterfeit founded on his own fatal inability to discriminate, to *see;* he becomes the mimicry of an image of limitlessness, of abstraction, of unreality. Incapable of self-reflection, confuted by hapless strivings originating in his own inattention, unequipped for governance or propriety, Pentheus is fit at last only for the grisly dismantling we are compelled to witness.

Two

Some Americana

The two vignettes that follow may serve as a reminder that the issue of "substance abuse" in America has had a long turbulent history and that a voluminous body of literature has accumulated around it.

Walt Whitman's 1842 novel *Franklin Evans, or The Inebriate: A Tale of the Times* is an exercise in what David Reynolds calls "dark temperance" or "immoral reform"—the use of moralists' pretexts and vocabulary to shock, titillate, or arouse through "a gloating over the grim details of vice" (Reynolds, 1988, p. 68). If *Franklin Evans* retains a capacity to surprise us at first acquaintance, it is less because of the sensationalist content as such than because of its apparent distance from the mature work of our venerated standard-edition Whitman. Yet, as Reynolds points out, Whitman used just such projects as *Franklin Evans* at this early stage of his writing life as "a training ground in zestful, defiant writing," exploring the "*imaginative* rather than the *political* possibilities of reform rhetoric" (p. 107). (We will see intimations of the later work as a spirit of bright festivity briefly shimmers forth from the dank confines of *Franklin Evans*'s dominant mood.) The novel may be both a finger-stretching exercise in self-creation and a cynical manipulation of immoral reform sensibilities, but it is important for our purposes to draw a third perspective as well: *Franklin Evans* affords an opportunity to observe a connection among the narrative process, the mechanisms of alcohol addiction and recovery, and the dark themes of temperance literature.

The motifs of temperance fiction—domestic violence, self-destructiveness, shame and guilt, deviance, futility—have remained with us, reiterated in fiction through the present century. The temperance novelists contextualized and externalized these motifs in the archetypal dark city, the site of symmetrical escalation par excellence, where self-estrangement is evinced in the war of all against all: ruthless business practices, corrupt politics, deceitful alliances, inhospitable architecture, mean convoluted streets, and all the other signs of urban dysfunction. The Washington Temperance Society linked recovery with festivity in their practice; as we will see, Whitman shows in his novel how that linkage was accomplished in part through narrative. Abetted by the vision of the Washingtonians, Whitman, the poet of the gift, imagines another kind of city—a city of complementarity, of eros, of community—and begins to conjure a pathway to it.

Exploring some of the same issues seventy years later, Jack London attempts a leap to legislated temperance, using the springboard of a dark version of his own life story. But this, too, is pretext: London may have a grand instinct to paint his life onto a national canvas, but the details of his drinking experience are tangled, private, claustrophobic, and unsusceptible to political intervention. Perhaps it is an oblique recognition of his political agenda's underlying lack of credibility that causes London to devote so few words to it.

In Alcoholics Anonymous a kind of master story is presumed that conforms to a model of alcoholism as a disease with a predictable course. But generalized pathology is an insufficient form of knowledge; it is left to individuals to flesh out the armature of diagnostic synopsis with their own particular histories. Symptomatology must be combined with personal experience; it is only to the embodied illness that curative techniques may be applied. Regular meetings and the exchange of stories provide a means for individuals to match private understanding against broadened forms of knowledge, and to draw strength from the leveling recognition of common experience. AA provides a field in which deforming feelings of isolation can be defeated.

London is condemned to a hapless bipolarity: he can examine his psyche tirelessly or he can project himself against national and even cosmic events—but there, not surprisingly, he finds only a grotesquely towering replication of his own inner contradictions. He moves between a microscopic privacy and a depersonalized vastness, but there is really no space for social interaction and symbolic exchange. Between his own inner torments and a universalized inflation of those torments there seems to be no room for any real responsiveness to the actualities of other inner lives.

John Barleycorn stands at a midpoint between the overwrought and sentimental posturings of dark temperance and the morbid self-scrutiny of late modernist literary fiction, and perhaps represents a developmental stage. But its major interest for us is the vision Jack London provides of the insidious pervasiveness of addictive thinking, and the cautionary glimpse he affords into the thickets of self-deception.

Down and Out in Mannahatta

The nineteenth-century temperance tale is a distinctive literary genre shaped in conformity with the multifaceted social movement that was an energetic agent in American culture and politics for well over a century. A climax of sorts was reached in the history of American temperance reform during the Prohibition decade of the 1920s, but legacies of the movement are very much with us—in public debates about the legal status of psychotropic substances, in the exhortations of television evangelists, in the propaganda of congressional alcohol and tobacco lobbies, and in the rhetoric of drug czars, Mothers Against Drunk Driving, and the agencies that create beer and liquor advertising.[1]

Historians variously assign the beginnings of the temperance movement in America to the publication of Benjamin Rush's *Inquiry into the Effects of Ardent Spirits upon the Human Body* in 1784, or the founding of the Moreau society in 1809, or the appearance of Lyman Beecher's *Six Sermons on the Nature, Occasions, Sins, Evils, and Remedy of Intemperance* in 1826, or the formation of the American Temperance Society that same year. But what we want to take particular note of at this point is the coincidence of public concern over alcohol problems—circulated in forms other than simple religious injunctions—with the social disorders and realignments arising out of the unprecedented growth in American cities.[2] City life created complex new problems and at the same time forced a reassessment of previously accepted (or overlooked) forms of conduct that became insupportable in close quarters, or ungovernable when separated from the regulatory sanctions of everyday life in agrarian family and community settings.

Uses of drink diversified and adapted to emergent conditions. Loneliness, estrangement, and the sense of menace experienced by city dwellers were relieved by the narcotic itself and, among men at least, by the milieu in which it might be consumed—the saloon.[3] Family and community attentions that might have remedied or concealed chronic addiction disorders or patterns of intermittent excessive drinking episodes proved inadequate in the new context. The incompatibility of habitual alcohol use in the workplace with the requirements of mechanization became apparent. Agricultural workers' customary beer-breaks and old-time artisans' unannounced days and hours of idleness were inappropriate in urban shops and factories under the spur of intensifying rationalization—for both humane and pragmatic reasons. The new conditions enabled refined conceptions of anti-social behavior to crystallize, and drunkenness—whether defined in theological, moral, political, commercial, or medical terms— was widely recognized and condemned.[4]

Issue-oriented reforming zeal became a distinguishing characteristic of the antebellum mind. Platform oratory, public demonstrations, and incendiary pamphleteering flourished along with tendentious fiction; causes—whether puritanically reactionary or quixotically progressive—must have seemed to compete in the measure of their greediness. For many, the problem of alcohol abuse assumed priority, subsuming other important issues.

> Temperance reform . . . as the period advanced, became one of the most popular causes. As drunkenness lay demonstrably at the root of other social ills, or at least symbolized such aspects of rampant pluralism as immigration and the roughhouse lifestyle of the American West, the attack on intemperance appeared particularly important. How, for example, could the nation logically promote better care for the mentally ill or the imprisoned if it allowed people to drink themselves to insanity or to a life of crime? Why reform public education when children returned each day from school to besotted parents, or end poverty when the poor squandered their pay on liquor? It seemed impossible to cure national ills without acknowledging the centrality of what Rush had pointed out long before: The elimination of drunkenness would prove crucial to avoiding internal civil disruption—thus literally preserving the republican experiment itself. (Lender and Martin, 1982, p. 66)

The temperance reform movement displayed a totalizing force that was congruent with the role of alcohol in the lives of drinkers and their families. As the drink problem pervaded all aspects of personal lives, appearing to be the root cause of every conceivable social ill, so did temperance advocacy suggest that social ills would at least diminish dramatically if the reform were enacted universally. This globalist impulse was a crucial part of the movement's profile. It is no accident that the temperance exponent's depiction of the interdependence of societal and individual vitality resembles American Protestantism's own institutional vision of itself as a set of typologically nested domains; before 1840, temperance reform was most vigorously advanced by the clergy—supported in silent partnership by entrepreneurial capital.

The emergence of the Washingtonians, the organization to which *Franklin Evans* is consecrated in its concluding chapter, shifted the emphases in temperance advocacy from religious to secular, and from social and political to individual and personal.

> The Washingtonians were unlike other regiments in the antidrink army. Their emphasis was on saving individual alcoholics, not general social reform. To them, alcoholism was a problem of the isolated drinker, not part of a broader social malaise or a matter of ideological neorepublicanism. Helping the drunkard was the end in itself. At a time when the formal temperance movement was advocating prohibition, the Washingtonians remained cool toward legislatively oriented solutions to the problem. Indeed, to keep the focus on alcoholics and their problems, Washingtonians often closed their meetings to clergy and to members of other temperance organizations. (P. 75)

The resemblances between the Washingtonians and contemporary AA are compelling. Like AA, the Washingtonian movement was not "allied with any sect, denomination, politics, organization or institution"; and, while by no means exempt from controversy in its few short years, its avowed purpose was only to achieve and maintain sobriety among its membership, and to "help others to recover from alcoholism." Groups organized regular "experience meetings," borrowed from English working-class temperance practice and comfortably similar to familiar Methodist procedure, where powerful narratives of debauchery and reform were related by their very protagonists (Tyrrell, 1979, p. 163). "Sometimes these were humorous and amusing; but more frequently they portrayed scenes that touched the feelings, and often drew tears from the eyes. They were simple unadorned histories of real life, told by the participants in them, and often with an eloquence of tone and manner that stirred the heart to its very depths" (Arthur, 1871, p. 27). Women in the Washingtonians formed an active participatory auxiliary, extending the base and focusing attention on the effects of alcoholism on families.[5] The autonomous class orientation of the Washingtonians is also noteworthy.

> The Washingtonian movement was not socially homogeneous; it embraced lower-middle-class as well as lower-class people, employers as well as employees, ex-alcoholics and men and women who were lifelong abstainers, the thoroughly respectable and the not-so-respectable, evangelicals and those of a more secular disposition. . . .
>
> What distinguished the Washingtonians of the early 1840s . . . was the relative absence of the older evangelicals and wealthy and upwardly mobile captains of industry from controlling positions in the new societies. These people—by and large the leaders of the old temperance movement—were either entirely missing from the Washingtonian movement or else they took a back seat for a time in the early 1840s. The Washingtonian movement was essentially a creation of the artisan classes. (Tyrrell, pp. 160–167)

The society was a vigorously democratic endeavor suffused with a spirit of festivity and confident self-celebration. Shaped partly in response to deepening economic depression, the Washingtonians sought to provide alcohol-free recreations, entertainments, and diversions for a membership beset not just by alcohol problems but also by the enforced idleness of hard times. Parades, picnics, concerts and recitals, and participatory musical events were routine Washingtonian fare—all these in addition to the sheer entertainment value of luridly titillating, heart-wrenching experience stories. It has been suggested that an "almost obsessive . . . exuberance" must be numbered among the causes of the society's decline (Wilentz, 1984, p. 309).

As the movement's character is clarified, Whitman's attraction to the Washingtonians begins to seem less peculiar, more in keeping with his subsequent development. Whitman would have admired the drama, the narrative drive itself, behind the rhetoric of renascence and self-determination. He would have applauded the democratic base, including the efforts on behalf of women, and the implicit celebration of diversity: here was an egalitarian society which also encouraged idiosyncrasy. And he would have endorsed the group's secular emphasis that opened an aesthetic spillway for the myths, images, and symbols that would help him to establish an innovative poetics.

Two potent images control the dynamics of *Franklin Evans*. The first is the pervasive figure of the city of secrets; the second is a vision of diversified humanity commingled in a festival of liberation, as set forth in the bizarre and formally dissonant twentieth chapter. (I do not quarrel with editor Thomas Brasher's assertion that the chapter was "inserted for padding" and provides "evidence . . . of the pot-boiling haste in which *Franklin Evans* was written" [Whitman, 1963, p. 219]; but I think the chapter remains indispensable to an understanding of the novel's interior tensions and feeling tones.)

The figure of the city of secrets was not a capricious or ephemeral conceit; it was a refined and widely circulated literary image representing some of the emotional and cognitive dislocations shared by a population in the midst of rapid and profound social change. Cultural historian Alan Trachtenberg describes its lineage:

> Within the traditional image of the fallen city lay another image, less of moral condemnation and more of fear and anxiety: the image of the city as mystery, as unfathomable darkness and shadow. Best understood as a trope, a figure of speech, mystery had attached itself to the very idea of a city, as opposed to the countryside, from earliest historical times. . . . As cities throughout Europe began to expand and change their character with the coming of the industrial revolution, the trope of mystery also changed; more secular, it focused less on sin and more on a new inexplicableness in city crowds and spaces, a new unintelligibility in human relations. . . . With denser crowds, more intricate, bewildering divisions of space, sharpening contrasts between rich and poor, the nineteenth-century industrializing city seemed a ripe setting for Gothic romance. . . . (Trachtenberg, 1982, p. 103)

The city in *Franklin Evans*—the "great emporium" that will be celebrated in proud and expansive meditations in Whitman's later work—is unconditionally the malevolent city of secrets, offering neither succor nor remission. This is no "stately and admirable . . . mast-hemmed Manhattan," nor yet the euphorically exalted Mannahatta with its "million people—manners free and superb—open voices—hospitality—the most courageous and friendly young men" (Whitman, 1973, p. 475). It is instead the defining and original source of dissimulation, mendacity, swindles, masks, traps, disguises, and frauds. There is a kind of negative charisma in the energetic potency of the promise of evil; but the underlying anxiety provoked by the trope is equally real, and uncontaminated by allure. ("It is," critic Leslie Fiedler remarks, "quite what one would expect from the perpetual mama's boy, as obsessed as Dreiser by the image of the enduring mother, and the refugee from a small town, breathless before the big city with its infinite possibilities of sin" [Fiedler, 1960, p. 260]).

The antiquary Stephen Lee, one of Evans's first acquaintances in the novel, puts the case against moving to the "wicked" and "deceitful" city of secrets plainly: " 'There will be a thousand vicious temptations besetting you on every side, which the simple method of your country life has led you to know nothing of. Young men, in our cities, think much more of dress than they do of decent behavior. You will find, when you go among them, that whatever remains of integrity you have, will be laughed and ridiculed out of you. . . . It is indeed a dangerous step' " (Whitman, 1963, pp. 145–146).

Intemperance is not merely grafted onto the enigmatic city as a symptom, but likewise unfolds as a trope: city and disease act metaphorically for one another. The quality they share is dissimulation. In drunkenness as in the experience of the city, nothing is what it appears to be. This is temptation's most potent weapon, the device by which the city robs, cheats, and disfigures, and by which the demon alcohol accomplishes its seductions. Drink and the city both induce forgetfulness, so that lessons go unremembered, leaving no trace of consequence. Drink and the city are both labyrinthine—one temporal, the other spatial. The temporal labyrinth of drink draws the drinker into a present and future where the past, concealed at each subsequent turn, is made continually unusable. The labyrinthine city draws the spellbound passenger into progressively meaner streets: the "looker-on" becomes a participant, the participant becomes an enthusiast, the enthusiast becomes habituated, debilitated, and finally a corpse—the last word in worthless simulacra.[6]

In an explicitly didactic sequence, Evans visits a theater. Any affirmative metaphorical baggage is discarded as the theater here is made a sign of pure meretriciousness. Subordinated and diminished, the theater bears the same relation to the figural city—as symptom and evocation—as confusion to drink.[7] Evans is momentarily infatuated by an actress who plays her role "very agreeably" and whose beauty excites his "admiration to no small degree." After the performance, during a visit backstage (amid "dungeon walls, castles, and canvas palaces"), Evans observes this scene:

> At a little table sat a woman, eating some cheese and thick bread, and drinking at intervals from a dingy pewter mug, filled with beer. She was coarse—her eyes had that sickly bleared appearance, which results from the constant glitter of strong light upon them; her complexion was an oily brown, now quite mottled with paint, and her feet and ancles [sic] were encased in thick ill-blacked shoes.
>
> Mitchell went up to the table, (I leaning on his arm,) and engaged in chit chat with the delectable creature. He introduced me. I was thunderstruck! *She* was my charmer, of the hoyden in the farce! Her voice was coarse and masculine, and her manners on a par with her voice. (P. 158)

The eyes themselves are contaminated by the devitalizing labor of producing deception; and the language of sexual inversion marks the degree of anxiety produced by the encounter. (In the last lines of the book, Whitman writes: "I have known more than one young man, whose prospects for the future were good—in whom hope was strong, and energy not wanting—but all poisoned by these pestilent places, where the mind and the body are both rendered effeminate together" [p. 239]. At least some revulsion at boundary violation must be understood.)

"The occurrences of the night," Evans ruminates, "taught me to question the reality of many things I afterward saw; and reflect that, though to appearances they were showy, they might prove, upon trial, as coarse as the eating-house waiter [earlier mistaken for a gentleman of fashion], or the blear-eyed actress" (p. 158).

Theatrical performance and its trappings focus and essentialize life in the secret city, and both theater and city metaphorically express grievous epistemological errors. These errors are repeated in alcohol abuse. The medium is internalized—literally—and the responsibility for misconstrual is shifted from external conditions to the perceiver; but the net result is the same:

> There seems to be a kind of strange infatuation, permanently settled over the faculties of those who indulge much in strong drink. It is as fre-

quently seen in persons who use wine, as in them that take stronger draughts. The mind becomes, to use an expressive word, *obfuscated,* and loses the power of judging quickly and with correctness. It seems, too, that the unhappy victim of intemperance cannot tell when he commits even the most egregious violations of right; so muddied are his perceptions, and so darkened are all his powers of penetration. And the worst of it is, that even in his sober moments, the same dark influence hangs around him to a great degree, and leads him into a thousand follies and miseries. (P. 206)[8]

The tropes of dissimulation come to permeate the narrative itself, controlling its shape and development. Whitman's announced intention of creating instructive parables is nothing less than an invitation to enter a labyrinth of narrative secrecy, to be prepared—for all the good it does—for duplicity, obstruction, and veiled reference.

Although there is no question that *Franklin Evans* is a work of compositional patchwork, the embedded stories nevertheless have thematic affinities to the main body of material. In fact, the presence of embedded stories is, itself, a thematic transmitter, for these functionally ambiguous narrative channels obstruct, delay, and mislead, like the culs-de-sac of a labyrinth. The revenge tale of the death of Wind-Foot, the most conspicuously irrelevant of the stories, hinges on the lethal consequences of mistaken identity and misplaced trust, and brings to bear a peculiar perspective on the bonds between parents and children. The lure to destruction here is a murderous counterfeit father who simulates loving paternal protectiveness in order to secure the compliance of his victim. In another instance, disclosure that the protagonist is indeed the narrator is reserved till the telling is finished—obscuring both the tale's intrinsic meaning and its relevance to the whole (p. 200). In still another story, the explanatory function of intoxication is held back until the last lines: "But all too soon did the fatal truth come to his knowledge, that *ardent spirits* was the cause of that pallor and that lassitude. His wife was an habitual gin-drinker!" (p. 231).

The controlled withholding and disclosure of information enthralls and then confounds the reader in a formal manipulation that corresponds with recurring themes; and this congruence underscores the unity of forms and ideas. Narrative has the capacity to exert the same destructive forces as drink and the city, and has at its disposal the same labyrinthine machinery to do so. Language at

every level is capable of equivocation. Just as "seductive enchant-
ments" have been "thrown around the practice of intoxication,
in some five or six of the more public taverns," so is their very
name—" 'musical saloons' "—intended to "hide their hideous
nature" (p. 238).[9]

To find the way out of this maze of seductive intoxicants, malevolent cities, and linguistic vertigo is not easy; but with patience,
commitment, abstinence, and the cultivation of specialized interpretive skills, the way can be found. One must learn to be a reader of
clues, the elusive traces of empirical and historical truth, and then to
recast them in a compelling, new, admonitory narrative that will
subvert and supplant the malignant old one.

A clue to the epistemology of the clue is given at the conclusion
of the episode of Margaret, the murderous mulatto. Phillips, the
plantation overseer called upon to solve the puzzle of Mrs. Con-
way's mysterious death, is "shrewd," "clear-headed," and gifted in
"ferreting out a mystery." Like a rustic Dupin, he allows "no incident to escape him, small or large."

> Many of what the people would have called trifles, were noted down by
> this man; and the sum of these trifles presented an array dangerous
> enough to warrant the suspicions even of the most incredulous. The
> strange appearance of Mrs. Conway's body was remembered—how the
> bed was all disordered, as if from a violent struggle—the livid spots upon
> her neck—the open window—and the tracks of some person's feet from
> the grounds without, through the next room—even the fact that Marga-
> ret's couch had the next morning borne no sign of occupancy the pre-
> ceding night—were hunted out by the indefatigable observer. Many
> other minor and corroborating incidents were also brought to light—
> the whole making the case of the suspected woman a dark one indeed.
> (P. 228)

The dark case, developed by a clear head, is an appropriately
effective counternarrative devised to ward off the predatory dark
woman who lurks in shadows, scheming and watchful—and plainly
kindred to the novel's other markers of lightlessness, secrecy, and
deception.[10] The dark case is a mode of comprehension: it sees and
grasps-all-together, successfully interpreting a jumble of otherwise
bewildering and unusable fragments.

In his long dream of the triumph of temperance, Evans had
earlier witnessed an alternative vision of "a fair female, robed in

pure white. Under her feet were the remains of a hideous monster, in whose grapple thousands and millions had fallen, but who was now powerless and dead. The eyes of the female beamed benevolence and purity of heart; and in her hand she held a goblet of clear water" (p. 222). A welter of images are thus collapsed into one during a lengthy central set piece experienced by Evans in "a kind of trance, beholding strange things, and abstracted from all which was going on around [him]." Feverish and densely allusive, the trance is reckoned "a species of imaginative mania, which led to giving full scope to my fancy" (p. 220). The episode produces a remedial conception of the city as well:

> Methought I was wandering through the cities of a mighty and populous empire. There were sea-ports, filled with rich navies, and with the products of every part of the earth, and with merchants, whose wealth was greater than the wealth of princes. There were huge inland towns, whose wide and magnificent avenues seemed lined with palaces of marble—and showed on every side the signs of prosperity. I saw from the tops of the fortresses, the Star-Flag—emblem of Liberty—floating gloriously abroad in the breeze!
>
> And how countless were the inhabitants of that country! . . . It was almost without boundary, it seemed to me—with its far-stretching territories, and its States away up in the regions of the frozen north, and reaching down to the hottest sands of the torrid south—and with the two distant oceans for its side limits. (P. 220)

These cities of empire are the dream antithesis to the city of secrets: they are rectilinear, prosperous, free, and accessible by means of an unbound imagination. Here is a clear anticipation of the later Whitman who "contains multitudes" by virtue of poetic fiat and a spirit as expansive as manifest destiny. The white woman holding a goblet of pure water is a nurturing lyric from the unacknowledged repertoire of infantile imagery, detached from sexuality and yet wholly fulfilling of it; opposed is the crabbed, menacing figure of a dark mulatto slinking through the humid involutions of toxic narrative, obsessed with lust and destruction.

The clue must be sought out, and previously unremarked elements realigned in a serviceable configuration. The new configuration, informed by the values of purity and truth, can guide us out of the city of secrets, out of the labyrinth of intemperance. Alcohol addiction; the pernicious, convolute city; and precisely the kind of story in which we have been involved for the duration of *Franklin Evans*—these may all be left behind by the painstaking and virtuous exegete. Malevolent tropes are discarded; the forms of narrative themselves modulate. Gin and port wine are abandoned for cold water. Urban renewal turns the treacherous city into a playground. *Franklin Evans* gives way to *Leaves of Grass*.

Narrative is not a cure, but it is a method, a path toward redemption. Redemption itself lies in abstinence and better understanding —an improved epistemology—including the development of a talent for recognizing counterfeit, seeing through duplicity, and resisting snares and seductions. Like the Washingtonians, the poet of the gift offers narrative to "act as a beacon light" (p. 168), to guide the supplicant's footsteps out of the dark metropolis of addiction and into the light of communality, freedom, and imaginative prospect.

One-on-One with John Barleycorn

The critic Alfred Kazin has commented that in all the repetitions of Jack London's attempt to write "the story that he lived," he "never succeeded fully, because he never mastered himself fully" (Kazin, 1970, p. 112).

Indeed, "self-mastery," as a term denoting a bifurcated personality with one "self" that governs and another that is unruly—the two separate and yet bound in chronic enmity—correlates neatly with Gregory Bateson's description of the disorder underlying alcoholism; *John Barleycorn*, in fact, could be viewed as an extended gloss on "The Cybernetics of 'Self.' " That there was a sociocultural environment in which such a disorder could be shaped to advantage and exploited for gain helps to account for both London's extraordinary commercial success and his undoing, a suicide at forty. He was rewarded in public for exhibiting and even aggravating precisely the private faults that caused him misgiving and pain.

London borrowed the name John Barleycorn from British folk traditions where it personifies the natural history of fermented spirits, from the cultivated grain through tomorrow's hangover.[11] For London, the name comes to betoken a split-off other self, a *doppelgänger*, a secret sharer with a philosophical bent: he is a relentless truth teller, and a rhetorical chameleon who is able to convince the author to drink in spite of the primary self's best judgment. The Barleycorn-self is partly disowned, made into an oppositional not-self who wheedles and deceives, and cobbles irresistible incentives to drink out of a relentless lucidity. John Barleycorn—his instrument the White Logic, his empire the Long Sickness—is a fascinating elaboration of what Bateson has characterized as "a real or fictitious other" who goads and cozens the sick alcoholic.

The book is framed by London's decision to vote for the womens' suffrage amendment in a California election because "when women get the ballot, they will vote for prohibition" (London, 1981, p. 4). London's wife is surprised:

> "But I thought you were a friend to John Barleycorn," Charmian interpolated.
>
> "I am. I was. I am not. I never am. I am never less his friend than when he is with me and when I seem most his friend. He is the king of liars. He is the frankest truth-sayer. He is the august companion with whom one walks with the gods. He is also in league with the Noseless One. His way leads to truth naked, and to death. He gives clear vision, and muddy dreams. He is the enemy of life, and the teacher of wisdom beyond life's vision. He is a red-handed killer, and he slays youth." (Pp. 4–5)

In the space of a few short phrases we are transported from the polling place to the scene of disorderly primal perceptions. Images of mutilation and tyrannical authority are intermingled with a longing for transcendence that, though it may originate with infantile conflicts in the primal family, is reconstituted autonomously in the ontological domain. Casual scrutiny of the human condition—perhaps motivated by the traces of incompletely resolved infantile conflict—leads to the desolating discovery of limitation; relief is temporarily won by the ingestion of chemicals, but only at the cost of a weakening of critical faculties and the production of phantoms, themselves determined by the return of repressed contradictions, which are then reprojected onto the chemicals and influence the ways in which they are interpreted.

London does not render John Barleycorn in full allegorical array, yet "he" is kept a sufficient distance from the realm of abstraction and critical analysis to enable the writer to resist comprehending "him" as internal or systemic. Of course London means to dramatize the awesome power of alcohol—but here is precisely the issue:

the dramatization has already happened, not as an artistic act but as an epistemological error supported by the popular culture. Intoxication has already been identified as a quantifiable substance outside the self, an external thing that resides in bottles and barrels, with its own life force and the will to compel submission.

Early on there is an intimation, a recognition of the more correct mode of understanding:

> And, as John Barleycorn heated his way into my brain, thawing my reticence, melting my modesty, talking through me and with me and as me, my adopted twin brother and *alter ego,* I, too, raised my voice to show myself a man and an adventurer, and bragged in detail and at length of how I had crossed San Francisco Bay in my open skiff in a roaring southwester when even the schooner sailors doubted my exploit. Further, I—or John Barleycorn, for it was the same thing—told Scotty that he might be a deep sea sailor and know the last rope on the great deep sea ships, but that when it came to small-boat sailing I could beat him hands down and sail circles around him. (P. 51)

But the perceptual challenge is not taken up, and the full consequences of identity between speaker and rhetorically embodied "force" are never explored; even in the passage above distancing figural usage is not wholly relinquished: the "adopted twin brother" is too fully and firmly personalized to allow for productive vivisection. It is significant, too, in this single passage where the fiction of otherness is glimpsed, that John Barleycorn is at his facilitative best, furnishing the means for accommodation to the adult world; here, instead of shifting the blame for transgressions to John Barleycorn, London graciously shares with him credit for the harmonious interactions achieved.

Actually, alcohol is credited in large measure with enabling the young London to win his "manhood's spurs" (p. 91) and the reputation of being a "good fellow . . . buying drinks like a man" (p. 93). *John Barleycorn* is surely a key document of the ethos of male camaraderie, with as much of its content celebrating men in exclusive groups as remonstrating against excess:

> A newsboy on the streets, a sailor, a miner, a wanderer in far lands, always where men came together to exchange ideas, to laugh and boast and dare, to relax, to forget the dull toil of tiresome nights and days, always they came together over alcohol. The saloon was the place of congrega-

tion. Men gathered to it as primitive men gathered about the fire of the
squatting-place or the fire at the mouth of the cave. (P. 7)

But camaraderie is the obverse of isolation, and an excess of one
may betoken an excess of the other. As we have seen, alcohol has
been able to "thaw" London's native, presumably chronic, reti-
cence: "I was not a forward child" (p. 40), he tells us, but "it is
ever the way of John Barleycorn to loosen the tongue and babble
the secret thought" (p. 52).

Nothing if not precocious, little Jack gets drunk for the first time
at age five, and again at seven, his second "bout" at a party with
Italian farm workers: "Dominick had never seen an infant of such
heroic caliber" (p. 29). In fact, whatever is not heroic in the child's
life is at least extravagant. The life of the mind, for example, while
not neglected in these early years, seems to verge toward an obsessive inwardness: "I read everything, but principally history and adventure, and all the old travels and voyages. I read mornings,
afternoons, and nights. I read in bed, I read at table, I read as I
walked to and from school, and I read at recess while the other
boys were playing" (p. 41). Shyness, isolation, precocity, and a rich
imaginative life set him dramatically apart: "When I come to think
it over, I realize, now, that I have never had a boyhood" (p. 171).
Alcohol smooths over the fissures in sociability left by these omissions and abnormalities.

Although protesting that in these early years he did not need
alcohol, London nevertheless becomes habituated to its use, becomes, like those he describes below, a "devotee" of John Barleycorn:

> When good fortune comes, they drink. When they have no fortune, they
> drink to the hope of good fortune. If fortune be ill, they drink to forget
> it. If they meet a friend, they drink. If they quarrel with a friend and lose
> him, they drink. If their love-making be crowned with success, they are
> so happy they needs must drink. If they be jilted, they drink for the
> contrary reason. And if they have n't anything to do at all, why they take
> a drink, secure in the knowledge that when they have taken a sufficient
> number of drinks the maggots will start crawling in their brains and they
> will have their hands full with things to do. When they are sober they
> want to drink; and when they have drunk they want to drink more.
> (P. 101)

In addition to recognizing the consequences of his own drinking —including sickness, injury, and narrowly escaping death from overconsumption and drink-induced suicidal indifference—London takes note of harbingers. Again, however, the language of competition derails lucid analysis. Between the poles of victory and defeat, only some form of cheating seems to represent for him a middle ground. Nowhere does he consider discarding the metaphor of competition altogether and trying to think beyond or outside these destructive oppositions:

> In the forecastle, the oldest man, fat and fifty, was Louis. He was a broken skipper. John Barleycorn had thrown him, and he was winding up his career where he had begun it, in the forecastle. His case made quite an impression on me. John Barleycorn did other things beside kill a man. He hadn't killed Louis. He had done much worse. He had robbed him of power and place and comfort, crucified his pride, and condemned him to the hardship of the common sailor that would last as long as his healthy breath lasted, which promised to be for a long time.[12] (P. 147)

If the idea of *not* drinking—of denying the validity of the competition altogether by side-stepping it in voluntary sobriety—is ever brought forth, the hazards and unpredictabilities of sobriety are quickly adduced to ratify intoxication. In one anecdote, a physician —characterized as a sententious prig—attending London dies suddenly in his prime by the unforeseen onset of a fatal disease:

> "You see," said John Barleycorn. "He took care of himself. He even stopped smoking cigars. And that's what he got for it. Pretty rotten, eh? But the bugs will jump. There's no forefending them. Your magnificent doctor took every precaution, yet they got him. When the bug jumps you can't tell where it will land. It may be you. Look what he missed. Will you miss all I can give you, only to have a bug jump on you and drag you down? There is no equity in life. It's all a lottery. But I put the lying smile on the face of life and laugh at the facts. Smile with me and laugh. You'll get yours in the end, but in the meantime laugh. It's a pretty dark world. I illuminate it for you. It's a rotten world, when things can happen such as happened to your doctor. There's only one thing to do; take another drink and forget it." (Pp. 280–281)

This is the White Logic, the terrible clarity that joins the sense of futility with its short-term remedy, intoxication, in an inescapably persuasive manner. Whether the White Logic is to be understood as a symptom of addiction or its cause is never altogether clear; and it is not certain that London himself sees the way that elements of his cognitive universe act upon each other.

Although the contemporary disease model of alcoholism had not yet achieved full flower when London wrote *John Barleycorn,* he is nonetheless aware of what alcoholism professionals call *progression:* the onset of irreversible symptoms in predictable stages as alcoholism runs its course. One such symptom is the growing need to drink in order to negotiate routine social interactions.

> When I was in company I was less pleased, less excited, with the things said and done. Erstwhile worth-while fun and stunts seemed no longer worth while; and it was a stupid torment to listen to the insipidities and stupidities of women, to the pompous, arrogant sayings of the little half-baked men. It is the penalty one pays for reading the books too much, or for being oneself a fool. In my case it does not matter which was my trouble. The trouble itself was the fact. The condition of the fact was mine. For me the life, and light, and sparkle of human intercourse were dwindling. (P. 259)

London fails to connect his malaise directly with alcohol in this passage; the ennui, the subversion of social fictions, is attributed only to the special clarity associated with the White Logic. What is not specified here or elsewhere is the precise relation of the White Logic to intoxication. At times London seems to imply that the White Logic precedes, and therefore helps to create the need for, intoxication; at other times the White Logic seems more a consequence or adjunct of drinking. This kind of circularity—a logic of self-reference that fosters the continuation and acceleration of an irrational desire—is typical in alcoholism, and is one of the more formidable obstacles to sobriety.[13]

Only a few pages later, however, London does seem to make a connection between drink and his increasing sense of social estrangement. Perhaps the two sets of symptoms were separate in London's own mind: the punishing clarity of the White Logic with its mood of special ontological insight could easily have been in a different register—more momentous and of a superior order—from the secondary discomfort of encroaching day-to-day social irritability.

One result of this regular heavy drinking was to jade me. My mind grew so accustomed to spring and liven by artificial means, that without artificial means it refused to spring and liven. Alcohol became more and more imperative in order to meet people, in order to become sociably fit. I had to get the kick and the hit of the stuff, the crawl of the maggots, the genial brain glow, the laughter tickle, the touch of devilishness and sting, the smile over the face of things, ere I could join my fellows and make one with them. (P. 279)[14]

London also finds himself taking the significant step of beginning to drink alone: "And right there John Barleycorn had me. I was beginning to drink regularly. I was beginning to drink alone. And I was beginning to drink, not for hospitality's sake, not for the sake of the taste, but for the effect of the drink" (p. 270). And, as if acting out his own remarks on the tenuousness of justifications for drinking occasions, London finds himself fabricating excuses:

It might be the assembling of a particularly jolly crowd; a touch of anger against my architect or against a thieving stone-mason working on my barn; the death of my favorite horse in a barbed wire fence; or news of good fortune in the morning mail from my dealings with editors and publishers. It was immaterial what the excuse might be, once the desire had germinated in me. The thing was: I *wanted* alcohol. At last, after a score and more of years of dallying and of not wanting, now I wanted it. And my strength was my weakness. I required two, three, or four drinks to get an effect commensurate with the effect the average man got out of one drink. (P. 276)

Finally, he begins to experience sleep disorders—another of the potent disincentives to sobriety that plague alcoholics and the therapists who want to help them. This is one of the few passages in *John Barleycorn* in which London sounds a note of real distress uncontaminated by arrogance. Perhaps the signs of physical dissolution have moved the disease onto a plane where it is not so easily reached by the facile elaborations of denial. Perhaps London's complacency is unequal to the task of bridging the space between fanciful system-construction and an experiential reality dominated by ineffectuality, sickness, and injury.

My sleep, always excellent, now became not quite so excellent. . . . I found that a drink furnished the soporific effect. Sometimes two or three drinks were required.

So short a period of sleep then intervened before early morning rising, that my system did not have time to work off the alcohol. As a result I awoke with mouth parched and dry, with a slight heaviness of head, and with a mild nervous palpitation in the stomach. In fact I did not feel good. I was suffering from the morning sickness of the steady, heavy drinker. What I needed was a pick-me-up, a bracer. Trust John Barleycorn once he has broken down a man's defenses! So it was a drink before breakfast to put me right for breakfast—the old poison of the snake that has bitten one! (P. 297)

But the White Logic maintains its hold on London, and even at the end of *John Barleycorn,* when only one conclusion seems admissible, London declares he will continue to drink moderately—much to the dismay of his friend Upton Sinclair and others who had hoped for an unequivocal, positive reformation. To pledge anything but abstinence in the face of such a record, so much evidence pointing toward sobriety, seems lunatic. London claims that the White Logic has been laid to rest, together with the Long Sickness—the deep pessimism that ensues from too much reflection under the White Logic's sway. But this harsh methodology appears to persist, protean, exerting itself by cunning.

The White Logic is "the argent messenger of truth beyond truth," London writes, "the antithesis of life, cruel and bleak as interstellar space, pulseless and frozen as absolute zero, dazzling with the frost of irrefragable logic and unforgettable fact." The White Logic is sent by John Barleycorn, who "will not let the dreamer dream, the liver live. He destroys birth and death, and dissipates to mist the paradox of being, until his victim cries out, as in 'The City of Dreadful Night': 'Our life's a cheat, our death a black abyss.' And the feet of the victim of such dreadful intimacy take hold of the way of death" (p. 308).

The White Logic teaches that intrinsic value is absent in the cosmos and that human value systems are cobbled together out of social fictions, aesthetic illusions, and the falsifications of need. Man the White Logic tells London, is a " 'flux of states of consciousness, a flow of passing thoughts, each thought of self another self, a myriad thoughts, a myriad selves, a continual becoming but never being, a will-of-the-wisp flitting of ghosts in ghostland' " (p. 328).

There is no new thing under the sun, not even that yearned-for bauble of feeble souls—immortality. But he knows, *he* knows, standing upright on his two legs unswaying. He is compounded of meat and wine and sparkle, of sun-mote and world-dust, a frail mechanism made to run for a span, to be tinkered at by doctors of divinity and doctors of physic, and to be flung into the scrap-heap at the end. (P. 13)

These utterances, having the forcefulness of hysteria despite their common theme are pressed upon the clear-sighted, upright drinking men among us, who are then driven by the unremitting abjection of it all to more drink, suicide, or inauthentic behavioral modification. Why certain constitutions and not others are especially susceptible to encounters with the White Logic, London does not say; he does intimate that these encounters are a badge of strength, or honor, or virtue. The paradox of the White Logic is that it undercuts such ideas as honor and virtue—even strength is not to be made much of in the face of overwhelming futility. These are the "fatal intuitions of truth that reside in alcohol" (p. 305).

In other contexts such thoughts as these might be turned to religious purpose; alternatively, they could facilitate controlled, purposeful meditations on the tensions that do, indeed, inform human endeavor.[15] Mostly in London they seem a venting of anger—the product of a kind of rage against brute facts that runs, in some sense, contrary to the dispassion a prolonged immersion in futility might be expected to induce. Further, these ideas are turned to the service of art and thereby mobilized constructively against themselves in a kind of rhetorical immunization procedure intended to strengthen both writer and reader as it dilutes the toxin of terror and solitude.

The stridency, the figurative excess, the sheer quantity—there are pages and pages of the same stuff—all suggest obsessions whose essence we will never know. London's prolific literary output and—before his success as a writer—his tireless capacity for unrewarding labor suggest the goading presence of standards that can never be attained, of goals that cannot be met, of an inner ideal that is always receding despite the bounty of effort to reach it.

The White Logic cuts away superstition, reputation, and estate; its bedrock honesty might prepare the heart for a serene accommodation of the vanity of interminable striving, but instead there is only rage. This is no mind of winter, consoled by a geometric silence; there is instead another kind of whiteness—a whiteness that eclipses definition.

White men in the tropics undergo radical changes of nature. They become savage, merciless. They commit monstrous acts of cruelty that they
would never dream of committing in their original temperate climate.
They become nervous, irritable, and less moral. And they drink as they
never drank before. Drinking is one form of the many forms of degeneration that set in when white men are exposed too long to too much white
light. (P. 288)

This moment of digression into the heart of whiteness, this meditation on the disease-bearing character of tropical light, recalls a
celebrated passage in American letters on the same matter by a
spiritual progenitor of London's. In another setting we might draw
an extended correspondence between *Moby Dick* and *John Barleycorn*—with London, of course, the obsessive mariner simultaneously deformed and strengthened by the unspeakable object of his
quest. There are similarities of structure: an innocent voyage turns
ineluctably by marked stages into a consuming, malignant one; and
similarities in homoerotic subtext: London's beloved saloons replicate world-wide the Pequod's claustral intimacies. Melville's meditation on "The Whiteness of the Whale" cannot be felicitously
reduced or abstracted, for its power is largely dependent upon the
weight of detail and the force of rhetoric. But in its essence it tries
to point beyond the "pasteboard masks" that are the world's visible
things and toward the quality of the "outrageous strength, with an
inscrutable malice sinewing in it" that is Ahab's description of what
animates the white whale (Melville, 1972, p. 262). Ishmael calls it
"the demonism in the world," and speaks of an "indefiniteness"
that "shadows forth the heartless voids and immensities of the universe, and thus stabs us from behind with the thought of annihilation" (p. 295). There is an "elusive quality" which "causes the
thought of whiteness, when divorced from more kindly associations,
and coupled with any object terrible in itself, to heighten that terror
to the furthest bounds" (p. 288).[16]

For London, the terrible object with which malignant whiteness
is coupled is reason itself, and the "clarity" and "illumination" that
reason yields when applied unremittingly. The White Logic is reason
intensified far beyond its customary uses, magnified to the limit of
a nihilistic extremity—like a newspaper disaster photo enlarged to
seem merely a field of large dots—where human purpose is deprived

even of the values framed arbitrarily within communities, denied even the tragic dimension in a seizure of absurdist revulsion.

It is a logic of excess, superfluity, redundancy; it is a logic of self-consumption and endless replication, suggested by the sheer visibility of proliferation and decay in the tropics but transposed by synecdoche to comprise all of life through all of time; it is a logic, finally, less of the estrangement of distances and abstraction than of immersion and disgust.

> "He [man] shuffles atoms and jets of light, remotest nebulae, drips of water, prick-points of sensation, slime-oozings and cosmic bulks, all mixed with pearls of faith, love of woman, imagined dignities, frightened surmises, and pompous arrogances, and of the stuff builds himself an immortality to startle the heavens and baffle the immensities. He squirms on his dunghill, and like a child lost in the dark among goblins, calls to the gods that he is their younger brother, a prisoner of the quick that is destined to be as free as they—monuments of egotism reared by the epiphenomena; dreams and the dust of dreams, that vanish when the dreamer vanishes and are no more when he is not." (London, 1981, pp. 328–329)

One may listen carefully and hear again the voice of the child, creating a system of redress by inversion: the child strives, in his endless imagination, to surpass what is great and to expand what is tiny; to tear away the masks that are on received things; to turn the social order upside down; to enact the romances of storybooks; and to build an epistemology based on Chuang-Tzu's parable. " 'Once upon a time, I, Chuang Tzu, dreamt I was a butterfly, fluttering hither and thither, to all intents and purposes a butterfly. . . . Suddenly, I awaked, and there I lay, myself again. Now I do not know whether I was then a man dreaming I was a butterfly, or whether I am now a butterfly dreaming I am a man' " (pp. 321–322). In an inverted world appearances imply intoxication and drunkenness bestows pellucidity; the "intoxicating show of things" and the "cheats and snares" of the symbolic world of human construction —the received world—are remedied by the leveling, the controlling effect of draining them of color: the White Logic neutralizes differentiation, affect, resistance, spontaneity. By means of an entirely symbolic manipulation, the symbolic is deprived of its constructive power.

What remains, or returns, in the end, is memory, reverie. In the final pages of *John Barleycorn* there is a curious ramble through noteworthy saloons of the past, recollected in tranquility. Praise to fellowship is offered ("Fellowship and alcohol were Siamese twins"), and an earlier passage of the book comes to mind, describing the first drinking days, before the advent of the White Logic and the long march into debilitation. London speaks of the power of alcohol in this first encounter, and it is precisely the kind of power that a writer might want to tap, for it yields insight and emotional guidance; it is, in fact, everything that the White Logic fails to be— and its invocation helps to provide some perspective on values that seem to have been scuttled over time. This John Barleycorn, with its inscriptive power, its curiosities and harmonies, its ability to craft remarkable emblems of the human world, should be remembered as an alter ego too:

> And yet—and here enters the necromancy of John Barleycorn—that afternoon's drunk on the *Idler* had been a purple passage flung into the monotony of my days. It was memorable. My mind dwelt on it continually. I went over the details, over and over again. Among other things, I had got into the cogs and springs of men's actions. I had seen Scotty weep about his own worthlessness and the sad case of his Edinburg mother who was a lady. The harpooner had told me terribly wonderful things of himself. I had caught a myriad enticing and inflammatory hints of a world beyond my world, and for which I was certainly as fitted as the two lads who had drunk with me. I had got behind men's souls. I had got behind my own soul and found unguessed potencies and greatnesses. (P. 60)

The California women's suffrage amendment was passed in 1911, with Jack London's vote supporting it. But his hopes for an era of benevolent prohibition under female auspices have not come to pass.

Three

Rehabelletration

The three contemporary writers to whom we now turn write from personal experience of alcoholism, orthodox treatment modalities, and Alcoholics Anonymous. These writers drank the same spirits, and disorders in their lives developed along similar lines; but explanatory and artistic strategies are different for each of them—and so are outcomes.

John Berryman, I think, tried earnestly to find a way out of the alcoholic labyrinth but failed. An attempt to understand this failure is necessarily speculative, but a look at *Recovery*, the novel built out of his rehabilitation experiences, will allow us to venture a suggestion or two. Frederick Exley, it seems to me, rejected AA and therapy in general on the argument that therapy is necessarily in the service of the deforming powers of hegemonic dominance in the present social order. (Exley, it should be noted, would have disdained this vocabulary, if not the sentiment expressed.) This position offered him a vantage from which to launch powerful social and cultural criticisms, and also a set of reasons to continue to drink.[1] Donald Newlove, in memoir as well as fiction, has detailed his own history of alcoholism and recovery, and writes with zeal about the transforming power of Alcoholics Anonymous. His work will act as a link between the literary works examined in Part One and the oral AA narratives of recovery taken up in Part Two.

John Berryman

John Berryman's 1972 suicide, bearing still a residue of grievousness, must inevitably affect if not control any consideration of his work. Suicidal motives together with less decisive forms of self-destructiveness generate the central tensions in *The*

Dream Songs, so that the act becomes integral—an essential interpretive index, and not a supplemental gloss. Berryman was at once
intimately personal and intensely theatrical—at times almost exhi-
bitionist—inviting our scrutiny, sympathetic or not, of the contradictions he lived and displayed in public forums.[2]

In an essay dealing with alcoholism, it is impossible to discard
the interpretive purchase afforded by Berryman's suicide; and it is
difficult to resist assessing the suicide in the terms of a diagnosis
that, admittedly, may be reductive, misleading, or simply wrong.
There are at least two alternatives to the view that Berryman's
terminative act was undissociable from his drinking: the first is that
insurmountable psychiatric problems at depth preceded and motivated both the alcoholic drinking and the suicide; the second is that
the suicide was somehow a dignified, rational transaction within the
elaborating structure of a life in which maintaining conformity with
unalterable inner determinants had become so disagreeably complex
as to be untenable. Suicide is not generally reckoned an "acceptable" choice in our culture—but its unacceptability seems to be
founded on such radically subjective conceptions as courage and
faith, or such radically subjunctive conceptions as the fulfillment of
promise, potential achievement, reconciliations, redemption, and so
on. But if suicide may be sanctioned on grounds of intense bodily
pain or physical nonviability, then surely that response to equivalent
conditions in mental life should warrant acquiescence.

I am not competent to appraise John Berryman psychiatrically,
but the evidence as I know it points to alcohol abuse as an inseparable factor in the suicide, even if we are disinclined to try to locate
the drinking in some sort of causal hierarchy. Nevertheless, there is
considerable room for dispute over both the philosophical questions
raised by the manner of his death and the exact character of the
evidence manifested in Berryman's writings.

Berryman is a poet of ambiguity, contradiction, opacity, and play
—qualities that are installed in the poetry by Berryman either will-
fully, in the service of his art—to forestall interpretive finality, for
example, or to emphasize his own insistence upon irresolubility—
or compulsively, in servitude to complex pathology. These qualities
may be taken for signs of perversity, or nuance, or disease—or
perhaps all of these, serially or in combination. The occasional appearance of a highly lucid Berryman persona—especially in some of

the late poems of alcoholism, though sporadically in earlier work as well—further complicates interpretive surety.[3] The voice contrasts starkly with that of the sometimes impenetrable Dream Song poet —but is this transparency to be taken at face value, or is it a defense, or a new experimental pose, or a subterfuge? Is clarity in Berryman a touchstone, or a deliberate canard? Along with the disintegration of our dearest conventions of realism and sincerity, we must contend with Berryman's sheer pervasive deviousness. We are back with Jack London's Chuang-Tzu: the inspirited poet wakes up to find himself an earnest penitent. . . .[4]

In order to be able to go on at all, we will take Berryman at his word—at least some of the time—and place trust in the late poems and *Recovery;* these will be understood as the writings of a man who has chosen to try to overcome his alcoholism because it carries a lethal prognosis and because he realizes finally that he has lost control of his life: valued personal authority and artistic accountability have become problematic.

Berryman was not helped in his confrontation with alcoholism at this point of crisis, or, for that matter, during the decades-long preparation for it, by the complex imagery and rhetoric of the Dionysian which he seems to have swallowed along with barrels of scotch. The regressive longing for dedifferentiation, the fantasy of repairing a "dissociated sensibility" with linguistic adhesive tape, the antithetical promptings of his own White Logic—Berryman may have suffered these urgings deeply and authentically; but that suffering was shaped and countenanced by cultural sanction and public acclaim, and Berryman was seduced by stereotypes perhaps most vividly enacted for him in his own time by Dylan Thomas.[5] Celebrity status—exemplified by the 1967 *Life* photo essay with text by Jane Howard—seemed to come to him as a reward not for his work but for a willingness to behave badly in public.

Even after his death Berryman provided the pretext for displays of ignorant folly. In reading Saul Bellow's introduction to *Recovery,* it is a shock to come upon this perverse analysis: "Inspiration contained a death threat. He would, as he wrote the things he had waited and prayed for, fall apart. Drink was a stabilizer. It somewhat reduced the fatal intensity" (Berryman, 1973, p. xii).[6] Bellow cleverly inverts the accustomed order in the Dionysian recipe, works a romantic-aestheticist transformation of the "underlying psychiatric disorder" position on alcoholic drinking. In either instance, psychiatric or romantic, the drinker must continue to drink, whether forced by mysterious compulsions intermingled with the disorder/inspiration, or to prevent the disorder/inspiration from running out of control. The drinker is self-justified through fear of losing touch with the inchoate—access to the unconscious for healing or art—or of allowing it to madden or kill; the drinker's friends collaborate in the fiction and thereby abet the drinker's destruction.

Another problem is the presence throughout *Recovery* of many passages that are manifestly self-serving, just as in AA stories there are occasional instances of boasting—about "heroic" drinking exploits, degradation, or criminality—that seem intended to shed a potent Satanic luster around the speaker. Berryman projects an intellectual's hubris, eager to tell of the miraculous healing application of his own insights to the lives of fellow patients, or the aggrandized torments of his own striving for self-knowledge. Indeed, there is a curious kind of presumption in the stroke of fictionalization that transforms poet and English professor Berryman into protagonist Alan Severance, a medical scientist who seems to be on the brink of a major breakthrough in cancer research. That Severance also writes fiction and teaches occasional Shakespeare seminars at the local college marks Berryman's refusal to disavow completely the religion of art and his humanist's faith in the superiority of controlled intuition over empiricist violence.

Nevertheless, the interactive metaphor of scientist for poet seems to take Berryman away from "correct" thinking, in Bateson's sense of an epistemological reordering, and deeper into the intricacies of duality; it seems to permit the selective emergence of a positivist persona, a distancing technique that obstructs productive self-analysis. Thus, in his journal, some years before the time of the main narrative, Severance had written, under the heading *"Recognition of 'Self,'"* this fragment: "The whole question of how the body recognizes some substances as 'self' and others as 'not self,' which has a vital bearing on the problem of transplanting tissues and organs from one individual to another—." Reexamining this issue in the novelistic present, Severance brings home the point: "Both ways. Science, Recovery. The point is to learn to recognize whiskey as *not* my 'self'—alien, in fact, to be rejected by the desire-center in the forebrain. Job no easier than—just the same as—cancer cure"

(p. 22). Rather than helping to locate the problem systemically where it may be better understood, this language seems directed toward a logic of violent behaviorist reformation or quasi-mystical rites of expulsion. In either case the literalist rendering of the "dis-ease" of alcoholism as an entity susceptible to excision or tissue transplant is a hazardous misconstruction.

Recovery is unfinished and essentially plotless, though it is di-rected by design toward an ultimate assertion of strength and seren-ity in sobriety, and the promise of a coherence imposed by that assertion through a retrospective logic. The episodes now are a string of exploding kernels with little accumulation of weight, power, or interactive resonance. Berryman's major tactic is to have Severance confront one of his "delusions"—a key word in the book —then analyze and explain that delusion, only to make the further discovery that his explanation is factitious, a defensive masking of still deeper truth. This scheme of exfoliating disclosures veers close to a technique used in detective fiction—the elaborated erroneous denouement—and serves the same purpose: the postponement of a decisive revelation. In detective stories such a postponement usually raises the stakes and enhances suspense by diverting attention from the real villain; and, in some sense, that's just what happens in *Recovery:* Severance moves in erratic circles from apparent insight to blindness to "authentic" insight, from exhilaration to despair to the glow of welcoming truth, while his alcoholism persists unaf-fected. Severance's hospital recovery is structured like fiction, per-haps a story collection—or, more exactly, like a progression of narratively ordered confessional lyrics, hewn to the same shape but never wholly unified. As in *The Dream Songs,* language is privatized and equivocally self-referential; knowledge is mobilized to obstruct comprehension; and isolation feeds upon its own distress.

A revealing sequence finds Severance detailing a dream to his therapy group. He has written it out in advance and insists on reading the account rather than extemporizing as the therapist sug-gests. This underscores Severance's conception of the dream itself as a literary artifact, "the drama of his spectacular dream, which enshrined . . . at least three concerns": the dream is instantly a play, a spectacle, a memorial, and perhaps an essay, but always a kind of text, never a symptom or upwelling of feeling-states. Language, in multiple degrees of removal, separates the dreamer from an affective core syntax which should be the rightful quarry. Part of the dream occurs in a theater and, surprisingly, this is what the therapist focuses on at the finish—not on Severance's overt "concerns." "Do you think you could *be* the amphitheatre?" The group leader asks him. During this exercise Severance feels "remote, austere, interested but uncommitted, semi-circular, almost empty, expectationless, patient." In the course of later self-exploration, he works with his journal:

> 'It is true that I am only an amphitheatre,' he began. 'But I have a certain power of criticism over the shows that are put on in me. I don't allow shows that are merely entertaining; in fact I insist on shows that are so interesting or difficult that they are put on again and again. Only certain spectators are willing to come so often, but that is quite all right; I am a very ambitious and demanding but not a *greedy* amphitheatre. How about the seats? Not too comfortable, lest somebody drowse. Adjustable? Yes, decidedly; so long as' Here he broke off bored. (P. 94)

As well he might: the conceit has grown top-heavy. But due to unspecified causes—perhaps it is precisely the analogical hypertrophy—Severance experiences a breakthrough:

> 'Now I'm struck by: Amphitheatre *never sleeps*. An amph., it's true, doesn't *need* sleep, but I am *not* an amphitheatre
> *'I am a human being*—Alan, in rags, "thin, woebegone"—arriving where he was *"supposed"* to be—Alas! (self-pity)
>   'This dream was supposed to be a picture of my true life; but all it is *is a picture of my illness* and delusions (grandeur etc).' (Pp. 94–95)

Severance expresses surprise at his earlier comfort in the amphitheatre role:

> 'I was *surprised* Friday by my *surprise* at being so comfortable as
>   an amphitheatre; since "that is what I am."
> 'Yesterday and today, I *am still* surprised, but for a very different
>   reason: didn't the deluded son-of-a-bitch *recognize* his delu-
>   sion?!' (P. 95)

By means of a flash-forward, Berryman is able to construe the dismantling of the "amphitheatre" as a real progress in Severance's recovery:

> Many months would pass, not until one rainy morning nearly ten months later would he be able to write, with sudden realization: '. . . So long as

I considered my self as merely the medium of (arena for) my powers, sobriety was out of the question: no care for self ("You were not responsible for *yourself,*" as Vin said).

'The even deeper delusion that my science and art *depended* on my drinking, or at least were connected with it, could not be attacked directly. Too far down. The cover had to be exploded off, then the undermadness simply withered away, for lack of sustenance and protection.'

. . . Severance was a conscientious man. He had really thought, off and on for twenty years, that it was his duty to drink, namely, to sacrifice himself. He saw the products as worth it. Maybe they were—if there had been any connexion. (P. 96)

At the end of this episode, Severance—except by virtue of the flash-forward, to which we will return—is left only with a sense of failure at having misconstrued the referent of a metaphor extrapolated, under therapeutic prodding, from the written recollection of a dream. The layers are peeled away and the amphitheatre is finally interpreted as nothing more than an emblem of what in AA is termed "grandiosity"—the inflated sense of self-importance that commonly afflicts alcoholics. This may be a virtuous insight, particularly in the framework of a rehabilitation exercise; and it may be a deft stroke of textual analysis, something to enhance the credibility of a poet and critic even though in its manifest content the analysis deflates him. Indeed, such a setting may produce the paradox of an inverse relation between self-esteem and self-abasement: in his eagerness to excel at rehabilitation, Severance seems almost competitive in his avidity for degradation. But throughout the explication, there is nothing to suggest a restructuring of the relationship to drink.

And even in the advanced reflections of "ten months later," the language of opposition persists: delusion is "attacked," its cover "exploded off." Drinking remains separate from a self that can engage in combat or root for delusions as if they were truffles. What Severance perceives to be the underlying causal delusion, the interdependence of drinking and art, is represented as lying at the base of some sort of sedimented structure, or at the bottom of a deep container—always concretized to accommodate distancing. And absent and unremarked is the idea that the putative interdependency is neither cause nor root delusion, but an aftereffect, a postformation of the addiction. The responsibility of the poet, as conceived by Severance/Berryman, is derived from a refurbished, nuanced, and modernized version of the fable of the Dionysian; the fable is pressed into the service of a relentless craving and named its cause. Severance is brought perilously close to a recognition of the redundancy of drink in these last paragraphs, but will not commit himself. The "if" overhangs his progress, leaving him in a sort of speculative limbo. He is able to confront isolated moments in the past and disconnected crises in the day-to-day routine—and perhaps gloat over exegetical triumphs, or enjoy the occasional cathartic sob. But it is all without the needed unifying theory, the sources of which reside in the restructuring that AA identifies as "spiritual awakening."

Incoherence and an intensified sense of estrangement are the consequences of this deficiency, whether in regard to literary production or an evolving sense of self. The morbid capacity to isolate temporal kernels (a liability masked as a skill), the ability to deny the cumulative force and interactive purport of moments in his life history and to refuse to acknowledge recurrence and pattern—these elements that simultaneously circumscribe the protagonist's condition and preclude the development of plot in *Recovery*—are consonant with Severance/Berryman's own sense of profound isolation from available human communities. The sense of isolation is virtually universal in middle stage alcoholism, and is often referred to by the term "uniqueness" in AA. In addition to a range of practices and patterns of speech, the very fact of AA as a social entity is predicated on redressing the damaging consequences of these pathologically heightened feelings of uniqueness.[7]

Severance, in his journal, makes a list of "reasons" for repeated "slips" in his efforts to remain sober. He includes "false pride," "teen-age instability and overconfidence," "despair," "lifelong rebelliousness vs all programmes (AA) and rules and superiors," "refusal to admit failure," "grandstanding," and "whim." Each of these may be taken as an aspect or outgrowth of the sense of isolation, with the drinker placing himself in a relation of contrasting extremity against a uniform mass, whether local or universal, of his fellows. Again, Severance is uncomfortably close to a truth but unable to make the step of recognizing his "reasons" as symptoms of addiction rather than causes. Isolation is a corollary of addiction —and the primacy of addiction is persistently evaded in *Recovery*.

The qualities that set him apart as a poet, presumably, are felt to be continuous with the qualities that determine his slips and make him unsusceptible to the curative properties of Alcoholics Anonymous—or any other sobering influence. "Almost unbearably depressing," he writes, and then carries the same insufficient logic over into self-fulfilling prophecy: "I need a programme of iron. AA will never do it."

But if AA's shabby, quotidian spirituality—small-scale and bereft of passionate amphitheatricality—and the necessary anonymity of AA's democratic mutuality are inadequate to Severance's rarified need, he will nevertheless entertain the therapeutic possibility of a wholesale religious and cultural transformation: "Maybe becoming a Jew?" (pp. 132–133).

"The Jewish Kick"—the projected title of an unwritten chapter—is a leitmotif in *Recovery* and a key emblem for the hapless, diffuse, unproductive striving that gives the novel its only real unity of feeling. Becoming a Jew, for Severance, seems to hold the promise of an end to estrangement and the fulfillment of auguries (*"All* has pointed HERE," p. 73). In his journal Severance lists a set of affinities to Jewish culture, history, and theology, and adduces as well his taste for *Commentary,* "Jewish girls," and Isaiah Berlin. An early Berryman short story, "The Imaginary Jew," is attributed to Severance and placed in evidence. In the story, a Gentile narrator is mistaken for a Jew and forced to recognize thereby the irrationality of persecution and the arbitrariness of social alignments; he assents to his exclusion as it becomes more real to him than the benign (to Gentiles) but equivocal order to which he has submitted in the past. Written in 1945, the story pleads for recognition that the virulence of bigotry can never be directed or contained, but saturates and infects whatever it comes near. In his notes on the making of *Recovery,* Berryman says of "The Imaginary Jew," "I identified at least with the persecution" (p. 241).

It may be that, by 1970, this was the significant attraction of Judaism for Berryman. As a signifier for oppression, exile, and separation, Judaism had become merely a bloated emblem of Berryman's drunkenness—the persecutory misconstructions of a backsliding alcoholic metaphorically inflated to global dimensions in a grandiose rhetorical gesture as pathetic as it is presumptuous. Berryman/Severance casually embraces the erroneous popular belief in Jewish exemption from alcohol problems ("And: Jews *don't drink!*," p. 73), but this has the character of an afterthought; it is really the promise of continued exclusion that attracts. Berryman must maintain a problematic, antithetical relationship with his cognitive environment, and the solitary, intransigent god of symmetrical *lex talionis* (the law of punishment in kind) meets his need to press for a religious accommodation that cannot be satisfied. "I feel apprehensive—joy but—can I? Will He receive me? I know I must prepare, be ready for all" (p. 73). "The Jewish Kick" transparently replicates the poet's painful, intricate, and multivalent relationship to his father, a suicide: "Mercy! my father; do not pull the trigger/ or all my life I'll suffer from your anger/killing what you began," Berryman writes in Dream Song 235 (1969, p. 254).

The father, like the primal Jewish god, is harsh, punitive, uncommunicative; desired and unattainable; simultaneously source and reciprocation for a mercurial malaise compounded of terror and guilt. The Jewish Kick, then, may be seen as a regressive impulse transposed to the register of historical aspiration. Longing for assimilation of the self to a culture of antiquity acts as a mirror to the imaginative lost bliss of an infantile utopia, and a ground for the reconciliation or amendment of the tortuous paradigms of contemporary disjunction. The Jewish Kick is, finally, only an emblem of persisting unrealities, and is probably efficacious only as a channel of diversion.

None of this is to suggest that Berryman's psychological dilemmas were unreal or somehow trivial; there is no way of knowing what outcomes might have been possible had Berryman found his way to a comfortable abstinence from alcohol. It may be that his suicide was an inevitability; but perhaps self-torment could have been diminished and the germ of self-annihilation successfully confronted, contained or negated, in a psychic ambience purged of fragmenting, deceptive, isolating addiction.

We can be fairly certain from *Recovery* and the later poems that all of Berryman's considerable skills were mobilized in subtle defense of the addiction itself—sometimes apparently in the cause of burrowing deeper, sometimes in the name of art, and sometimes through an obscurely motivated but willful process of mystification.[8] Representation of the full complexity of lived experience, poetic overdetermination, psychological explanation at unlimited depth—

each of these activities may generate exactitude and luster, but may also be pressed into the service of obfuscation, diversion, or delay. Berryman built and inhabited his own labyrinth, but obsessive complexity at length outdistanced utility and aesthetics; maps became useless in time, precluding either access or escape. The refuge became a prison and, finally, a tomb—one of those hulking, ungainly monuments that catch the eye in cemeteries and provoke bemusement at the folly of unfathomable ideals, and pity for the vanity of human endeavor.

Frederick Exley

"Why does man feel so sad in the twentieth century?" Walker Percy asks at the start of *The Message in the Bottle*. And again: "Why do young people look so sad, the very young who, seeing how sad their elders are, have sought a new life and freedom with each other and in the green fields and forests, but who instead of finding joy look even sadder than their elders?" Part of Percy's response is this: "There is a difference between the way things are and saying the way things are" (Percy, 1975, pp. 3–45).

With linguistics and semiotics as his pretext, Percy is revisiting the charred landscapes of the White Logic—London speaks of "cosmic sadness"—bearing witness to the chronic bewilderment engendered by a symbolic order's pasteboard masks, suffering again the consciousness of secrets and deceptions that dispirited a youthful Whitman. William James too spoke of the problem not in terms of violence or extremity but of *sadness:*

> Old age has the last word: the purely naturalistic look at life, however enthusiastically it may begin, is sure to end in sadness.
>
> This sadness lies at the heart of every merely positivistic, agnostic, or naturalistic scheme of philosophy. Let sanguine healthy-mindedness do its best with its strange power of living in the moment and ignoring and forgetting, still the evil background is really there to be thought of, and the skull will grin at the banquet. (James, 1982, pp. 140–141).

It is sadness that governs Frederick Exley's *A Fan's Notes*. I want to make only a few observations about the ways Exley refigures the problem of the disjunctions among factual and symbolic structures —the sources of sadness—and to try to get some sense of how these disjunctions and the weird logic of alcoholism collaborate with one another in the production of a peculiar kind of despair. The narrator of *A Fan's Notes,* "Fred Exley," is a contemporary epitome of the "sick soul," and James would have been proud to display him alongside other examples of spiritual torment in the specimen-case of *The Varieties of Religious Experience.* The richness of Exley's artistry does not require a modification of the diagnosis: it might be argued that the dense, rigidly well-crafted prose is, itself, a sign of retaliatory aggression from the depths of this wounded writer's heart and mind—in the same way that a mirror-gloss on the shoes might portend sadistic proclivities in a policeman.

A Fan's Notes is an intricate machine of redress and reprisal; an afflicted artist's apology; an analytic attack on educational, thera-peutic, and business institutions; a stained and laminated section of the mind of an alcoholic who is also perhaps paranoid; a senti-mentalist re-creation of willed defeats and invited humiliations; a celebration of literature and football, or literature *as* football; a collection of jokes; a poison-pen letter to the American popular culture; and a failed accommodation of a dead father. Exley's verbal precision—and it is often possible to admire his elegantly built sentences on the strength of architectonics alone—enables him to move freely among modes and genres, to collapse parody, confes-sion, encomium, and critique together, or to overlay irony with romance and pathos. His manner felicitously subsumes a startling variety in content, and holds multiplicity, even contradiction, in suspension.

The novel opens as Exley suffers a seizure in a bar just before a televised football game; it ends with the "infinitely sad" dream of a violent encounter between Exley and a cluster of loutish American youths who mock him. The related paradigmatic themes of compet-itive violence and compulsive self-destruction control almost all of the intervening incidents, whether ludicrous or pathetic. Football, for Exley, is "an island of directness in a world of circumspection."

> In football a man was asked to do a difficult and brutal job, and he either did it or got out. There was nothing rhetorical or vague about it; I chose to believe that it was not unlike the jobs which all men, in some sunnier past, had been called upon to do. It smacked of something old, some-thing traditional, something unclouded by legerdemain and subterfuge. It had that kind of power over me, drawing me back with the force of

something known, scarcely remembered, elusive as integrity—perhaps it was no more than the force of a forgotten childhood. (Exley, 1968, p. 8)

Football is atavistic, nonverbal, violent, manly, competitive: we are back on Oedipal turf, it seems, a bounded field of fantasy on which Exley can enact a complicated identification with his charismatic dead father by means of an obsession with Frank Gifford and the New York Giants. Exley calls parodic commentary and runs plays amid the stools and tables in bars, but burlesque reduction is the most he can make of his aspiration. Earl Exley—overestimation shimmering even in his royal name's contrast with the prosaic "Fred"—is forever out of reach, and the son must endure a condition of irreversible eclipse. The guilty overextensions of filial ambition must be, by their very nature, dismembered through disease and failure—and so they are: throughout *A Fan's Notes* Exley is stricken and sickened and ridden with disease; he is beaten, abused, humiliated, imprisoned, hospitalized, shocked with electricity and insulin, made insane, impotent, dysfunctional, and vicious. Near the end, Exley suffers an epiphany. Having involved himself unnecessarily in a street fight, he recognizes that he has been part of a long-term "conspiracy against anonymity," a conspiracy with no hope of success.

> The knowledge caused me to weep very quietly, numbly, caused me to weep because in my heart I knew I had always understood this last and most distressing reason, which rendered the grief I had caused myself and others all for naught. I fought because I understood, and could not bear to understand, that it was my destiny—unlike that of my father, whose fate it was to hear the roar of the crowd—to sit in the stands with most men and acclaim others. It was my fate, my destiny, my end, to be a fan. (Pp. 356–357)

The dream of fame motivates *A Fan's Notes,* from an epigraph on that subject out of Hawthorne's *Fanshawe* through the concluding recognition of obsessive disaccord. But while the germ of the dream is in the tense triangulations of the primal family, the agent of its confirmation and nurturance is the despised American popular culture—with its greed and compromises and petty villainies that Exley sees on every hand and reviles without respite.[9] Exley recognizes the deforming potency of received culture, evidenced, for example, in the formulaic insipidities of television, the moral depravity of cigarette manufacturers, and the commodification of sexuality with its attendant challenges to personal integrity; but he seems incapable of any response but invective.

Perhaps invective is the only conceivable channel for the transformation of his frustrated rage, controlled as he is by the combined force of the toxified culture he detests and an irreconcilable psychosexual principle—an eroticized, murderous, infantile envy. If, somehow, the fame he craves were to be thrust upon him, it would be conditioned upon accommodation to the very commercial culture that he loathes and reviles without quarter, demanding the renunciation of the critical capacities which have allowed his individuation and informed his artist's malaise in the first place. In either sphere, the resolution he craves would entail the ultimate erasure of the subject himself. The situation—the nested set of situations—is wholly untenable, and Exley is driven into a remorseless circularity in the effort to break free.

His rejection of therapeutic solutions is vigorous. In order to maintain his integrity during terms of residence in mental institutions he adheres to "Exley's Law of Institutional Survival." "It was simple. It involved leaving the mind as malleable as mush and letting them impose any inanities upon it they wished" (p. 76). A mask of docility is worn to protect the damaged but still-precious self.

> Was I, too, insane? It was a difficult admission to make, but I am glad that I made it; later I came to believe that this admission about oneself may be the only redemption in America. Yes, I was insane. Still, I did not despise my oddness, my deviations, those things which made me, after all, me. I wanted to preserve those things. To do it, I had to get out of that place. Then—as quickly as the rage had come over me—I suddenly knew how to do it. I would be the kind of man I suspected the world wanted me to be. I played the game with all the loathing the benevolent doctor had put at my command. (Pp. 88–89)

To resist therapeutic compromise is, in fact, to resist insanity, in the inverted formulation we have seen played out in recent years through countless documents, fictions, and events.[10] This position has merit but, with the added complicating factor of addiction, it overlooks a crucial point. In addiction, all of the resources of the organism are drawn upon for the protection and gratification of the craving. Addiction will make use of skills and talents, of circumstances of birth and education, and of modes of deviation as well, whether manifested as neurotic misery, ordinary unhappiness, or voluntary transgression. No dimension of the subject's being is exempt from subversion to the primacy of the addiction, and the addiction will be served unless that primacy is deposed, often at grave peril or cost. Addiction often prevails over existence itself, much to the dismay of counselors and therapists—whether or not they concur with a radical analysis of the politics of psychotherapy.

Exley recognizes his own compulsion to repeat acts of a violent or at least emotionally painful, self-destructive character, but he seems unable to grasp that his addiction in some measure structures this repetition, that it short-circuits rationality and self-interest, that it lends itself only to the reinforcement of existing "reasons" for drinking and supports the work of generating new ones.

His "reasons" tend to collide. At one point he writes, "I lived in many cities . . . and with each new milieu my jobs grew less remunerative, my dreams more absurdly colored. To sustain them I found that it took increasing and ever-increasing amounts of alcohol" (p. 71). Elsewhere his explanation veers toward the neurasthenic hypersensitivity model we saw advanced by Saul Bellow to explain John Berryman's alcoholism. "After a month's sobriety my faculties became unbearably acute and I found myself unhealthily clairvoyant, having insights into places I'd as soon not journey to. Unlike some men, I had never drunk for boldness or charm or wit; I had used alcohol for precisely what it was, a depressant to check the mental exhilaration produced by extended sobriety" (p. 26).

Out of the muck of his first thirty-five years, Exley does, however, fashion *A Fan's Notes,* and much of the novel chronicles his painful journey toward artistic control, from the first imitative efforts contrived out of a hapless love of literature, through the tedium of painstaking exercises in prose construction and the drama of torched manuscripts, to the promise of a preliminary version of the very book in hand. But even this achievement is tainted as Exley, at least sporadically, regards his own literary inwardness with contempt. Writing seems to him at times to be a kind of reaction formation, characterized most significantly by its inappositeness to the sporting worlds of Gifford, Steve Owen, and Earl Exley; membership in the "sickly aristocracy of letters" (p. 67) is small comfort for condemnation to life in the bleachers.

At other times, however, Exley recognizes gratifying therapeutic and diagnostic dimensions of his writing. He is able, at last, to examine dispassionately the causes of his repeated institutionalization, to treat seriously a fellow inmate's advice that he look inward for the circumstances of his "malaise," and not heap the full burden of accountability upon a defective social order:

> For the first time Paddy the Duke's smug admonition that I had best ask myself what I was doing at Avalon Valley had begun to haunt me, and taking a deep breath, I started fearfully into the past in search of answers. In many ways that book was this book, which I wasn't then ready to write. . . .
>
> I was on a writing kick and was by then unable to stay the rush of words. I wrote in joy and in anguish, wrote giggling like a madman and with the tears streaming down my face, wrote at times so exhilarated that I daren't move for fear of discovering I was incapable of what I seemed to be getting down on paper. (Pp. 329–331)

This is the critical event in Exley's autobiography, the point of synthesis toward which his story has been tending, and around which all the preceding bits of narrative now coalesce; it is a point where relief from the past is afforded and direction for the future indicated in a fearful and exultant simultaneity. Teeming with presence, and uttered in the language of religious conversion, this is the supreme moment of comprehension, the "taking all together" in which the mysterious disjunctions between experience and language are erased, errors redeemed, vagaries contained, and utopian longings made susceptible to realization.

Exley enjoys this narrative apotheosis without relinquishing his drinking and, presumably, *A Fan's Notes* is the happy issue. By the end of the novel, Exley seems to have achieved a kind of self-assurance based not in a false identification with celebrity novelists and screen stars spun out of fantasies of debauchery and adulation, but in the emergence of his authentic writer's identity. Still, the final words of the novel reassert obsession and the compulsion to repeat, dreamed but vivid brutality, and an overpowering sense of futility; redemption itself is contaminated.

Exley's rejection of Alcoholics Anonymous is explicit. He has attended AA meetings under duress while a patient in the mental hospital:

For a time, when I was incarcerated in the nuthouse, I had gone at the "request" of the authorities to the meetings of the hospital branch of that organization, but . . . the "confessions" had embarrassed me. . . . though AA professed to the contrary, it was evangelical in character; and . . . I could not bring myself to call daily upon God for help in abstaining, feeling that if there were a God I'd like to hold him in reserve for more lovely mercies than my own sobriety. Quite frankly, it was more than this: I wasn't sure I *wanted* to live without an occasional binge. (P. 26)

Alcohol for Exley, although justified as a tranquilizer, fuels the rage and frustration that in turn appear to be the generator of his art —and in this sense, it *is* his inspiration. Without the alcohol-induced discontinuities, obsessions and repetitions, oscillations of mood and affect and intention, the "perspectives by incongruity" to which he gains access, Exley would have no subject worthy of his craft, no drama of a vitiated life around which to fold the elegant fabric of his discourse. Alcohol carries with it a guarantee that intimations of bad news will come true, then dulls sensitivity to the point where bad news can be borne. The Dionysian mythology is propagated, and the supply of contradiction at the heart, sufficient to underwrite the status quo, is insured by locating all responsibility outside the self-system. A sort of pure or primordial self—a reference self, a complaining self, a damaged, artistic, transcribing self—is felt to be helplessly imprisoned at the very heart's core by the intersecting trajectories of capitalism, consumerism, philistinism, greed, shame, and lust.

Or so Exley would have it; and even if we find his explanations implausible, we are obliged to reacknowledge the potency of the myth. Beyond that, there are only speculations over imponderable questions, and evaluations based on the most subjective of standards. Can substance abuse be legitimated or even understood on political grounds? What might have characterized Exley's achievement in an alcohol-free parallel universe—or would there have been any achievement at all? Must therapy mark the death of an authentic, intransigent literary art?

At this juncture—Exley's personal variants on the dilemmas confronted by any addicted person at the prospect of relinquishing the addictive substance—we are propelled back to where we began with Exley, perhaps no wiser than before. But there is still an uncanny effect produced by the rediscovery of these words, exchanged between Exley and Paddy the Duke as the latter is ending his hospitalization in order to resume ordinary life on the outside:

> At this point he did a ludicrously dramatic, profoundly unsettling thing. Looking slowly over his right shoulder, then over his left—and in either case there was nothing there but blank wall—he brought his head down close to mine and whispered, in the most chillingly solemn tones, and almost choking on the words:
> *"I've discovered what alcoholism is."*

Here Paddy the Duke and Exley pause to allow suspense to build. At last, Paddy reveals his discovery:

> "It's sadness."
> *Sadness?*
> "Sadness?" I exclaimed gleefully. "Why, Paddy! You're a goddam drunken Irish poet!"
> I laughed and laughed and laughed.

Exley is lost to the truth of Paddy the Duke's insight, in part because it is rhetorically unsatisfying, but primarily because it directs his attention to complementarity—a mode Exley is unprepared to accept.

> "I'll never drink again!" he said, perfectly exultant. "Don't yuh get it? And in that way I'll never cause another's sadness!" Then he rose and looked directly at me. "And tell me, wise guy—ain't that enough?" . . .
> . . . I will live my life a lesser man . . . for having walked away from him. Despite his arrogant ignorance, Paddy *was* a poet. It was when he was leaving the next day that I discovered this and understood that Paddy had come to a kind of truth, the truth for himself, a truth that to this day will not let me divorce the term *alcoholism* from *sadness.* (Pp. 113–115)

Sadness is the signifier of absolute contradiction and the act of philosophical resignation that accompanies a willingness to dwell alongside that contradiction. Alcohol actually drives a wedge between a subject and its sense of embodiment or systemic emplacement while counterfeiting a capacity to bind men together: what might have become ordinary sadness is transformed to mawkish self-display, aggressive rage, or suicidal abandon. Sadness is transferred from the drinking self to others who witness, and who must then confront the contradiction between the unhinged drunk and the potential or remembered entity presumed lost, perhaps past salvation, within. Contradiction feeds on itself, shape-shifting and mercurial, until it is arrested by the redemptive gesture of capitulation.

Donald Newlove

In Leo and Theodore, the Siamese twin protagonist(s) of *Sweet Adversity,* Donald Newlove has crafted a remarkable vehicle for the concretization of the self-division, multivocality, and sense of estrangement that characterize alcoholism. The dialogic twins, whose story carries them from cooperative long-term bibulousness to enduring, harmonious sobriety in AA, embody along the way most of the common forms of resistance to sobriety—the varieties of denial, the shrill assertions of autonomy and freedom, and the fatalistic embrace of self-hatred. By contrasting the twins' respective degrees of advancing sobriety—and it is advancing even in spite of temporary relapse—Newlove is able to examine a nuanced range of attitudes and behaviors, and circumscribe a typical alcoholic career. *Sweet Adversity,* for all its eccentricity, is a paradigmatic account of alcoholism's progress according to the standard AA model, and represents the dialectic of recovery as it is described—or prescribed —by AA. As such, it may be seen as a kind of antitype of *A Fan's Notes.*

Thus, Leo, sober, late in the book, chides a fellow artist about drinking and composition: " 'Creative boozing. Gibberish with haloes. Slumping in your chair, year after year, plunged into yourself, a few witticisms now and then, a bit of charm, but always with the creative mind working its auroras. Religious boozing, really spiritual. I'm familiar with it' " (Newlove, 1978, p. 599). What is debated here is the question of the priority of an alcohol problem— whether any psychological disorders can be addressed adequately when complicated by addiction. Newlove elsewhere affirms his position in restating an AA maxim: "When alcohol chooses *you,* you drink because you drink" (Newlove, 1981, p. 111). Leo's words, again in response to the resistant artist, might be deliberately contrived to oppose Exley's rejection of sobriety:

"I was always sayin' if I could just have one hit song—I'm a songwriter —and get some clothes an' have enough to squire some chick around . . . or land a rich widow or a grant or fellowship, *then* I might take care of my drinkin' problem. After all the other problems, right? After cigarettes and fat and the rent. I didn't know that if I took away the bottle problem, the others'd evaporate—if I can get over my self-defeating *yes, but's* and *poor me's*. If you take the bottle outta your life, you *won't* get canned . . . you will regain your sexual vigor, you may gain partial custody of your children, your constant depression and nameless anxieties will lift, *and* the deetees, and what's absolutely sure is that your composing will get a helluva rise. Alcoholic composers do their best despite their booze habit, not because of it." (Newlove, 1978, p. 603)

Much of the second volume of *Sweet Adversity* may be taken as an ethnographic collage of Alcoholics Anonymous in contemporary New York City, with special attention to a debunking or inveighing sort of rhetoric, whether uttered by the twins or by any of the legion of minor characters.[11] The ideas about alcohol, the tone of knowingness, polemical and sometimes abrasive, and many phrases and formulas in the passage above are typical of spoken language as it might be heard at any AA meeting marked for "beginners" in the program. Persuasive principles are transformed to personal anecdotes in the effort to enlist recognition and identification; in the above passage Leo performs in small for the composer what Newlove enacts for the reader in narrativizing his own self-division, addiction, and recrudescence.

The author's unequivocal, enthusiastic partisanship and his desire to bear encyclopedic witness to the effectiveness of AA are of considerable interest for nonliterary reasons; nevertheless, *Sweet Adversity* seems occasionally to veer out of artistic control. A key purpose for Newlove—like Whitman and some other temperance advocates of an earlier time—is the subversion of a popular conception of sobriety as prosaic, flat, anti-ecstatic, inhospitable to play and fantasy, unsusceptible to eros; it is to this end that Newlove places before the reader a novel that both endorses sobriety and is energetic, goofy, theatrical, ardent, and broad. But, despite its dexterity and brilliance, *Sweet Adversity* at times feels bloated and maundering. The incessant chatter between the twins may tire and disorient the reader; hyperkinetic, exclamatory prose, laced with improbable, sometimes surreal images, runs toward a kind of redundancy under the burden of its reiterated themes and sheer quantity. In this, it may be said, the novel re-creates rather than reports the AA experience.

In this final edition, *Sweet Adversity* is already a revision of two earlier novels, *Leo and Theodore,* and *The Drunks.* As Newlove tells the story in his memoir, *Those Drinking Days,* he becomes obsessed with achieving an ever-intensifying stylistic density for his manuscript novels:

> *More light?* I decided to read through the entire manuscript on pot. . . . The first page fell apart. Too many words! My God, this is very dull. You've got to compress down to the tightest telegraphic style that will still carry the life of the sentence. . . .
>
> . . . The published volume was light-filled to bursting, enormously lively, and for most readers unreadable without great attention to every syllable. If the reader tried to skim even one page, he'd fall asleep. (Newlove, 1981, p. 100)

With the passage of sober time, however, the obstacles placed before the reader begin to disturb Newlove, and he seizes happily upon the opportunity to revise again for paperback reprint, this time clarifying and "loosening" his prose: "With joy I set to and loosened the telegraphic style with several thousand corrections, titled the work *Sweet Adversity* and at last saw in print the drug-free novel about alcohol that sprang from my life's earliest memory . . ." (p. 101).

Those Drinking Days recapitulates in just over one hundred pages the story told in *Sweet Adversity*'s 665 pages, and does so in language that, while energetic, is altogether lucid and direct. In this third revision—counting two versions of *Sweet Adversity* as the first and second—Newlove represents himself alone, an un-twinned speaker before an imaginary convocation of writers who are "companions in alcohol" and possess a "genius for self-deceit" (p. 10). He is, then, addressing an assembly of his peers in a gesture of professional accord, and his "talk" is a cautionary exhortation, contrived both to solidify his own position and to enlist the sympathetic emulation of others. He adheres to the proposition from the AA "Big Book" that has become a recipe for crafting a talk: "Our stories disclose in a general way what we used to be like, what happened, and what we are like now" (Alcoholics Anonymous, 1976a, p. 58).

Like most spoken AA narratives, Newlove's story dwells on what happened before the onset of sobriety; stories about drinking seem to be more interesting than stories about not drinking, and certainly contain higher levels of dramatic contrast, abjection, violence, unpredictability, and, occasionally, euphoria. Newlove's re-creation of his drinking days culminates in an astonishing and relentless seven-hundred-word sentence that describes with graphic particularity the predicament of the soi-disant writer as hopeless alcoholic:

> I was now almost two-hundred-and-fifty pounds, red-faced, losing my hair, given to cankers and bleeding gums, pissing so often I'd use the kitchen sink instead of the toilet, finding my teeth and nails loosening, a victim of boils, my eyes were pink, tired, dry and scratchy and the lids stuck together with mucal infections when I slept, my ears rang and were supersensitive to any scrape or screech, I gave off a staleness no soap could reach, my crotch and privates were forever raw and cracked, I was losing the hair off my shins and pubis, my bellybutton stank and I shaved my armpits to no avail, my nose enlarged and capillaries split, the insides of my ears were raw from flaking, my tastebuds wore smooth at the rear and grew apart up front so that I oversalted everything and could awaken before breakfast only with a tablespoon of salty redhot pepper sauce, my skin eroded in the creases and rubbed off in balls, I had a relentless belch for years from an ulcer, a liver that was trying to get out of me and die somewhere, shitty shorts and wine gas that ate holes in them, breath that even I couldn't stand, sweaty cold soles and shoes I hid under the bed or in a closet if I had a girl overnight, I gasped during any kind of work and could not get a full breath even while typing, I began waking up nightly on the floor having convulsed out of my bed, wine trots were common and many hours spent near tears trying to wring out my bowels on the toilet, my pulse seemed to clog and dribble, I had false angina in my upper left chest regularly, someone was going to shoot me in my rocker so I moved it away from the window, but I had a waking dream for ten years of my brain exploding on impact, I would lie unable to wake up but not asleep while strange men moved about my kitchen and livingroom (they weren't there), I could not sit comfortably in any position, I smelled of stale semen between my weekly or biweekly baths, my gut bubbled day and night and I'd try to overfeed it to sleep, I had a two-year sinus cold and special flu attacks that laid me out near death, I was hoarse and kept grenadine and lime syrups and pastilles for my hack, my memory self-destructed on the phone and I'd hang up wondering whom I'd talked with or what arrangements we'd made, I often cried out 'I'm coming!' when no one had knocked and I answered or heard

the phone ring when it was long gone for nonpayment, I felt fungoid and sexually impotent for two years, I slept poorly and kept a pot by my bed in case I couldn't make the sink, I heard people laughing while I was trying to read and metallic sounds that echoed, my overswollen brain rolled liquidly in my skull, I got dizzy rising from chairs or picking up a handful of spilled coins, must I mention mere headaches and hangovers, my bloody morning shaves with safety razors, the mental fog that had me leaning on the table trying to remember my middle name, my age or where I just laid down my glasses, my rage over a dropped spoon or lost paper lying before me on my desk or the endless drinking glasses snapping to pieces in the sink, my poor handling of kitchen knives, and the strange yellow bruises that wandered up and down my arms and biceps, my harsh nerves and weird fugue states on paralyzingly gruesome images of loved people, the living dead people standing around my bed for hours on end (they're worth two mentions), and just normal things everybody had like wanting to sob all the time, especially over the sunset beaches and bathers in the vodka ads, divorced wife and kid, any lost piece of cake or life or unearned joy as a pretext for just letting go with a thirty-minute screamer on the couch, and such clinical loneliness that my cat talked to me. (Newlove, 1981, pp. 65–67)[12]

The progressive revisions tell a story of parallel aspirations toward sobriety and narratability; or of the striving toward a single state of mind that is marked by clarity, consistency, integrity, purposefulness, and full possession of an operative memory and wakeful receptivity, all of which contribute to a capacity for the coalescence of meaning from acutely observed succession and resemblance. Although Newlove declines to abandon a transcendental impulse, made most evident in his effort to assimilate to sobriety some of that privileged intensity earlier reckoned the genius of alcohol—and this primarily by means of a continuing desire for compression—his language in *Those Drinking Days* is largely freed from figures and arabesques of the sort that inform *Sweet Adversity*.

Intricate metaphoric sutures are repudiated. The complex baggage of twinship and its host of dependent allusions and associations are tossed aside in favor of telling directly and precisely what happened; lyricism gives way to reportage; interpretation takes a back seat to self-sufficient detail. The change of conceptual and stylistic priorities coincides with what is called "getting honest" in AA—deciding, or learning, or being somehow compelled, to recognize and expel the resident processes of denial, dissimulation, rationalization, and self-deception. *Those Drinking Days* represents a therapeutic advance over *Sweet Adversity*, a rejection of meticulously developed literary strategies that have become likewise the means of alcoholic self-justification. Movement toward "the thing itself," however faltering, is seen as the rhetorical equivalent of probity in self-evaluation.

Newlove's inventory of liabilities is the pivotal point in his memoir; this prose culmination attempts to replicate the moment of recognition of limitation, the deposition of the primacy of addiction, the defeat, in a word, that AA calls "hitting bottom." In Newlove's story this is not a single dramatic event—as it may be, according to AA case literature—but rather the achievement of critical mass that produces a qualitative change at a precise but unspecifiable moment in the accumulation of horrors.

The story finally achieves conformity with AA orthodoxy, but also retains the shape of the life itself, and neither narrative form nor the historical record are desecrated in the process. "Reality" is served, and so are the competing claims of the personal and the social, and the ideals of consonance and persuasive conviction. In serving the needs of the group, Newlove reinforces its structures and, at the same time, consolidates his own integrity, not telling the story dissidently, but telling it well; marking himself as representative and therefore, for the moment at least, exemplary.

Two

AA Narratives
of Recovery

Four

Paradigm and Form

The life story of AA's charismatic co-founder William Griffith Wilson has been told many times in works of varying scope, insight, and complexity; by biographers with different perspectives and degrees of sympathy; and often by Wilson himself, both orally and in writing. There are book-length accounts, such as Robert Thomsen's popular *Bill W.* (1975) and AA's collectively prepared "official" life, *'Pass It On'* (Alcoholics Anonymous, 1984). Ernest Kurtz brings the discipline of a trained historian to bear in *Not-God* (1979), his superb interpretation of Wilson's life and work and the growth of AA. More recently, in *Getting Better: Inside Alcoholics Anonymous* (1988), journalist Nan Robertson has retold the story acknowledging Wilson's personal shortcomings—his egocentricity, his "womanizing," and his moodiness. Robertson projects a credible "contemporary" Wilson for readers taught by popular psychology and mass media that wealthy, powerful, and celebrated figures must be inwardly troubled and less than exemplary.

Wilson told his own story at AA meetings and frequently shared it with outside groups as well in the course of his unabating pursuit of acceptance for the fellowship; printed versions of his talks appear in *Alcoholics Anonymous Comes of Age* (Alcoholics Anonymous, 1957) and the pamphlet "Three Talks to Medical Societies" (Alcoholics Anonymous, n.d.), as well as in the Big Book.

These versions of Wilson's autobiography, and the manner in which he customarily delivered it, have percolated throughout the secondary literature on alcoholism and treatment, sometimes with misleading consequences. Hostile or ill-informed critics of AA have been willing at times to attribute Wilson's idiosyncrasies to the membership at large. His personal dramatic white-light conversion, for example, continues to trouble even some in AA, who regard it as inconsistent with their own conceptions of dignified spiritual bearing, if not frankly embarrassing. Robertson mentions Wilson's "old-fashioned" prose style, his use of "outdated slang," and "a boosterist tone of onward and upward with George Follansbee Babbitt" (Robertson, 1988, pp. 72–73). Critics of AA seem disposed to believe that this manner is current, widespread, and obligatory.

Clues to specific influences on Wilson's development as a writer and thinker are sparse. His prose style is a mid-1930s transformation of a popular inspirational strain in American writing, dating from the early eighteenth century or earlier, bearing the marks of Franklin's influence (perhaps traceable to Bunyan), codified in the mid-nineteenth century by, among others, T. S. Arthur (*Ten Nights in a Bar-Room*, 1966; *Six Nights with the Washingtonians*, 1871), and carried on in our own time by legions of authors of self-help and popular psychology tracts numbering among them such figures as Norman Vincent Peale, Fulton J. Sheen, Joshua Loth Leibman, M. Scott Peck, Leo Buscaglia, and Dr. Joyce Brothers.[1] The style is aggressively plain with frequent irruptions of a kind of oafish "poetic" excess to signal a surplus of emotion.

Wilson's manner of speaking and writing bears an interesting correspondence to that of the advertising executive Bruce Barton; indeed, a suggestive affinity is evoked by a glance at the two men's roughly contemporaneous careers. Both were schooled in American ideals of entrepreneurial success and pursued those ideals uncritically and without cynicism; and both seem to have felt an insufficiency at the heart of the dream. In *The Man Nobody Knows* (first published in 1925, the same year that saw the publication of *The Great Gatsby*), Barton reinterpreted the life of Christ for the instruction and profit—both spiritual *and* fiscal—of modern businessmen. "Every one of His conversations, every contact between His mind and others, is worthy of the attentive study of any sales manager," Barton said of "the most popular dinner guest in Jerusalem" (Barton, 1952, pp. 12, 72). Wilson, too, would link therapy, persuasion, and the bottom line, and bear witness in his writing to a confluence of the pragmatic and the inspirational in the language of modern advertising. The key difference between the two may be that Wilson ultimately discovered a product he really believed in.[2]

"Jesus hated prosy dullness" (Barton, 1952, p. 94). Justified by this proposition, Barton provided a recipe for effective communication in business that includes conciseness, simplicity, sincerity, and repetition—values that also inform AA stories. Whether Wilson was acquainted with Barton's work is uncertain, but we may be sure that he knew Franklin, the novels of Horatio Alger, and had at least passing familiarity, from his small-town Vermont Protestant upbringing, with the available range of popular Christian inspirational literature.

Wilson's life story has attained a certain canonical character in AA, and acts as an important reference point, both historically and structurally. There is an agreeable congruence between the story of Wilson's recovery from alcoholism and the story of AA's origin. The founding of the program was no afterthought, conceived by Wilson subsequent to becoming sober, but rather was integral to his attainment of sobriety: the precise moment of AA's conception is said to have occurred when Wilson, feeling that his own sobriety depended on communicating with another alcoholic, located Dr. Robert Smith in Akron, Ohio, and pressed upon him the message of submission and spiritual regeneration. At this juncture—according to the celebration of these events in the literature—Wilson's own sobriety was reinforced, Dr. Bob's was inaugurated, and Alcoholics Anonymous was set in forward motion. A complex typology will henceforth obtain.

The hard-won principle of complementarity seems to require an externalization or enactment in order to be made complete; while symmetry thrives on isolation, complementarity entails interactivity, communication, the realization of systemic self-definition. The historical moment of the formation of the fellowship—the bonding of the two founders in Akron—becomes analogous to the moment of commitment to the group in the life of the individual alcoholic, whether that individual is Wilson or a contemporary. As the world before the formation of AA was without recourse for suffering alcoholics, so is the individual before commitment to AA desolate, hopeless; and as the world since AA came into being is a place where the alcoholic may now find a happy alternative to institutionalization and early death, so is the individual subsequent to commitment to AA liberated from degradation, mental chaos, and despair. The story of the group's origin is a historicized and globalized version of the story of personal recovery; a subject telling his or her own story according to the pattern set out by Wilson is making a complex affirmation of identification with the founding member, with others who align themselves in the same pattern, and with the group as an emergent entity in the social world. Pivotal biographical and historical decisions coincide and inform and deepen one another.

It is appropriate that we should look at the first telling of Wilson's life, "Bill's Story," from *Alcoholics Anonymous* (1976a), originally published in 1939. We might hope to find here a certain ingenuousness and freedom from political and propagandistic motives that could have contaminated later tellings. As with our earlier readings, this task should provide useful historical and conceptual data as well as interpretive leverage.

The Big Book, as *Alcoholics Anonymous* is universally known among the AA membership, was first published only four years after the founding of the program. Wilson wrote the expository first section of the book, to which "Bill's Story" acts as prelude and representative anecdote, and carefully edited the rest—a collection of twenty-nine first-person stories of recovery by other AA members —for consistency of content and tone (Alcoholics Anonymous, 1984, p. 200). Since 1939 the Big Book has been modified twice— personal stories were added or deleted—"to represent the current membership of Alcoholics Anonymous more accurately, and thereby to reach more alcoholics," but "Bill's Story" and opening arguments have remained unchanged (Alcoholics Anonymous, 1976a, p. xii).

Alcoholism is, among other things, a disease of authority; that is, centers of power and patterns of hierarchy are misperceived or displaced; existing social and political structures are repudiated or ignored; the texture of human life—situated, interwoven, dependent—is denied; phantom authority is arrogated to the self, and a potent illusion of control is contrived to maintain the false edifice. It is a therapeutic commonplace that "alcoholism is a family disease," that in the lives of the children of alcoholics there is no center, no certainty, no trust, and often a consequent disposition to seek remedy for these omissions, ironically, with drink and other drinkers.[3] It is not coincidental that the theme of disrupted relationships between fathers and children has appeared often in the substance as well as the circumstances of the literary productions we have looked at, and that social criticism by our writers has tended to take the form of self-marginalization—a disconsolate withdrawal from the field of conflict. Such withdrawal seems to entail the hazards of encroaching mental dissolution and a deepening of social isolation by exclusion or institutionalization.

Euripides' Pentheus most clearly exemplifies diseased authority at a certain exaggerated allegorical pitch: in the presence of the new god, whom we have likened to the deforming power of the compulsion to drink (either within the subject or pervading the subject's mental ambit), Pentheus rejects both the majority voice of his constituency and the traditional wisdom of antiquity in deference to the dictates of, first, his inadequate, solipsistic version of organizational propriety and, then, his own hallucinations. If Thebes were conceived as the mind of an active alcoholic, Pentheus could be likened to a mental process that insists on its ability to exert control, all evidence to the contrary. Authority here is diseased because its self-reflexive capacities are shorted-out, and false lines of demarcation are drawn.

Bill Wilson's craving for praise despite his avowal of the need for "the destruction of self-centeredness" (Alcoholics Anonymous, 1976a, p. 14) and his struggles between anonymity and celebrity, humility and self-aggrandizement, are well documented, often reported by Wilson himself. It is not difficult to understand why "Bill's Story" has pride of place in the Big Book. By virtue of its position as well as its name, the primacy of "Bill's Story" and of Bill himself within the fledgling fellowship is asserted; "Bill's Story" becomes, as if by fiat, *the* paradigmatic story for AA—at the same time that the singularity of its author is emphasized. Bill writes his personal evolution as a chronicle of the reapportionment of authority—and it is not inappropriate by AA standards for the renovated self to affirm its own worth as refurbished moral and behavioral principles strengthen in recovery. But at the same time the story bears traces—perhaps necessarily—of those defiant gestures of repudiated "self-centeredness," an inescapable residue of persisting conflict. An apparent contradiction develops in the paradox of "prideful humility." This problem in one form or another is often examined in the course of AA discussions, and is often confronted by AA speakers as they experience a tension between the ambiguities of self-display and the commitment to service.

"Bill's Story" begins during the First World War, a time made emblematic here by virtue of social dislocation and stark polarities. "War fever ran high in the New England town to which we new, young officers from Plattsburg were assigned," Wilson writes, "and we were flattered when the first citizens took us to their homes, making us feel heroic." Worldwide military conflict mirrors Bill's doomed, escalating efforts at inward self-determination; "fever" immediately suggests loss of control. There may be a measure of justification in war itself, but "war fever" denotes discord overlaid with delirium, hallucination, rashness, and the unpredictability of high heat. "Flattery" makes note of the capriciousness, the mutability of social definition, and the narrator's susceptibility to it; he is made to feel heroic, but the feeling is without depth; his situation is altogether spurious.

"Here was love, applause, war," says Wilson. "I was part of life at last" (Alcoholics Anonymous, 1976a, p. 1). But definition is supplied from without; the sense of participation in "life" is felt to be a social fabrication, false as flattery—although even a false sense of participation provides recompense for intimated antecedent lone-liness. Loneliness and estrangement are only suggested here, and the recognition of any possible underlying social dysfunction is barely a whisper of implication. The role of social pathologies in the genesis of individual alienation will never become a powerful theme in AA: the restoration and maintenance of sobriety and the develop-ment of autonomous moral responsibility are reckoned sufficiently formidable tasks from which, within the framework of the group, engagement with social and political critique could only prove a distraction. This is not to suggest that AA members are incapable of, or enjoined from, social activism—only that platforms for it must be found outside of the boundaries of the program. Nothing in AA precludes activism of any sort, provided it is not chemically buttressed, but this is beyond the reclamatory therapeutic AA pur-view and irrelevant to it. There is, of course, a quietist strain in AA philosophy that might br construed as socially prescriptive; but probably more to the point is the utopian content of "mere" sobri-ety: survival of passage through active alcoholism renders humble acquiescence to everyday life contrastingly so superior to dissonance of any sort that willful disruption is, for many, wholly unthinkable.

Still, almost all AA stories contain at least germinally the suggestion of radical social dysfunction.[4]

Throughout the first part of "Bill's Story," a terminology of reciprocal motion is employed—both vertical (rising and falling) and horizontal (arriving and departing)—corresponding to repetitions of the cycle of sobriety and relapse. In the opening paragraphs Bill goes away to the war in Europe and returns to enter the world of Wall Street. The rise and fall of stocks and money values becomes a leitmotif, replicated in the fluctuations of commercial enterprises, in business successes and failures. As the story progresses, the alternation between sobriety and drunkenness reflects these first oppositions, but then absorbs their force and takes on a life of its own. A qualitative change in Bill's drinking coincides with the stock market disaster of 1929; as before, institutional history and personal history coalesce, this time in the single image of the Crash: "I was finished and so were many friends. The papers reported men jumping to death from the towers of High Finance. That disgusted me. I would not jump. I went back to the bar. My friends had dropped several million since ten o'clock—so what? Tomorrow was another day. As I drank the old fierce determination to win came back" (Alcoholics Anonymous, 1976a, p. 4).[5]

The movements of alternation and opposition persist. Bill and his wife leave New York and return twice (pp. 3, 4); Bill repeatedly makes and loses money, finds and loses jobs (pp. 4, 5). He begins to follow the course described by Bateson: prideful periods of "fierce determination" are inevitably succeeded by demoralizing drinking bouts; symmetrical patterning is established, and a predictable intensification, which is deterioration in social and therapeutic terms, occurs:

> Liquor ceased to be a luxury; it became a necessity. "Bathtub" gin, two bottles a day, and often three, got to be routine. Sometimes a small deal would net a few hundred dollars, and I would pay my bills at the bars and delicatessens. This went on endlessly, and I began to waken very early in the morning shaking violently. A tumbler full of gin followed by half a dozen bottles of beer would be required if I were to eat any breakfast. Nevertheless, I still thought I could control the situation, and there were periods of sobriety which renewed my wife's hope. (P. 5)

The alcoholic tremor itself becomes emblematic of the forward and backward movement that dominates Wilson's life. He refers to his diminished capacity to "surmount obstacles," and refers to his worsening condition as a "plunge into the dark" (p. 8). Despair is likened to a "morass" and to "quicksand" (p. 8). Bill apprehends his newly sober friend Ebby in terms of retroaction: "escape" and a "recapturing [of] the spirit of other days" (p. 9); Ebby looks to him like someone "raised from the dead" (p. 11). Even after he attains sobriety, Bill is bedeviled by oscillating apprehensions: "waves of self-pity and resentment . . . sometimes nearly drove me back to drink" (p. 15). But the emergent AA program, "the path that really goes somewhere" (p. 15), cuts at the perpendicular across the futility of tidal repetition.

"The path that really goes somewhere" denotes the breaking of the patterns of symmetrical escalation, and also implies a new construction to be placed upon the idea of success. Success, for Wilson, had been a version of the common received American ideal: "My talent for leadership, I imagined, would place me at the head of vast enterprises which I would manage with utmost assurance" (p. 1). "Business and financial leaders were my heroes" (p. 2).[6]

The success Wilson craves is, of course, meretricious; things are not what they seem. "Unhappy scenes" are enacted behind the façade of Bill's "sumptuous apartment"; the boom of the twenties, "seething and swelling"—like something about to explode, or like a nest of larvae—is built on "paper millions" (p. 3); both are symptomatic of an erroneous system of values based in misperceptions. Like the deceptions that lured Franklin Evans into the tortuosities of a corrupt city, success, for Wilson, is a lethal illusion. The initial false materialist utopia of "vast enterprises" is counterbalanced, by the time we reach the end of "Bill's Story," with a realized utopia of a starkly different character: "We have it with us right here and now. Each day my friend's simple talk in our kitchen multiplies itself in a widening circle of peace on earth and good will to men" (p. 16).

The friend referred to is Ebby, a former drinking buddy who had achieved sobriety in the Oxford Group, a Christian revival fellowship with Lutheran pietist roots;[7] the "simple talk" is Ebby's presentation of the Oxford Group's "simple religious idea and . . . practical program of action"; and the practical program of action, which had yet to be filtered and codified as the Twelve Steps of

Alcoholics Anonymous, was a rudimentary and somewhat folksy six-point procedure:

1. We admitted that we were licked, that we were powerless over alcohol.
2. We made a moral inventory of our defects or sins.
3. We confessed or shared our shortcomings with another person in confidence.
4. We made restitution to all those we had harmed by our drinking.
5. We tried to help other alcoholics, with no thought of reward in money or prestige.
6. We prayed to whatever God we thought there was for power to practice these precepts. (Alcoholics Anonymous, 1957, p. 160)

Bill searches out elemental images to convey Ebby's overwhelming impact. In his conversion, Ebby's "roots grasped a new soil" (Alcoholics Anonymous, 1976a, p. 12), and not the quicksand or morass of before; his arrival is "an oasis in this dreary desert of futility" (p. 9); Ebby is "on fire" (p. 9), his effect "electric" (p. 14). Ebby enables Bill to stand "in the sunlight at last" (p. 12), to make contact with the "Father of Light who presides over us all" (p. 14). "Scales of pride and prejudice fell from my eyes," Bill writes. "A new world came into view" (p. 12). "How blind I had been" (p. 13). Unifying, clarifying images of light replace dissonant figures. Bill's language stabilizes, takes on a compelling self-assurance. "There was a sense of victory, followed by such a peace and serenity as I had never known. There was utter confidence" (p. 14).[8]

The final third of "Bill's Story" is taken up with a presentation of the Twelve Steps in a nonprogrammatic, anecdotal manner. For example, Steps Eight and Nine, in their present, codified form, read:

8. Made a list of all persons we had harmed, and became willing to make amends to them all.
9. Made direct amends to such people wherever possible, except when to do so would injure them or others.

In "Bill's Story" these Steps are narrativized: "My schoolmate visited me, and I fully acquainted him with my problems and deficiencies. We made a list of people I had hurt or toward whom I felt resentment. I expressed my entire willingness to approach these individuals, admitting my wrong. Never was I to be critical of them. I was to right all such matters to the utmost of my ability" (Alcoholic Anonymous, 1976a, p. 13).

At last on that "path that really goes somewhere," Bill celebrates the "fellowship [that] has grown up among us of which it is a wonderful thing to feel a part." Families are reunited, "feuds and bitterness of all sorts" have been wiped out, and "business and professional men have regained their standing" (p. 15). Out of the abjection occasioned by ever-accelerating alcoholic degeneration, a new concept of success emerges based on the fellowship of complementarity rather than symmetrical competition, sympathetic human interaction rather than self-serving instrumentality, voluntary gift giving rather than compulsory market exchange, unity rather than fragmentation based on misperception. In prospect is the restoration of an Edenic natural harmony—not unlike the proto-Dionysian moment in Nietzsche—uncongenial to greed and the hunger for power.

"Bill's Story" falls into three parts, anticipating and enacting the narrative formula that Wilson will provide in Chapter 5 of the Big Book ("How It Works"), and establishing the pattern for almost all stories of addiction and recovery to come: "Our stories disclose in a general way what we used to be like, what happened, and what we are like now" (p. 58). This is not the first occurrence of trichotomy.

The phrase "love, applause, war," in the opening paragraph of "Bill's Story" is the first of a succession of Wilsonian triads that often seem to control his rhetoric and his thought. He writes of "remorse, horror, and hopelessness" (p. 6), of "happiness, peace, and usefulness" (p. 8), of struggles that are "strenuous, comic, and tragic" (p. 16); he studies economics, business, and law (p. 2); on a camping trip he carries "three huge volumes of a financial reference service" (p. 3). He describes three similar failed attempts to control his drinking before learning the impotence of will power against the craving for alcohol—an important premise in AA doctrine. There are deltoid icons, as well: Wall Street is a "maelstrom" (p. 2), and financial speculation is like a "boomerang" (p. 2).[9] At a moment of illumination, Wilson feels the melting of an "icy intellectual mountain" in whose shadow he has lived (p. 12). His victorious sobriety is like a wind from a "mountain top" (p. 14). Images of trajectory form a subset of the imagery of triangulation. Bill's health declines "like a ski-jump" (p. 7); he is "catapulted" (p. 8) into a "fourth dimension" of existence—which, presumably, subsumes and transcends the first three.

Trichotomy does not stop with "Bill's Story," but seems to saturate the program. The AA "Preamble," read at the start of every meeting, characterizes the fellowship as composed of men and women who share "experience, strength and hope" with each other for the sake of sobriety. "Experience, strength and hope" may be understood as a recipe for story production in speaking before groups, each element matching a phrase from the more explicit Big Book story formula, "what we used to be like, what happened, and what we are like now." A bit of AA folk wisdom has it that each speaking occasion consists of three parts—the message you planned to give, the message you gave, and the message you wish you'd given. Some members like to recite a three-part figure, playing on the language of Step Two, that claims to summarize a probable line of spiritual development in AA: "I came; I came to; I came to believe" (a triplex variant of the duplex "bring the body and the mind will follow"). A similar model of progress is elaborated by Wilson in a chapter of *Alcoholics Anonymous Comes of Age* called "The Three Legacies of Alcoholics Anonymous: Recovery, Unity, Service." The words *recovery, unity,* and *service* are identified with the three legs of an equilateral triangle inscribed in a circle, a standard AA emblem, often with two triangular *A*'s in the center.

Several common AA slogans are made up of three words: "Easy does it"; "First things first"; "Keep it simple"; "Keep coming back"; "Listen and learn." New members are told they would do well to avoid "people, places, and things" associated with their drinking habits. The main points of the Twelve Steps of AA are sometimes reduced to three and rendered formulaically, as "I can't; He can: let Him," the third-person pronouns denoting, of course, the Higher Power. The Serenity Prayer, now generally associated with AA and cognate entreprises, has frequently made its way into the printed literature of the program and is reproduced on one side of a widely distributed wallet-sized card produced by AA World Services. The prayer is often recited in unison by a group, sometimes as an alternative to the Lord's Prayer, to close their meeting.

The Serenity Prayer, too, is tripartite: "God grant me the serenity to accept the things I cannot change, courage to change the things I can, and wisdom to know the difference." Acceptance, wisdom, and courage are congruent with experience, strength, and hope, and name qualities or attitudes of mind that may be rightly aspired to with respect to the past, the future, and the present; the suggestion of a rudimentary but unitary approach to a method of deliberation over warring ideas is also present.[10]

Alcoholism is characterized throughout AA as "a threefold disease—physical, mental, and spiritual." "The clear message," Ernest Kurtz writes, "is that there is a unity in human life, ill or healthy. The parts of the human experience are so interconnected that to suffer disturbance in one is to suffer dislocation in all; and in recovery, all must be attended to if any is to be healed" (Kurtz, 1979, p. 202). (In characterizing the AA speaking process, one AA member remarked, "This is just pure religion, medicine, and psychology.") By Kurtz's account, the comprehension of this triform creates the basis in a receptive subject—the alcoholic in defeat—for the idea of the "wholeness of accepted limitation." This wholeness is conceptually near-of-kin to what we have identified as epistemological reintegration under the principle of complementarity.

In "The Number Three in American Culture," Alan Dundes (1980) has documented the pervasiveness of trichotomy as an important principle in the occidental cognitive landscape, operative in every expressive and regulative mode, from the rhymes and games of children to the most rigorous rules of "scientific" procedure. The play of this native category in "Bill's Story" and throughout AA is normative, then, somehow deeply familiar, in no way odd or exceptional; a similar array of triforms could probably be produced using everyday-speech-based evidence from any ideologically informed institution or association. In AA, however, trichotomy seems to play a special, integrated, structural role.

To put it succinctly (and in only three words): trichotomy subverts symmetry. In a list of generalizations about the uses of the number three as a native category, Dundes observes that "a third term may be the result of splitting a polarity," or that a third term may be formed by the "merging or combining of two terms so that one has *A, B,* and *AB.*" It is then only a short step to the production of a third term that depends upon the two members of a polarity but is not contained by them, or even necessarily and specifically implied by them. The third term may be qualitatively distinct, a synthesis that is something other than a mean or a sum, but is perhaps a transcendence. Analogies from genetics or chemistry might be suggested, but they would fail, as always, to convey the intricacies of symbolic process, especially in its characteristic ability to elude or defy categorical rigidity. Transcendence, in the imagination, is not answerable to falsifiability strictures, or even to brute facts.

I want to suggest that the imposition of a dynamic trinary structuring process on the relentless binary alternation of alcoholic hopelessness creates the possibility for new patterns of cognitive practice to develop through accustomed linguistic channels, primarily the narrative modes. We have witnessed the deterioration of binary opposition when a distinction between symmetry and complementarity was approached; similarly, the mere introduction of trichotomy as a concept to be comprehended in a binary framework challenges the very utility of that framework and forces an expansive renovation of the cognitive system. Similarly, the process of reformulating the materials of experience according to the three-part story format encourages retroactive overhaul of the meanings of the experience. Duality may continue to inhere in the recollected materials of experience; but trichotomy, introduced as a function of the narrative discourse, becomes the mainspring of reinterpretive options.

In the pragmatics of alcoholic progression, "hitting bottom" compels the recognition of a need for a term beyond the two terms governing the malevolent machinery of symmetry and escalation. Optimally, the term "sober" will transcend and replace the opposition "drunk/not drunk," and an entire new range of possibilities will become available for the creation of an amended life. Wilson's defeat is total in "Bill's Story"; the binary schema in which he has operated confidently at first and then with diminishing faith is finally undone even before the propitious advent of Ebby: "I had met my match. I had been overwhelmed. Alcohol was my master" (Alcoholics Anonymous, 1976a, p. 8). At this point, Wilson has "taken" the First Step, and is on the way to "working" the all-important Second and Third, a triangulation that points, like an arrowhead, toward the further particulars of AA practice. Trichotomy has been superimposed upon the dualistic world, opening it up, offering the possibility of liberation from the bondage of dualist epistemology.

Further, trichotomy in its transcendence of dualism now comes to represent a new unity; a sense of personal integrity accompanies the new cognitive amplitude. Dundes recalls the "special case" of trichotomy, the triune, or "three-in-one." Christian theology furnishes our best and most familiar example in the Trinity, of course, but other instances might be mentioned: the *Moirai* of the Greeks —Atropos, Clotho, and Lachesis, the "Fates"—or Freud's early model of the mind. It may be that trichotomy is a cultural and not a natural category, but there is a fact of physical structure underlying the symbolic force of the triune: the immutability of the triangle. Given sides of a determined length, the triangle alone among polygons can assume only one shape. Its unity is its strength, which is unassailable, granted the integrity of the limbs. The rigid three-part structure of the AA narrative forces upon the narrator a restriction of scope and limitation of focus; benevolent but austere confinement to a particular form and direction is imposed. The structure encourages an evocation of AA's utopian ideology without concession to any alternative narratorial designs.

AA story structure is strikingly like the narratologists' definition of the "minimal story": "A narrative recounting only two states and one event such that (1) one state precedes the other state in time (and causes it); (2) the second state constitutes the inverse (or the modification, including the 'zero' modification) of the first" (Prince, 1987, p. 53). Adherence to this structure in AA is virtually irresistible, not only because of the weight of AA convention, but, underlying that, because of the structure's conformity to a "natural" conception of narrative and communicative felicity. As Dundes abundantly demonstrates, the play of threes may be noted in our everyday suppositions about causality, and in our ideas of dynamics and individual and corporate success.

In "Bill's Story," the initial state is the dualistic world of binary thinking and symmetrical drinking behavior with all of its concomitant disasters and pains culminating in total abjection; the modifying event is a succession of educating experiences resulting in a "spiritual awakening" that allows Bill to understand that he may choose his own conception of a Higher Power to which to relinquish his impotent and now defeated will; the second state is the "widening circle of peace on earth and good will to men" inhabited by Bill as a consequence of submission to the Higher Power. That circle expresses the unifying power of complementarity, offering a conceptual alternative to the jagged symmetricality of the initial state, in consequence of the restructuring of basic cognitive categories. An intensity of crystalline light symbolically erases the shadows of false discriminations enjoined in binary perception; trichotomic process points the way to the remedial attitudes, symbolic strategies, and cognitive positions that we have subsumed under the idea of complementarity. The emblem of the triangle inscribed in a circle becomes an instruction concerning how to think: trichotomy or dialectic is to be employed within a horizon of inclusiveness, community, integration, and acceptance.

The shape of an ideal AA narrative is easy enough to chart on the basis of what we have determined so far. The representation of the first state, "what we used to be like," must illustrate the qualities and repercussions of alcoholic drinking, and suggest the untenable situation devolved around the speaker as a consequence of symmetrical thinking. Important themes must include the sense of isolation, and the amelioration of loneliness initially provided by drink; the recognition of false conviviality; the material and spiritual privations of addictive drinking; the development of despair and the fear of madness based in the inability to reverse what has become an obviously suicidal progression. The middle-term event, "what happened," must emphatically if not dramatically represent the mental changes that led the speaker to discover AA, the growth of a willingness to comply with the ideology of AA, and the advent of authentic, unbroken sobriety. The second state, "what we are like now," should evince in some measure its own inverse relation to the first state. Now composure has replaced mental disorder; material losses have perhaps been replaced, but these gains are understood to be far less valuable than the spiritual enrichment which has occurred; real conviviality is discovered in fellowship and service through the enactment of AA principles.

Schematically, the story looks something like this (the conditions above and below the central event, "spiritual awakening," mirror each other):

1 Salutation ("Hi, my name is X and I'm an alcoholic")

2 First state
(what we used to be like):
$\left\{\begin{array}{l}\text{isolation/self preoccupation}\\ \text{false conviviality}\\ \text{reasons for drinking}\\ \text{privations}\\ \text{despair, fear of madness}\end{array}\right.$

3 Event (what happened):
$\left\{\begin{array}{l}\text{discovery of AA—skepticism, slips}\\ \text{"spiritual awakening"}\\ \text{acceptance of AA—authentic sobriety}\end{array}\right.$

4 Second state
(what we are like now):
$\left\{\begin{array}{l}\text{serenity, rule of reason}\\ \text{material and spiritual restoration}\\ \text{reasons for not drinking}\\ \text{real conviviality}\\ \text{service/community orientation}\end{array}\right.$

5 Coda

The content of "first-state" representations, "what we used to be like," may be, to some degree, quantified, itemized, and pressed into a scheme of narrative functions after the manner of Soviet folklorist Vladimir Propp (1968). First-state narrative often matches the classical models of alcoholic progression that have been deployed from Benjamin Rush to E. M. Jellinek. Rush showed alcoholic deterioration on a descending scale, like marks of decreasing temperature on the "Moral and Physical Thermometer" he devised for graphic impact; an 1846 Nathaniel Currier lithograph depicts "The Drunkard's Progress from the First Glass to the Grave" in nine steps; Arthur's 1854 novel *Ten Nights in a Bar-Room* (1966) measures alcoholic decline at the community level in the intervals between the narrator's successive visits to the intemperate Cedarville; Jellinek counts out forty-three characteristic symptoms divided according to degree of severity among a Prodromal, a Crucial, and a Chronic phase. The triplet follows on the heels of a prealcoholic period.[11]

Predicated upon the speaking subject, the forty-three symptoms of Jellinek's phase model act as a tentative inventory of functions for the construction of AA stories. The predictive value of the list for narrative analysis is limited in that there is no obligation on the speaker to include any function or cluster of functions; the list is like a menu from which the speaker may "select"—in harmonious patterns, capriciously, or not at all. Many stories told by "high-bottom" drinkers—that is, those who were able to achieve sobriety before experiencing extreme degradation—are structured as if functions had been selected only from the Prodromal phase; others range throughout the list, apparently at random, and certainly without regard to an idealized model of progression. Most AA stories are top-heavy with occurrences of these functions. Still, the functions differ from Propp's kind of morphological schedule in two important ways: they are not bound to occur in any order and they do not, of themselves, produce a story.

Middle-term representations, the "event" or statement of "what happened," are rarely as abrupt, intense, and precisely framed as the moment in "Bill's Story" when Ebby's question, *"Why don't you choose your own conception of God?"* instantly liberates Bill from the "vestiges" of "prejudice," enabling him to build a private spirituality not bounded by rejected theological orthodoxy and to submit to an authentic Higher Power. "That statement hit me hard. It melted the icy intellectual mountain in whose shadow I had lived and shivered many years. I stood in the sunlight at last. *It was only a matter of being willing to believe in a Power greater than myself. Nothing more was required of me to make my beginning.* I saw that growth could start from that point. Upon a foundation of complete willingness I might build what I saw in my friend. Would I have it? Of course I would!" (Alcoholics Anonymous, 1976a, p. 12).

Wilson's "spiritual awakening" is presented with considerable restraint in its Big Book version. In *Alcoholics Anonymous Comes of Age* (1957), Bill tells of a moment of revelation that matches the dramatic conversions recorded in the *Varieties* of William James. James, in fact, has identified the appearance of vivid white light—"photisms"—as the distinguishing mark of a virtual subgenre of mystical experience. If we accept the *Alcoholics Anonymous Comes of Age* version, it is at this moment rather than during the dialogue with Ebby that Wilson's real "spiritual awakening" takes place:

"Suddenly the room lit up with a great white light. I was caught up into an ecstasy which there are no words to describe. It seemed to me, in the mind's eye, that I was on a mountain and that a wind not of air but of spirit was blowing. And then it burst upon me that I was a free man. Slowly the ecstasy subsided. I lay on the bed, but now for a time I was in another world, a new world of consciousness. All about me and through me there was a wonderful feeling of Presence, and I thought to myself, 'So this is the God of the preachers!' " (p. 63).

The modifying event, the "what happened" stage in AA narratives, may be related in tones that range from the gravity appropriate to a supernatural visitation, perhaps accompanied by upwelling tears of awestruck gratitude, to drier moods of analytic bemusement or detached irony. (While it is true that mystical illuminations occur from time to time in spoken AA narratives, they seem to be, in the urban Northeast at least, in a clear minority. Nearly one hundred "spiritual adventures," some as rapturous as Wilson's, are collected in an AA-approved publication, *Came To Believe,* 1973.) Most commonly, I think, "what happened" is represented not by a moment of abrupt change at a single point in the past, some catalysmic disruption of the cognitive universe, but rather by an account of gradual accommodation to AA folkways and a set of adjustments— some major, many microscopic—to everyday life without drink. The narrative location of a moment of surrender is probably in most cases a retrospective contrivance, an interpretive interpolation in what seems to be a long and faltering journey toward present stability.

> I went, that night I . . . stood up and I told who I was and I was an alcoholic. I think that's when I completely surrendered to the fact that I was powerless over alcohol. So I started making meetings there pretty regular. But I wasn't making their Step meetings. I was going to meeting meetings, and I started making [meetings at] New Humbert. I was down there for around three months and I wanted to belong to a group—so I asked whoever it was [that had the meeting], uh, how much dues did I have to pay to be a member. And they told me you paid your dues way before you came here. I said, "Well, what does that mean?" So they explained to me what it means and I started going down to New Humbert and I got to know quite a lot of people and I grew to love very much. Uh, they were always there for me, when I needed help, I always could call there, call one of them and they were always there to help me.

The description of "what we are like now" is often a condensed, allusive coda to the first two parts of the story. Cindy, for example, says only this of her "second state": "This program has really given me a lot; and I have a, a sense of self back. Um, still have a lot of trouble with self-esteem but it's gotten so much better. And, uh, I have a lot of trouble with a lot of defects but I'm, I'm on a road now, and I have a direction now, and, uh, things are steadily getting better, and it's all from this program. Thanks a lot."

Phil's second state inversion is even more tightly compacted: "But I don't drink and I go to meetings. And I, I try to put these Steps in my life." Susie's peroration is similarly terse. Spike concludes with a humorous anecdote which, although it seems on its face to celebrate attainment of a nonspiritual kind, should probably be taken with a pinch of metaphorical leavening.

The concentration of most AA stories is on the depiction of "what we were like." And while there is a disapproving category in AA aesthetics for the recitation of unevaluated prideful drinking exploits—the reviled "drunkalogue"—it is possible to satisfy an AA audience with only the smallest spoken homage to the boundless rewards of sobriety. Overly effusive self-proclamations of inner harmony, tranquility, and emotional growth—especially in a national cultural climate of mistrust and cynicism—veer too close to the display of pride or complacency for the liking of AA audiences; and a structured story, drawing attention to its own clever parallelisms and repetitions, could imply a dualistic thought pattern that shadows too closely the transcended restrictions of binary opposition. It may be simply that the past drinking life, for all its liabilities, is more interesting—taking that term to suggest the capacity to generate funny or lurid anecdotes—than the sober present. For St. Augustine, history ended and exegesis began at the moment of his conversion; and so it is with the alcoholic who has entered AA. A period of purposeful commentary is inaugurated that coincides with the beginning of a time of mental restructuring based on the principle of complementarity; the production of new tellable incidents is brought to a close—although the raw materials of good tale-making remain in stock.

The real weight of "second-state" representation comes not from the words of the narrative, but from the presence of the speaker. The effect of this presence is most powerfully experienced at meetings, of course, during the delivery of the stories; but even given a story separated from its speaker in time, space, and discursive community, the *idea* of the living speaker continues to inform the text. Some knowledge of the source is vital to the judicious evaluation of any personal narrative; this is especially important to remember when the very existence of a narrative is the primary demonstration of that narrative's truth, and the animate presence of the speaker its embodiment.

In response to a general question about intentionality and sincerity in AA stories, Margaret offered this recollection: "one of the most effective speeches I've ever heard was from a guy who couldn't talk. I mean, he got up and he said, 'I . . . uh . . . ,' and a tear rolled down his eye, you know . . . and then he said, 'I mean, they picked me up out of the gutter,' he said . . . that was approximately the content of his speech. But he so obviously was trying to say it, and obviously was so happy that he was where he was instead of where he'd been, that it was a very effective speech."

When I repeated Margaret's anecdote to Hugh, he commented:

> That, I think, is a perfect example of, uh, of a talk with feeling. You know, where, I mean . . . even the physical aspect of it, the tear and that, you know, it's like . . . [sometimes] the emotion is much too powerful. They cannot speak. And you don't have to hear words to identify with where somebody's coming from, you know, it's like . . . if you printed that speech in the newspaper, you wouldn't move a lot of people, because there wouldn't be any words . . . but . . . it's not just the words, it's, uh, you're looking at the person, you're actually there, and it's actually a live event in a way.

Scott, in the course of responding at some length to my question about the relation between story-telling and sobriety maintenance, made the following comments regarding the substantive affective enrichment afforded by "qualifying"—telling one's story—understood as a speech act.[12] The act of commitment displayed in speaking conjures an additional level of dramatic complexity, structuring new tensions and refractive points of correspondence or antithesis.

> I can see in myself, and I think I experience it with others, that the telling of a story, uh, enriches the sense of the joint effort to be well. . . . The person who tells the story sort of commits himself to the effort; he's taking a risk in telling a story, and nobody really ought to believe other-

wise; it's not that you're there bathed with love and therefore you're perfectly safe. When you tell a story in an AA room, you're taking risks; you're, you're taking the risk that you may be misunderstood, that somebody may remember it later on in a funny way and if you've ever had somebody tell you two months afterwards that you said thus-and-so and you never said anything like it, you realize the kind of hurt that telling a story entails. . . . The person who's telling a story is taking a chance, and it's not just that it'll be misunderstood, it's the very risk of being intimate in a big room full of people. And so he's committed to doing something difficult . . . because he's been told it'll . . . help him to get well. And that commitment . . . engages the commitment of the other people in the room. I just know it does, and . . . aside from its content, the very act is a way of joining, as it was with me when I gave my first qualification.

It's a rite of passage . . . it's a commitment to this mode of therapy, or this way of life, or this . . . getting better, and . . . it's a big step. And everybody who listens accepts it as a big step, it's not considered a trivial thing. Because after all there are these thirty or forty people willing to sit there for a half an hour and listen to something that isn't television, isn't a movie, it isn't exciting, it isn't a ball game, and their act of listening is a form of sharing as well, because they're sharing his life and they're committing themselves to this whole methodology, in a way that very few people are prepared to commit themselves, that is by shutting up and letting someone else do the talking. And . . . everybody's casting their lot with the process when they attend a meeting where there's a speaker. And that's all a vote for sobriety and getting well, and I think it's a terribly unifying, mentally unifying experience. I know I've never left a meeting when I didn't come away feeling more purposeful, and my molecules, which lay at random up till then, are now organized until I need another meeting. It just gives me a sense of purpose and a sense of, um, of belonging to something, and a sense of direction; that is to say, I'm there to be well and that's the most important thing in my life.

Much of the third part—the second-state, the "what we are like now" segment—of the AA narrative, then, is implied or signaled by information that is, strictly speaking, outside of the narrative: the very presence of the speaker, the speaker's governing intention to enter into a compact with the group by means of the act of speaking, and the dramatic negotiations that this intention might imply, such as confronting the past and overcoming temperamental resistance. We will return to the question of intention in the next chapter.

Just as narrative is imposed upon brute fact at a point suited to the needs of a teller, so are particular schemes of narrative form imposed upon narratives—according to the goals of an interpreter. It should not, therefore, surprise us that AA stories may be shown to conform to other models. In the model of oral experience narratives advanced by Labov and Waletzsky, narratives are said to consist of six components. In an *abstract,* the speaker makes known, or implies, an ostensible purpose for the narrative act, or situates the narrative relationally in a continuing verbal interaction; the *orientation* locates the narrative in time and place, and identifies characters and causal linkages; *complicating action* tells or describes what happened; *evaluation* highlights key elements in the story or makes suggestions concerning interpretation by the hearer; *resolution* tells what happened to conclude the narrative sequence; and a *coda* may be present to reconnect the narrative to the immediate situation.[13]

The AA narrative form may be matched to the Labov-Waletzsky model by simply dissolving boundaries that would probably be unclear in an actual narrative in any case. Thus, Bill Wilson's "what we were like" might subsume the orientation and part of the complicating action; "what happened" would include more of the complicating action and the beginnings of resolution; and "what we are like now" could complete the telling of the resolution and provide a bridge to the coda. Refining his own earlier work, Labov (1972) has noted, in "The Transformation of Experience in Narrative Syntax," that the evaluation function is not confined to a specifiable location in the narrative structure, but may appear at any point, and more than once, according to narratorial discretion. Evaluation may be thought of as a free-floating function, able to surface—become explicit—as needed, and always underlying and informing the surface of the story. In long, complex narratives, we may expect subsidiary evaluative devices, perhaps in a relation of uncertain consistency with the main point and brought forth as secondary points are made.

An abstract is present in AA stories, but often it bears a strong evaluative function. It is not necessary for an AA speaker to state a purpose or summarize story content because these things are situationally implicit; and a speaker may move directly from salutation to orientation. Some speakers, however, feel impelled to state what might be described as an initial discursive situation—an abstract, if Labov's definition may be modified slightly here.

For example, Ross says: "My story is largely a bottle story; so, if you're offended by those I suggest you just sit back and take some inventory, indulge your fantasies, whatever. I . . . I need to hear about the, uh, the blood, the vomit, and the broken glass. And I presume that others do too." Ross is letting his listeners know that in his story he will concentrate on "what we were like"; that his story is realistic—or naturalistic—rather than romantic or pathetic or utopian; and that an extended spiritual excursus may not be expected. "Taking inventory" is AA vernacular, derived from the Fourth Step, and may be used to mean either constructive self-examination or, with an ironic cast, the self-righteous judgment of others. Ross is expressing a distaste for the sanctimonious.

The coda in AA stories is, precisely as Labov and Waletzsky have it, a "functional device for returning to the verbal perspective of the present moment" (Labov and Waletzsky, 1967, p. 39). Often, the speaker addresses the audience directly, linking the final moments of the historical account with the immediate present of the speaking situation. Susie says, "This program has given me back everything. You people are my strength." The coda is, in fact, a significant gesture of unity, bonding the past to the present, audience to narrative substance, speaker to audience, unalterable historical data to continuing interpretive process, subjectivity to objectivity.

The coda carries out a complex unifying operation and points to an ancillary principle of totalization. The idea of unity in AA bears the sense not just of solidarity or mutuality, but of the necessary integration of program principles into all aspects of the subject's life. Embedded stories of slips and failures are invariably interpreted as failures to adhere to an AA "suggestion," to follow an AA rule, to understand a simple principle. Ultimately, each AA precept stands in synecdochic relationship to the whole, and, similarly, seemingly casual utterances may be expressive of the entire body of suppositions, principles, implications, lore, and shared history.

The simple coda, then, is more than a structural afterthought and, like other components of the narrative pattern, may enact a signifying purpose supplementary to its ostensible content. The AA verbal universe aspires toward the anagogic, and analysis will be inadequate to the degree that it loses sight of that aspiration. Perhaps the figure of the triune is, after all, the most appropriate to impose upon AA stories, and the stories best imagined as units of verbal action that are themselves only atoms in the larger entity. A list of phase symptoms, the change of heart, and the presence of the speaker—these notations for representing the form and meaning of AA stories are incommensurate with the potency of the actual storytelling occasion. The correspondences, harmonies, and inversions in a multidimensional grid, together with the gravity and immediacy of the issues—the *fact* of something at stake—generate a highly charged performance. Scott summarizes the galvanic effect of a good speaker upon an AA audience:

> It's direct experience. You can squirm with his embarrassment, you can feel empathetic with his tears, or her tears . . . it's got a dramatic quality to it that's unmatched in church meetings; it's got nothing like it anywhere that I know of. And it's personal: . . . somebody said, "The more personal, the more universal." I don't know who that was, but . . . there's a lot of truth in it; if the speaker can get to the nub of his experience, can tell it as it really was, he's going to elicit responses, because he's talking about something that will be in that room a universal, a universally experienced thing. And I think after a good qualification, there's a great drawing together of the group.

Five

Intention and Reception

As a rule, speakers in AA are chosen from among affiliates who have succeeded in remaining sober for at least ninety days. Sometimes up to a year of continuous sobriety is required for speaking; customs vary regionally, and even from group to group within a region, but six months is probably average. A newcomer's sponsor may suggest—or insist—that the "pigeon" speak, or the newcomer may contrive independently to speak. Some affiliates enjoy speaking, and some find it painful; speaking may bring therapeutic revelations and personal gratification to some; for others it may seem only a program obligation, a duty to be discharged with no special expectations. Speaking careers range from one or two occasions to a span of years and hundreds of engagements. There are no fast rules; there is, I think, an idea held generally that anyone serious about sobriety should speak at least once.[1]

Within a region, AA groups often exchange speakers for open meetings by means of advance programming arrangements. When planned schedules break down—which they often do because of AA's exclusive reliance on regularly rotated volunteers for administrative routines—speakers are selected from the members available at the start of the meeting. Members who lend themselves freely to speaking occasions, often seem to develop a relaxed, confident, and engaging manner at the podium.

Open AA meetings usually last one hour. Within that compass there may be one speaker, one speaker followed by responses from the floor, or two speakers introduced by a leader who often provides a connective matrix of some kind, perhaps pointing to correspondences between seemingly unlike talks, matching his or her own experiences to those narrated, or specifying certain abstract or latent precepts based on the narratives.

There may be a natural history of the AA speaker to be plotted —a parabola superimposed upon the first few years of sobriety, peaking with frequent and energetic speaking activities, then declining to one or two annual engagements. In general, as individual accommodation to sobriety is deepened and secured, participation in AA subsides; and so too—inseparable as it is from other dimensions of the program—does speaking.

"Our primary purpose," states the Preamble, read at the start of every AA meeting, "is to stay sober and help other alcoholics to achieve sobriety." Even in the unthinkable circumstance of the omission of this reminder, AA affiliates would recall its authority. The idea of helping other alcoholics has been, as we have seen, fundamental to the program from the time of its inception in Akron. Step Twelve is explicit on the point: "Having had a spiritual awakening as the result of these steps, we tried to carry this message to alcoholics, and to practice these principles in all our affairs." So is the Fifth Tradition: "Each group has but one primary purpose— to carry its message to the alcoholic who still suffers."

AA rhetoric is saturated with the conception of helping other alcoholics, and that rhetoric permeates the thinking of affiliates, impinging upon the smallest verbal gesture, coloring every utterance. Next to avoiding intoxicants, helping is the major premise upon which the program is built, the suspension in which its discrete components are harmoniously maintained. The helping imperative is reiterated incessantly, its hegemony never foreclosed. A prescription appearing on much of the sanctioned literature reads: "When anyone, anywhere, reaches out for help, I want the hand of AA always to be there. And for that: I am responsible." For active members in good faith, there is no exemption from responsibility to this rule in the performance of AA activities and in the practices of everyday life.

Narratives must be comprehended within this context. Even when a helping intention is unstated, its informing presence must be assumed. The speaker and the audience both understand the conjuncture of narration and purpose within the matrix of AA principles, rules, and conventions.

It should come as no surprise, then, to find that AA speakers questioned about their intentions explicitly assert their desire to try to help others newly or potentially sober who may be present in the audience. But speaking is based almost entirely on the speaker's own intuitions and assumptions, not a set of protocols or even determinable standards, and it is in this sense an act of faith; audience composition is unpredictable, audience reactions are unfathomable, and the positive efficacy of AA narratives is, in any measurable sense, unknown. Patrick contrasts the hope-filled urgency of his own message with the inscrutability of reception:

> The thing I do try to give people the impression of, consistently, I hope, is that . . . and it's the truth, I've never seen anybody who followed all this—the principles of the program—who didn't get better. And, you know, you can call it a message of hope or something but it's also a fact, you know, it's not fiction, you know. I've seen the weirdest, craziest, most spaced-out people come in, and if they, you know, just follow the directions, they get better too, you know. Next week *they're* leading the meeting and you're sitting there going, "Oh my God, I'm hurting," you know? It's amazing the way it works. So that's, you know, one thing that I always try to convey to people. I've come to the conclusion, though, [that] you've really just got to say your story the way it is and, you know, don't expect, [with] fifty people in a room, don't expect forty-nine of them to identify with you. You're lucky if, you know, five of them do.

Dogmatic moral valuations at the podium, abstract judgments, and theoretical homilies are regarded by most speakers as ineffective as well as presumptuous, and hence avoided. Here, as elsewhere in AA, a congruence between pragmatics and right conduct is achieved. Bill Wilson wrote that "the 400 pages of *Alcoholics Anonymous* contain no theory; they narrate experience." "Being laymen," he told a group of psychiatrists, "we have naught but a story to tell" (Alcoholics Anonymous, n.d., *Three Talks*, pp. 29–30). Hence, exemplification becomes the persuasive strategy of choice. Patrick again: "I believe in leading a beginners' meeting by talking about myself a lot. And if someone has a problem, I talk about how I had what I consider to be something similar, and what I did for it. You know, I don't like to say to people, 'You should do this,' or, 'You should do that,' and I can't stand being in any other meeting where-[they do that]. . . ."

Margaret remembers the value of examples in her own history: "Once I was convinced that I was an alcoholic, I got a lot of hope from other people; from sober, happy people standing up and tell-

ing their story and indicating that they were sober and happy."
Elliot, too, values the demonstration of a dramatically changed life
willingly projected in exemplification: "And what I mean by a wonderful message. . . . I guess a message where I hear things that I
would like to convey to people: sincerity, humility, hope, gratitude,
sincere . . . [a] story where there was a hopeless life and now there
is hope, and a life where we're getting out of ourselves and are
reaching out to other people, which is to me a miracle, if you
can take someone who's self-centered and self-contained, totally
self-preoccupied, and . . . reaches out to people."

Margaret talks about the inclusion of essential details as a strategy
for forming a communicative link between herself as an embodiment of recovery and the hospitalized alcoholics to whom she sometimes speaks: "And I try, really, at that point to kind of dwell on the
alcoholic part of it, because these people are just getting over . . .
these are detox and rehab people. And I figure that I'm showing
them that I'm happy and sober and stuff, but I think that they can
relate more to the rotten details of my, of my drinking, because . . .
that's what they're nearest to."

Selena speaks of the importance of representing the idea that
"sobriety is rewarding." "I want people to think that I'm happy,"
she says. "I want to convey that I really enjoy my life sober." Selena
and Terry discuss tailoring their stories, like Margaret, to fit the
specifics of a meeting held in a rehabilitation unit, where patients
sober perhaps only a few days are likely to form their crucial first
impressions of AA.

> T: I'm sure it was important to me to convey that life was a hell of a
> lot better. You know? And that it was, regardless of what, of anything,
> it was—the one thing I wanted to convey was it was worth doing,
> you know.
>
> S: Well, I think you would keep it simpler.
>
> T. Yeah, maybe so, and maybe, if you had a tendency—say you were
> going through a hard thing or something and you wanted to talk
> about some of the problems you'd had in sobriety, you might want
> to censor that a little bit and not make it too frightening, you know.

It is not a question of misrepresentation or suppression, but of
propriety and judicious selection. The helping imperative determines how the selections are made, where emphasis is placed. Elliot
and Hugh both note the dissonant effect achieved by a speaker

insensitive to an audience's particularities. Elliot reports on an engagement in which he was paired with another speaker whose sense of "fit" seemed impaired; the prosperous amateur yachtsman was indifferent or oblivious to the realities of his down-and-out listeners' condition:

> . . . He was from Seaview and he was a big sailor, and these are captive people in the Salvation Army, and they were . . . we were an hour late to boot, so they were angry when we got there. . . . I know when he got up there he said . . . "I was getting so depressed, I hadn't had a drink in about six months before I came into the program, and I was getting so depressed I didn't even want to sail anymore." . . . I remember them sort of shifting in their chairs when they heard that. . . . Course, he had his Bass Weejuns on, and his khakis, his Brooks Brothers khakis.

Hugh—invoking the same prestigious trade name—says that he prepares differently when he is going to speak in a prison or hospital, or to "people that have just come out of a rehab, or just been swept off the street somewhere."

> I think then you have to be able to make it so that they can identify. You know, I mean, you don't go into a prison in a Brooks Brothers suit and a camel-hair topcoat and, you know, talk about all your problems, you know, with your income tax. Or, you know, that . . . you were really deprived when you were a kid because you, you know, you only had a . . . a sixty-eight Chevy or something. . . . You have to identify with your audience as well as hoping that they identify with your feelings. You have to identify with their feelings. You know, and it's affected me profoundly. I've only spoken in prison a few times, but that's affected me a lot. Because I could have been there real easy.

Sometimes story-shaping decisions are made according to a sympathetic calculation of needs based on the speaker's own AA education, and the speaker's role shifts from exemplar to instructor. Selena tells of her decision to repeat useful AA formulas, gnomic verbal recipes that identify and help to control recurring contradictions or ambiguities that may discompose the newly sober. Selena worries that as her sobriety has evolved her adherence to the helping imperative has weakened and her speaking has become vulnerable to the taint of complacency or self-indulgence. The formulas will serve her as a kind of personal mnemonic of humility at the same time they educate her audience.

> We were riding home from a meeting one night and I was saying, "You
> know, we need to get back to some of the stuff that we heard when we
> were newer that really hit us as profound—like that 'egomaniac with an
> [inferiority complex].' " You know, that you kind of go through . . .
> phases and . . . I've been sort of at this point in the last year or so where I
> think I'm too far along to say trite things that seemed so meaningful to me
> when I was new. And I kind of made a conscious decision lately that I'm
> going to start . . . like, "Alcoholics don't get married, they take hostages."

There is an AA joke that says, "If you can stay sober in AA,
you can stay sober anywhere." The joke sympathetically encourages
resignation in the face of a discontent that must challenge even the
most deeply committed affiliate from time to time. Many members
perceive AA as an absolute necessity for themselves, and they participate voluntarily in a fiction of compulsory attendance, complaining,
usually with comic irony, about program obligations and the injus-
tice of having to maintain this bizarre symbolic edifice. Humorous
commiseration among members is a virtual tradition in AA, and
words of consolation are sometimes joined to unmasking gestures.
Terry recalls his own hostile first impressions, and explains how he
constructively incorporates the memories when he is before newcomers:

> One of my first meetings I was at Step by Step, you know, and Fritz
> Grimble was down there dressed in some idiotic zoot-suit, you know,
> and he said, "Oh, we're going to go down after the meeting and go
> dancing at the Rendezvous, they're having Big Band Night," and I says,
> "Oh Christ . . . this is what they do to have fun, this is what I'm going
> to have to learn how to do," you know? These poor, pathetic jerks. . . .
> . . . That's one of the things that I try to include in my lead, is how
> much I hated it when I first came, because it was really important for me
> to hear that. Those, I, I really perked up when I heard people say that,
> because I could really relate to that when I was new. That sense of, you
> know, you don't want to drink but you sure don't want this crap either,
> you know.

Margaret, too, indicates a desire to balance the gilded prospect
merchandised by some AA propagandists. From the sympathetic
vantage of her own recollections, she hopes to disarm inauthenticity,
convinced that realism and recovery are not incompatible.

> I know that when I was a beginner and people got up and said, "I came
> to AA and I have never turned away from it"; "The minute I got there I

knew this was where I belonged"; "The desire for drinking dropped from me like a cloak"; you know, this kind of stuff—I don't believe them. But whether I believe them or not, that's not the way it happened with me. I slipped and I came back, and I slipped and I came back, and I slipped and I came back, and I think that's important to tell people, because it's harder every time.

Admonition as warning or dissuasion is not usually a baldly articulated feature of these stories for the same reason that moral injunction is avoided; but admonition is often an implication of story form and thematic emphasis. Phil (see Appendix) brings purposeful unity to his story with the recurring insistence that he did not know he was a problem drinker for the entire span of his fifteen-year drinking career. Following a recapitulation of each lamentable episode or interval, Phil reaffirms that he did not know he was an alcoholic. The repetition casts a thematic net over the whole and effects a dissuasive cohesion. An attentive listener enveloped in the same conceptual darkness that afflicted Phil might hear the proper cautionary clues within the story. The warning, while not explicit, is unambiguous.

Ross (see Appendix) does embed an explicit warning in his story. "Slips"—the AA term for "relapses" or returning to drinking after a term of abstinence—call for special attention because they are not locked into the unchangeable past but are implicated in the contemporary daily life of the program and coexist with the standard of continuing sobriety. Slips demonstrate the tenuousness of sobriety and the unremitting presence of temptation; they are important talking points in discussions, and often become crucial plot fixtures in qualifications. It seems likely that slips can elicit vigorous or even exceptional denunciatory language in AA because of the widespread and experientially validated conviction that slips pose unforeseen mortal dangers to alcoholics who have accumulated time in sobriety. Ross's account is typical.

> Several years, uh, in sobriety, I guess I was suffering from an excess of, uh, success—uh, it's a classic story: I stopped going to meetings and, uh, declared myself cured. And, uh, that worked for a few months, and then I got [in a] situation and took a drink, took another one, and . . . the worst possible thing the next day: nothing. There was no hangover, no remorse, none of that terrible cold feeling that you get; so, shit, I knew I was cured then. And six weeks later I was in detox. I don't

recommend slips as part of any treatment modality, because they can kill you. But for me, it tuned my ragged ass right up.

Ross goes on to define his "spirituality" as "rather ephemeral" —but the point is made that some attention, however spotty, to a spiritual dimension is essential; that complicity with the premises of the program, no matter how grudging, is vital. And the warning about slips is lodged: "They can kill you."

Self-help in AA is the obverse of helping others. Individual spiritual development rewards the practitioner and the group concurrently. AA defines no perfected state; desirable outcomes are defined in only the most general way. Perfectionism is, in fact, disclaimed in a well-known Big Book passage: "No one among us has been able to maintain anything like perfect adherence to these principles. We are not saints" but "we are willing to grow along spiritual lines" (Alcoholics Anonymous, 1976a, p. 60).[2] Perfectionism not only reflects a distorted appraisal of the human situation but, more pragmatically, poses a dangerous challenge to the alcoholic temperament. Scott provides a useful gloss on this issue, extemporizing on the subject of the use of the AA meeting as a forum for the promulgation of outside interests—in this case, religious orthodoxy.

> One of the things I don't like about a lot of the spirituality that I hear in the program is that it tends, even without being fundamentalist, to suggest that the closer you are to a traditional religious belief in a personal God who listens to you like someone answers the telephone and who sometimes writes out orders like a prescribing doctor; the closer you are to that view of the spiritual arrangement of things, the greater your spirituality is, and, I get a little acerbic sometimes on that, and insist that your spirituality is as complete as it needs to be at any given time and there's no greater spirituality than what you have at a given time, and that nobody is more spiritual than anybody else in his accomplishment. And that there isn't a fuller and a lesser version of spirituality, because the minute you concede there is then there's a place you're not yet at, and you better get there, you know what I mean? And what is that except more of traditional religion?

The capacities to help oneself and to help others are reciprocal, and neither can exist in isolation. As a teacher and an exemplar, one should be able to demonstrate continuing growth and development in one's own sphere; and that development in turn enhances one's persuasiveness and credibility. Since speakers and listeners are not generically segregated in AA, the opportunities for giving and receiving help are allocated democratically: everyone speaks, and everyone listens. The egalitarian distribution of narrative rights prevents escalation and runaway; no speaker—ideally—is heard from more than any other; and a narrative laissez-faire that might favor oratorical training or dramatic skills is enjoined by the rule of custom. A distinction here may be formulated in terms of complementary rather than symmetrical or competitive storytelling environments.[3]

Margaret notes the satisfactions inherent in this reciprocity: "When I have really . . . felt that I have exposed myself, that is a very gratifying feeling; that I have shared; that I have possibly helped somebody else; certainly cleaned my own stables—or whatever it is. It's a good feeling, you know, it's a feeling of, of . . . well, exactly what the program, what I consider the program: helping myself by helping others, or helping others by helping myself. Either way, it's, it's, uh . . . I think that's the heart of the program, and I think telling a, your story is, to me, a very important part."

Hugh, among others, ascribes a "cathartic" potential to the self-help dimension of the storytelling process: "I feel much, I feel incredibly good after speaking; it's like after leaving a meeting; it's like after, you know, really sharing anything: one . . . relief that it's over, but, two, you know, that, uh . . . it's just such a release, you know. It's wonderful . . . it's like really getting . . . something off your shoulders."

The nature of the "cathartic" here is not the unsticking and running-off of unwanted sediments built up on the inside of the personality, like deposits from an impure, fast-burning affect. Again, a more pragmatic construction obtains in AA: "catharsis" is the successful solicitation of community approbation. Mark had spoken earlier of his "sense of relief . . . at letting out something that's been there for many years . . . with all the distortions . . ." when he told his sponsor a hitherto guarded and guilty secret. "I thought I was going to die when I told him, and he, he just kept chewing his hamburger like I didn't say a word, you know, and that was, you know, instant trust was really developed." Now he speaks of a similar experience that occurs when his forthright disclosures before a group are felt to be understood:

Telling a bunch of people, um, about some of the insanity and . . . the events that happened as a result, or in connection with my drinking, it was really, um, something very freeing about it. It's nice to be able to talk about something, um, that you're not too sure of and suddenly a bunch of people, you know, laugh about it . . . that is like one of the greatest healing powers I've ever had, you know. Or, people don't have to laugh at it, I mean, you can talk about something and have somebody afterwards come óver and say, "Jesus, you know, something like that happened to me," and blah-blah-blah, you know. And, well, even for someone not to respond at all, you know, to be more self-centered about it, just in terms of what it does in terms of letting that out there and realizing that there's no repercussions as a result of it.

Psychic fissures are sealed over by means of symbolic submission to the will of the group. But in addition to this repair, or "healing," in consequence of storytelling, there may be the production of new cognitive material. This unbidden outpouring of unacknowledged or hitherto unwelcome truths in the course of a narrative is probably the closest AA practice comes to conventional psychotherapeutic process. Patrick puts the matter clearly:

Well, by speaking, I learned things about myself, like things came out when I spoke that I'm—it's almost like a, you know, a psychological thing where you're hypnotized or something and your unconscious speaks—but things came out when I spoke that, you know, like, for instance the thing about guilt about, uh, you know, Vietnam and what not. I believe there are things that are inside of me that are making me feel bad about myself, and some of them came out when I spoke, and I was able to deal with them and, you know, recognize them and, uh, help me not feel bad about myself, which consequently helps me not to, it takes away the urge for, uh, escape.

Hugh holds a similar point of view, and details the revelatory experience during his first speaking engagement:

I had a lot of secrets I was never going to tell anybody, and [the] first time I spoke I was . . . in the program about three months, and, you know, I had a wife who had died—she was in a wheelchair and all kinds of stuff and I was out carousing and drinking and . . . and a lot of things that I just wasn't going to share with anybody. Fine: I'll get my sobriety, I'll do all the other stuff, but I'm not going to . . . relay this to anybody. You know, I was thinking—that was my preparation, sort of: I'll speak at open meetings but I won't tell *this,* and I'm not going to put *that* in my

Fourth Step, I'm not going to talk about it in my Fifth Step. But in doing no preparation, I got up there and I spoke, and I . . . everything just came out. And thank God it did, because it's the first time, not only that I'd ever told anybody, really, but it's the first time I ever really verbalized it to myself. And it was almost like, like hearing from afar myself speaking.

The idea of hearing oneself speaking occurs with some frequency in AA, often in quasi-therapeutic terms, and sometimes wrapped in the diaphanous language of mysticism. Terry tells of advice received at his first qualification:

My sponsor told me to go in the bathroom before I went, before I did it, and say a prayer that I hear the things that I need to hear to stay sober. He told me that was what it was about. That it was so that I could hear the things that I needed to remind myself what it was like so that I could continue to stay sober. . . .

. . . I always say the same thing that my sponsor tells me, you know, what it's for is for you to hear the things that you need to hear, so in a sense you're not really in control of that process, you just have to go up and tell your story and then listen to your own story. Get your feedback off that, you know.

The object of hearing oneself speak is a concept that lies somewhere between the free association of psychoanalysis and automatic writing, between therapy and poetry. The double prescription of honesty and spontaneity in AA is universally endorsed, reckoned a sine qua non for "comfortable" sobriety; and the AA meeting, like the psychoanalytic session, becomes a "facilitating environment" for the nurturance of the "reflective self-awareness" that is required for generative explorations of the self. The wariness of everyday social life—hedged about by restrictive convention and internalized rules of evasion and self-defense—must be relaxed in opening oneself to the gift of insight, analogous to the influx of poetic inspiration.[4]

In the psychoanalytic dialogue, of course, exploration is managed by the analyst under constraints imposed by a substantive and delimited body of knowledge. Exploration of self in AA is governed to some extent by the ideology of the program but, as should be obvious by this time, that ideology is indistinct, haphazard, and susceptible to a wide sweep of definitions and motives. Psychoanalytic interpretations emerge as agreements painstakingly constructed by the collaboration of skilled analyst and vigilant patient; in AA validation of the speaker is instantaneous and virtually assured. As Selena says, "No one really cares that much except you. Not too many things you can do wrong, I don't think." With the compliant, almost invariably approving audience cast in the role of the therapist, or with the speaker enacting that part personally on his or her own behalf, critically challenging interventions are unlikely. Fortunately, for the most part, AA speakers are not afflicted by grave psychiatric dysfunctions, and the production of volatile material at the podium is unlikely to overwhelm their integrative capabilities.

Hugh, nevertheless, had a disturbing experience in disapprobation:

> I had somebody come to me once . . . probably a month after I spoke
> . . . and she said, "I really hated you after you spoke." I said, "Whoa."
> And she said, you know, "What you did to your wife, and what you
> did. . . ." And like, and that was, I mean . . . and all I could do with that
> was talk to a lot of other people about it and what . . . you know. It was
> more than just a slightly negative reaction. And I think I was able to
> handle that all right . . . it never occurred to me to ease off from what I
> was saying, you know, when I was talking and all that stuff. That's one
> person's . . . problem. That's her problem. She's, uh . . . it would sound
> wrong if I said she was a very strong feminist, but she's always very aware
> of, you know, the woman's, uh, often victimization in alcohol. And even
> though she's an alcoholic, that's what she latched on to, and she really
> gave it to me really good.

Because of the possibility of offending or disturbing a member of the audience, many speakers exercise watchfulness over their presentations, particularly in the selection of details and representative incidents, and avoid expressive vernaculars that are not universally sanctioned. Again, this is not a matter of denial or suppression, but a means of precluding the kind of experience described by Hugh.

The reconstitution of badly eroded confidence and the acquisition or redevelopment of social skills is another benefit that accrues to speakers of AA stories—a benefit that holds a considerably less volatile potential than spontaneous self-disclosure. Hank recalls:

> The process of speaking was very instrumental in my regaining confidence in, in public speaking. And I think that's one of the side benefits that is frequently overlooked in the recovery process through AA that, by overcoming our reluctance to talk about ourselves or even to talk at

all before a group of people, that, by doing it frequently or at least periodically, that it gives one a restored sense of self-confidence and certainly made it possible for me to resume a career that involved a fair degree of speaking. And I think that happens to a lot of people, although they may not acknowledge it.

Patrick echoes these sentiments, adding that speaking "gives people the feeling that they're not just . . . a spectator anymore, they're now participating, they're, you know, part of the show." Clearly, "the show" refers not only to the speaking activity at the podium, but rather to the AA meeting process in its totality: networks of regular participants, the decorative insignia that transform the meeting space, the preparation and restoration of the room, coffee and cigarettes, the din, the array of human variety. The larger world beyond the meeting rooms is of course implied too.

The self-discipline required to "work the program" is taken by some to be an ancillary benefit of speaking. Ross outlines his adherence to the helping imperative, and explains it in allopathic terms: "I . . . try to talk to another alcoholic every day, to remind me of who I am. And I try and make a genuine all-out effort to help people. Because it's alien to my nature. I am not a giver. I'm a taker. Those things help me to stay sober."

Scott tells us that we are justified in expecting a qualification that is neither incoherent nor endless from a speaker who has spent some time in AA. "A touch of discipline [should be] brought to the exercise," enhancing its value for speaker and audience both. "I don't think it's a weed spontaneously growing, or a flower spontaneously popping in front of us; I think that it's a controlled thing, and there are certain things that are appropriate to it and certain things that are not."

There is, further, a purely historical function in the AA narrative that is identified in the phrase, "Keep the memory green." The memory of the past must be recalled, revivified, and retained if the alcoholic is to remain attentive to the dangers of relapse.

Margaret finds that with the passage of time she has been able to recall more about the past and, presumably, find there shapes and meanings that help her to construct a coherent future. "I've become increasingly comfortable, increasingly . . . well, I've been able to tell more and more, I think. I've been able to remember more and more. That's another value that I didn't really mention. Just the act of telling stories makes you remember things that otherwise you might forget."

Terry intimates that historical reconstruction is the primary reason for storytelling; the privation of the properly remembered past becomes a compelling argument for sobriety. Explaining why storytelling is an institution in AA, Terry says: "Because . . . because of denial, I think. Because we need to remember, you know. . . . If you asked me to tell you what it was like, you know, then that forces me to go back there, and I think I have a natural tendency not to go back there. And that natural tendency not to go back there is what works against me. It's what's going to make me forget how bad it was. And I think the more that we rehearse, or that we explain to one another like what it was like, the more we remember what it was like."

Hugh, likewise, believes in the protective value of remembrance, and emphasizes the importance of proximity and verisimilitude:

> I think it's really important for me to keep telling my story, especially up to my coming into the program, so I don't forget. You know, because I can really forget really easy. I've been in, be going on eight years, and I don't want it to be in the dark and distant past. I got to keep it, you know, up close to me; because I could be back there tomorrow if I drink. And I would, you know. I had a slip once, you know, it was like *whoosh*. Straight back. Right where I came from. You know, I think that was because I didn't go to meetings, I didn't listen, I didn't identify.

Hugh theorizes, too, about repetition and its role in keeping memory active and vivid. Repetition functions in lieu of a dependable capacity to retain the important recollections:

> You know, it's a bit of a Chinese water torture method, it keeps your memory green, reminds you of where you're coming from, and it should remind you how precious recovery is . . . I think it's the accumulation of the effect, like I said before, of the speaking. You know, eventually it will all come out, and eventually you will hear, in meetings, everything you need to hear. It doesn't do me any good to hear something sometimes, because there . . . that night it may not really grab me; maybe a week later, or two weeks later, you know I can hear the same thing again, and it really has meaning—maybe because of what happened during that day, or what's happened in the meantime. . . . And I think that's the importance of hearing it and hearing it and hearing it over and over and over again. Um, because it's different every time. Similar, often the same,

but, you know, every time I go into a meeting I'm different. I receive different things.

A final crucial intentional function to note is the double gesture of pledging a personal commitment to AA and the individual group and, at the same time, of consolidating that group by becoming the center of its attention, reiterating common history, and reenacting protocols that are consonant with the group's expectations. Margaret contrasts the feelings of unity at an AA meeting with the spurious and in any case now impermissible conviviality of a cocktail party:

> The kind of connection I feel with an AA group is . . . much better, but also it's a much truer kind of a feeling, because it isn't fueled by, by some kind of a drug. I think for the audience being able to identify, and also . . . well, I think anything you do together, no matter what it is, binds people to each other. And here's a roomful of people listening to a person and, and kind of reinforcing their connections with each other. And I have come to believe, as I get old, that the only thing that matters, honestly, the most important thing is connections between people. I honestly think that that's what all this . . . this living is about. . . . I'm making it sound ideal. You don't feel very connected when you're in the middle of a sentence and somebody gets up and leaves the room to get coffee, but that's all right, that's part of the thing too. I think the value for me, even if I didn't . . . get any kind of response, would still be there —a lot of the value would still be there. Perhaps the more important value. But it's nice to be in a roomful of people all of whom are really pursuing sobriety together, in whatever ways they can.

Here, then, is a summary scheme of intention in AA narrative:

Purpose	Mode
1 help/others	exemplify
	teach
	console
	admonish
2 help/self	therapeutic
	purge
	explore
	social
	discipline
	embolden

3 remembrance   recall
                               revive
                               retain
4 aggregation   self: commit
                               group: unify

It should be clear at this point that there are no sharp lines of
categorical demarcation here. Intention and reception must necessarily be in symbiotic relationship to one another, but in AA the
unifying rather than the differentiating dimension of the symbiosis
is paramount since speakers and listeners are interchangeable at
literally a moment's notice. Most "acts" or attitudes of reception
will be in a clear relationship of complementarity with parallel intentional acts or attitudes. We have noted some of these relationships
above, but some peculiarities of reception warrant special attention.

"Don't compare," newcomers to AA are told, "identify." This
instruction for listening to speakers at open meetings and, indeed,
to anyone who may have the floor in AA, tells the listener to actively
search out points of correspondence between him- or herself and
the speaker rather than areas of differentiation. The implication is
that affects and patterns in one addiction story are very like those in
another, that enough points of correspondence predictably exist for
the effort to be worthwhile, and that deliberate attentiveness to
these identities will facilitate the formation of bonds of fellowship
and mutuality. As Terry says: "They say, I guess you've heard the
thing of, it's the speaker's job to qualify, and it's the listener's job
to identify. You know. But I can't say I always do that. . . . "

Most affiliates seem to take the responsibility of identifying
with a speaker seriously. Patrick claims, "I always find something to
identify with, no matter who's speaking, if I really sit and listen."
Margaret articulates the widely held conviction that emotional
patterns transcend circumstantial particulars:

Well, I listen to someone else's story as intently as possible. And I identify
with . . . well, I identify with their feelings of misery . . . their feelings, I
guess, that's what I have to say. Not an awful lot of people that I listen
to can I identify with as far as the actual details of the story's concerned,
because they just don't seem to relate to mine directly. I really wasn't
a housewife—well, the housewife who drank for a while and then
I stopped drinking; and then I went to work and then after a while I
started drinking and . . . I just can't seem to see any coherent pattern in

my life . . . that I can see in other people's lives when they're talking. . . .
But certainly, of course, all their feelings.

Patrick stresses that the role of the listener in identification is an
active one, and that internalized program obligations together with
simple force of will must sometimes be drawn upon:

A lot of times . . . I'll have built up prejudices about somebody and I've
never even met them before, you know, just by the way they walk in, or
the first thing they say, you know, and I have to say to myself, you know,
"That is ridiculous; that's part of your problem," or whatever, and there
must be something that this person's saying, you know . . . if, if nothing
else you can learn not to be like them; I mean, if you totally don't like
anything they say, you know, your lesson is, you know, don't be like
them or whatever. But there's always—I've never had that happen—
there's always something.

The process of hearing what one needs to hear by listening to
one's own story as it is spoken has its reciprocal in the experience of
hearing one's own story told by another speaker. Hearing an analog
story is a frequently reported occurrence and often produces a sense
of the uncanny; that sense, if not immediately rationalized and dissi-
pated, may be employed in support of the listener's best interest in
the conflict between alcohol and abstinence. In charged, enthusiastic language, Patrick reports an episode of this kind that appears to
have confirmed his sobriety:

The first time I heard speakers, I was at a meeting, it was a brother and
sister [who] spoke; and the brother had a story so similar to mine that I
—this was my first time I heard an AA speaker, and I honestly thought
this—and I was in a room where nobody knew me, I went to a place
where, you know, nobody took me there, and I know none of these
people knew me, but I honestly felt that this guy had been told stories,
things about my past, that he injected into what he was talking about.
Beause it was so exactly the same. You know, so the identification, you
know, was incredible; and when you can really identify with somebody,
and really, you know, just by their speaking you can put yourself right in
their place, and then you realize that this person hasn't drank in a long
time, it really gives you the feeling like, you know, if he can do it, I can
do it.

Terry and Selena, in response to questions about how to listen,
introduce what might be called a pragmatics of identification. These

two strategies represent the kind of small but purposeful self-corrective measures that affiliates take in the interest of program unity.

> T.   I'm enough of an alcoholic that I, that there's just got to be some common ground between me and anybody else who's an alcoholic somewhere . . . and when that common ground comes out, then I'm there, I'm in there. But I don't think I . . . one thing I do sometimes, if I find I'm not listening a lot lately is I try to sit up front. You know. That sort of forces me.
>
> S.   And I always thank the speaker. I remember my sponsor telling me that without the speaker there wouldn't be a meeting, so you always thank the speaker no matter what you thought of the speaker. And that's an action I make myself do, so . . . I feel better when I, even if I'm feeling angry and judgmental, I feel like I still did what I was supposed to do.

Hank encapsulates the issue of substantial audience responsibility. A "good AA audience," not merely a gathering of bodies, will participate actively as a receptive entity in the speaking event, accommodating itself to the affective content of the discourse from the podium.

> It's important to speak. But it's also important to, to hear the stories of others, and relate the feeling content of those stories to our own, and also, and I stress again, to provide the support and communication to those relatively new people that's necessary to their recovery. And that's an obligation that we have to the program and to them. Amen. I get . . . I get a little mad at the oldtimers wishing to be comfortable and becoming more selfish and less selfless, which I think is the heart of the program. I frequently disagree with people who say, "It's a selfish program." And I say, "Horseshit. It's a self*less* program." Amen, amen.

The responsibility of the listener to participate actively in the storytelling event raises the issue of a speaker's sincerity and authenticity, already discussed briefly in the preceding chapter, and leads us then to the question of aesthetics in AA.

The demand for honesty in representation is universally expressed, and the conception of honesty is often delimited by contrast to theatricality. Hank rejects the "acting performance"; Terry and Selena "react negatively to a show"; Hugh dislikes "posturing" and "travelogue type of talks"; the "jokester" presenting a "roadshow" is castigated by Scott; Elliot repeatedly condemns "entertainers" and "entertainment." Two interviewees find objectionable connotations in the word "audience" in reference to the nonspeaking participants in an open meeting.

We have noted that voicelessness and inarticulateness in speakers may be valued as markers of powerfully felt, sincere emotions. This is not to say that the converse obtains and voluble, articulate speakers are dismissed as fraudulent—Selena says "given my druthers I'd rather hear somebody that speaks well and is reasonably honest"— but that operative standards of narrative acceptability are different from those brought to bear in business, politics, or art. Plausibility in AA is independent of amusement value and persuasiveness in any tactical sense of these terms—as they might be used, for example, in evaluating the techniques of modern advertising. Hank, to whom "glibness" is a particular *bête noir,* reflects on the meaning of this value:

> I'm never particularly impressed with those who make a grand production and . . . and act as if they were performing on stage. It . . . it turns me off their internal feelings and their internal story, and therefore holds little instruction for me. . . . As one who has difficulty expressing deep feelings, especially to those closest to him, I'm always moved by those who are able to, and who do it, frequently, accompanied by tears, or . . . or breakdowns. Because they really are leveling in the truest form, and facing their own . . . their own pain.

Terry expresses the same sentiment more directly: "I'd rather hear somebody who is incoherent and doesn't speak well but who, you know, is being reasonably honest than, than somebody who speaks real well and is just full of crap, you know." As an antithesis to the idea of reasonable honesty, Terry supplies this anecdote of gross abuse of the AA forum:

> Like I heard a guy one time, he was sober about seven or eight months, at this meeting in Elmwood over here—a lot of young people go there, a lot of drug people and stuff, and he gave, you know, he gave like a really slick lead for somebody who was only six or seven months sober, you know. Real slick, it was like he'd picked up how to do it and he just did it. And after the lead was over I went up and thanked him, and I shook his hand, and he said, "Oh, thanks, yeah, man, if you ever need any carpet, man, I can beat any price in town"—he gives me a card, you know.

Brevity, too, is taken for a sign of sincerity in its respect for the tolerances of the group and the limits of the group's ability to accommodate—which are, after all, even in this utopian environment, finite. Elliot reveals an interactive dimension in even this small point: "Usually in these talks, by the way . . . the shorter the better. People love . . . you know, we don't like to be, we like to be talking, not listening. So, you, [if] you can get applause for a half an hour, you can get a standing ovation for fifteen minutes. I think I've gotten my, my best compliments when I've started speaking at ten of ten, when someone else had spoken for fifty minutes or longer, and I did a story in ten or fifteen minutes and I—they were raving about it. They'd say, 'That's all you needed, it was very concise.' "

Finally, the mutability of AA stories must be considered. Mutability, Scott tells us, acts for him as an indicator of sincerity:

> I'll tell you how I can judge a sincere or honest person is if I hear him three times, and I know that he's reaching for the truth of what he's saying, on each of those three occasions. If I hear the speaker three times and he says the same thing all three times, I suspect that he's got, now, a "correct" version of the world, and that's the version he's adopted and his sincerity should question that version, because life is changing all the time and you're never going to get at it unless you look beneath the last version to see what new thing you can find out. So I judge a person's honesty in AA by his willingness to uncover new material in public and tell about new things.
>
> And, above all, for a person who's been around a while, a person is insincere for me if he tells his whole story in the past tense. And he is sincere and honest for me, and interesting, if his story is an ongoing story, that includes present problems and—I know everybody's got problems, and yet a lot of people in AA deny that they have problems. They look at the world, at least in public, they say they look at the world as if since the day they got sober they haven't had a bad day. And that's a lot of bullshit; it just isn't true, and it turns me off, because I'm not interested in histories, I'm interested in present human life; and sure the qualification has history in it, but it leads up to now, and it also entails some time during sobriety, and if there isn't conflict and turmoil during that period of the story, then I know I'm getting bullshit and insincerity.

Typically, changes over time occur both in ways of speaking and in ways of listening. The same qualification could hypothetically produce two significantly distinct responses at two points in an auditor's career. Elliot's reactions shift according to predictable, "objective" standards and along a range of physical and emotional variables as well:

> When I'm twenty pounds overweight, and when I'm having sexual problems, and I'm, when I've been drinking caffeine or/and sweets, but not getting enough sleep, et cetera, or thinking about my mother, or guilty about my separation or divorce, or angry that my kids are not doing well —whatever life is—these are the negatives I'm talking about—my filter system is different. If I'm running, feeling good, if I'm doing all right in my sexual life, if I'm doing all right in my relationship, if I'm feeling more secure, my filter system is different for the same individual. It doesn't mean that I would take someone that chemically . . . I don't buy, and make him a tremendous positive, but I don't think I would be as critical.

Hugh suggests there are as many distinct responses to a story as there are listeners in the audience. He begins by imagining a project of the sort that might be contrived by a well-intentioned folklorist:

> Okay, somebody speaks, and then you would interview like ten people who just listened, and, like, "What did you get out of it?" "Well, I . . . I really, you know, I couldn't identify at all." And another person would think it was, like, great, the turning point in their life. And another person who got something completely different. You know, that's where it might be interesting to see really how speaking affects people. . . . You know, because, not only is the speaker at a different phase in his life, so are the people that are listening, and needing different things out of it. And maybe some of those speakers that I got up and walked out on really changed somebody's life. Who knows? You know, but, maybe changed the speaker's life, maybe changed the person that's listening's life. It's really hard to tell. It's hard to be judgmental. I guess you just operate on the premise everybody's trying their best or they wouldn't even be there.

There is no more appreciative, sympathetic, and grateful audience imaginable than an AA group, particularly in the presence of a new speaker ("in which case he's forgiven everything," Scott says), or a speaker who is palpably agonized by a disjunction between emotion and linguistic resources. Except for the minimal sanctions against excessive length and excessive artifice, the weight of convention bearing on an adherence to a rudimentary structure, and some points of propriety that would obtain in most mixed public assemblies, there are no powerful restraints governing speaking at AA. Of course there are traditions within individual groups, and there are quasi-political factions within groups that exert pressures; but the final authority in qualification strategies is the speaker. It is not part of the AA narrative's purpose to invite criticism, correction, or amendment. The story is presumed to be the most appropriate contribution a speaker is capable of making to the AA community at the moment of speaking—a confluence of group purpose and individual evolution. So deeply implicated as it is in the dynamics of complementarity, the logic of story making and story reception shows forth as naked circularity.

To supplement our schematic of purposes and modes, above, to include reception, we have only to add "identify" and "accommodate" as the receptive helping modes extended to self and other, respectively. "Accommodation" may then subsume the pragmatic elements of "presence" and "gratitude." Identification and accommodation are so intimately bound up with one another as the deliberate mental gestures are made in both directions that useful discriminations become elusive.[5]

The helping imperative governs every aspect of the program, storytelling as much as any other, and speakers and listeners are both bound by it. Resistance to the helping imperative must be understood as a display of disqualifying inner contradiction that, if not confronted and overcome, will invite a withdrawal of support by other affiliates and the dissolution of the participatory compact. Thus, the only real alternative to acceptance of this principle is resignation from the program—absence. Complementarity has no contrasting reciprocal on offer within the AA program; again, binary thinking is abjured.

Among the conclusions to be drawn from the material presented here is that narrative in AA is a mutable and multivalent medium; whatever propositions are advanced invite immediate qualification or contravention. But this is as it should be in a symbolic community where the "law" of non-contradiction has been abrogated in such formulations as "don't compare, identify," and even "live and let live." The underlying assumption is that polarities, too, are a human construction, and as such may be dispelled or transcended using the same signifying apparatus by which they were conceived.

Six

Meaning and Value

It is not the purpose of this inquiry to engage with hostile critics of Alcoholics Anonymous. Sympathies and outcomes notwithstanding, such critics do perform the service of raising issues that may indeed warrant more concentrated and disinterested attention than they have received in the past. An example is the question whether an active alcoholic who is unable to find a foothold in AA is in an advanced state of self-deception and denial or is simply unsuited for one reason or another to the AA program's approach. "Upon therapy for the alcoholic himself, we surely have no monopoly," the Big Book generously states (Alcoholics Anonymous 1976a, p. xxi); and yet, the dominant AA position, also affirmed in the Big Book, appears to be that men and women who "fail" in AA are "constitutionally incapable of being honest with themselves" and simply "seem to have been born that way" (p. 58). This contradiction may be dismissed as merely apparent by someone favorably disposed toward AA, while a critic might see it as evidence of a prejudicial disjunction between theory and practice—complacent rigidity mocking a pretense at catholicity. Debate, while producing no major revision of AA text, has nonetheless elasticized opinion within the fellowship over the last two decades, generating an increased willingness to respect alternative therapies on merit and sometimes to work toward collaborative accommodation. AA, while striving on principle to hold itself aloof as a corporate entity from participation in controversy, and especially from lending its name in disputes around addiction research, has nevertheless, as a responsive human population, profited from being the subject of vigorous debate in the past, and, it is to be hoped, will continue to do so.

Some unfriendly commentators, however, must be acknowledged

because they represent a segment of professional opinion that is at least tangentially pertinent to our discussion of narrative. The stage is set in "Alcoholics Anonymous as Treatment and Ideology" (1979), where Robert Tournier argues that successful early intervention in problem drinking may be virtually precluded by the AA precept that a drinker must reach an extremity of alcoholic degradation *before* any rehabilitative strategies can succeed. Tournier also observes that the widespread institutional acceptance of AA's conception of alcoholism as a unitary disease entity with a predictable course has obstructed innovative research—especially research in pursuit of alternatives to the goal of total abstinence.

Tournier's lucid and balanced presentation is hostile to AA only insofar as it must be in response to AA's own admittedly nonscientific orthodoxy; indeed, the characterization "hostile" is accurate here only vis-à-vis the sometimes self-protective insularity of that orthodoxy. But some variants of the same argument slouch toward disingenuousness. Herbert Fingarette describes AA this way: "There are frequent meetings, with a strong confessional element. Members are expected to search their souls and their memories, and they are expected to gradually discover therein a personal history that by and large conforms to the AA picture of the course of alcoholism. Members whose memories or understanding of their experiences are inconsistent with AA doctrine may be confronted and charged with denial" (Fingarette, 1988, pp. 87–88).

These are not straightforward falsehoods, but rhetorically unbalanced declarations tricked out as "objective" propositions.

> Not surprisingly, those who become regular AA members do learn to believe in an autobiography that exemplifies AA teaching and to gloss over or ignore experiences and feelings that are contradicted by the teaching. For them, AA often becomes an alternative way of life, which is as intensely focused on abstinence as their former lives had been focused on alcohol. This passionate and complete reorientation is not a unique phenomenon; it is rather like what critics of sects would call ideological re-education or a modest form of elective brainwashing. (P. 88)

Fingarette's polemic is based largely on the findings of David Rudy, a symbolic interactionist sociologist whose evaluations of qualitative data are frustratingly uneven. Rudy swims in the same interpretive waters as Fingarette when he discusses storytelling:

"Telling one's story" or "giving testimonial" is perhaps the best known aspect of AA's organizational dynamics. . . . The testimonial is made up of two parts: a story about how bad it was before AA and a story about how good it is now. AA members frequently refer to the drinking part of the testimonial as a "drunkalogue" and to the second part as a "sobriety story."

Students of conversion and commitment have sometimes pointed out the importance, for the commitment process, of a "commitment act" which symbolizes the initiate's incorporation into the group. . . . Speaking in tongues or receiving the baptism of the holy spirit may serve for members of the Pentecostal movement as the "bridge-burning act" that separates their old identity from the new; in AA, one acknowledges one's embracement of the alcoholic identity by telling one's story. (Rudy, 1986, p. 38)

Paul Antze, the symbolic interactionist anthropologist, uses language similar to Rudy's: "In truth AA does far more than to help the compulsive drinker shake off a troublesome habit. It also draws him into a community that globally reorders his life. It provides him with a new understanding of himself and his motives as an actor—in effect a new identity" (Antze, 1987, p. 149).

A kind of spiritual ancestor to these recent critics is the psychologist Arthur Cain, who, in the once notorious *The Cured Alcoholic* (1964), called AA "a movement which is becoming one of America's most fanatical religious cults" (Cain, 1964, p. 61). In the early 1960s, Cain thought he discerned "a disquieting change" in the program: "AA is now highly formalized. The meetings, believed to be absolutely necessary, are ritualistic. And any suggestion that The Program is less than divine revelation evokes an irrational outcry" (p. 62).

Insofar as these commentators are working to clarify research objectives, enhance public awareness, or refine definitions and motives, their participation in a dialectic of critique is legitimate. However, in several instances, they are guilty of factual misrepresentation and rhetorical manipulation.

"Giving testimonial," for example, may be standard usage in the region of Rudy's fieldwork, but it is not used in the Northeast; affiliates with whom I talked avoid locutions of this kind precisely because of the institutional religious connotations. (The terms "qualify," "lead," and "speak" are widespread.) Rudy's use of quotation marks around "telling one's story" causes an ordinary phrase to seem charged or exotic. "Drunkalogue," in my experience, is used not to describe the "drinking part of a testimonial," but rather as a pejorative description of a talk that recounts drinking exploits without interpretation or connection to the present. Fingarette's account of AA resorts to reckless generalizations, the use of suggestive language ("charged," "gloss over," "passionate," "brainwashing"), and a false reification, dependent upon deceptive use of the passive voice, of a totalitarian, controlling, monolithic "AA." Each of these writers draws an infelicitous parallel between AA and religious fundamentalism; and each insists upon the notion of the acquisition by AA affiliates of a "new identity."

"Identity," in all of these cases, is a term used carelessly—and used without precision, the term has little explanatory value. Identity should not be construed as a commodity that may be exchanged, even pursuant to a state of crisis, for a "new" equivalent. That superadded newness breaches the integrity of the concept, stripping it of its essential differentia: coherence and continuity. The rhetorically devious term "new identity" is tendered to emphasize both the supposed cognitive susceptibility of affiliates and the voracity and relentless coerciveness of the program—characterizations which are, in my experience, entirely untenable. If "identity" here refers simply to an individual's structural position in a group, these social scientists should say so. Most alcoholics, I think, take the word *recovery* seriously and literally in their self-descriptions. A recovering alcoholic is not a person with a "new identity," but someone who has reestablished those temporarily disrupted or disarranged thematic continuities that inform the significant plot lines of the life story. A strong conserving trend is integral to AA's rehabilitative dimension.

The analogy between AA and religious fundamentalism is drawn in a manner comparable to the "new identity" tactic. For reasons one may only surmise, AA is pressed into the mold of psychosocial deviance, depicted as a fanatic, alien, unwholesome world quite unlike the normative milieu of most readers of academic social science journals.[1] The idea of fundamentalism acts insidiously as a polar opposite to the prized "neutrality" of social science. Fundamentalism becomes a kind of antithesis to the "detached" and "objective" science of the textually occulted but covertly controlling inquisitor. That neutrality is itself never questioned, but it should be, for it is as pitiless and barren as the White Logic that tortured Jack London—half-truth that conceals its own insufficiency. In the course of the movement of this analogy, the object of study, Alcoholics Anonymous, is transformed into—or, more likely, exposed for what it has been all along—the scientist's enemy. When Rudy's paraphrases and interpretations are compared with his qualitative data, the "ordinary language" of his informants, a curious cognitive slippage may be witnessed.

These critics hold what Clifford Geertz calls a "flattened view of other people's mentalities"—the same outlook as that which leads some social scientists to proffer inadequate explanations of symbol systems. To these social scientists, the effectiveness of a cultural symbol is understood in terms of how well it either "deceives the uninformed" or "excites the unreflective." That the symbol "might in fact draw its power from its capacity to grasp, formulate, and communicate social realities that elude the tempered language of science, that it may mediate more complex meanings than its literal reading suggests, is not even considered" (Geertz, 1973, p. 210).

There is a cursory similarity between AA stories and "conversion" narratives: both describe one state followed by an event followed by a second state that may be in a kind of inverse relation to the first.[2] But, as we have seen, this structure defines any minimal story, and implies no special kinship between conversion stories and AA stories, except insofar as both are similar to many other types of stories as well—stories of reversal, metamorphosis, education, or unmasking. With respect to content, the AA story rarely reports the seeking and inducement of supernatural vision, and there is no solicitation for such a component, implicit or explicit, either expressed in AA literature or welling up out of the regulative force of the collectivity. Scott says, "Our spirituality . . . is very, um, 'deconstructivist'—it's because there's scarcely anything of it, except what you want to make of it, and . . . there's room for all types of spirituality."

Scott's remark points to the conspicuous absence from AA speaking phenomena of another key element of historical conversion narratives: the appeal for acceptance to a prepotent judgmental authority, such as a committee of superiors in a rigid hierarchical structure, with the gravest penalty for failure not rebuke or expulsion but the implanting in the confessors of morbid inner uncertainty concerning their own justification. Of course most speakers desire to please the AA audience, to garner laughter, signals of assent, and generous applause at the end; but these prizes are practically guaranteed in advance and, in any case, are surely incentives of a significantly different order from a deeply inculcated terror of eternal damnation.

Individuals do sometimes speak of returning in their sobriety to the religious denominations with which they were affiliated in childhood and youth, before the epoch of the disruptive prevalence of alcoholism; but I have not heard such rapprochements dogmatically prescribed. The AA distinction between religion and spirituality is almost universally appreciated, and theology as such is only rarely an ingredient in AA stories. AA's indeterminate spirituality is a zone where inner experiences—feeling-states, imprecise cognitions, awkwardly intermingled ideas and affects—may be articulated in nonsectarian language, made accessible to others across a range of aptitudes, habits, and codes. It is one of AA's virtues that people who do not share elaborated linguistic resources—the precise technical vocabulary of sociology, for example—may nevertheless communicate concerning the complexities of sobriety with enough clarity and a sufficient capacity for nuance to be intelligible and useful to one another.

As we have suggested, much of the AA repertoire of phrases and formulas, recipes and standards, is consecrated to the dismantling of habitual binary apperceptions. The term "dry-drunk," for example, denotes a commonly occurring state of extreme irritability, anxiety, and discomfort in an alcoholic who is technically sober—that is, not ingesting alcohol—but who has not experienced any of the vaunted liberating transformations of a serene sobriety. This paradoxical hybrid term disrupts the received oppositions drunk/sober and dry/drinking, eliciting a new concept that, in effect, takes alcoholism out of the bottle and relocates it in a system comprising substance, person, language, social frames, and affective vectors.

Another case where apparent simplicity conceals complex signification is the intricate speech act performed by speakers at the start of all AA narratives and, in fact, at the beginning of all formal speaking turns during meetings. The form, described earlier as a "salutation," is "My name is [Hank], and I'm an alcoholic," and, although it does have casual social utility, its more important functions are not so evident. The affirmation "I'm an alcoholic," at the start of a narrative, establishes with certainty the conditions under which the narrative to follow may be contemplated, just as the clues that arouse particular expectations in literary genres are contained in titles, first lines, and initial situations, not to mention packaging and marketing appurtenances. To say to an AA group, "I'm an alcoholic" is to affirm a commitment to the avowed purposes of the group, to claim credibility as a witness and participant, and to petition for the authority to admonish, exemplify, advise, and so on.

In the taxonomy of speech acts advanced by John Searle (1969, 1979), the statement "I'm an alcoholic" may, in fact, be understood as a member of each of the five discrete categories simultaneously. It is a *representative* (or *assertive*) in that it commits the speaker to the truth of the proposition as far as that truth is understood in good faith; it is a *directive* in that it enjoins the audience to full, responsive participation and sympathetic identification; it is a *commissive* in that it commits the speaker to continuing adherence to the shared principles of the program; it is an *expressive* in that it conveys the speaker's psychological state, presumably beginning with a sincere confidence in the unfolding narrative process and the AA process as a whole beyond that; and, finally, it may be construed as a *declarative* in that it reconfers the bond and privilege of membership in AA upon the speaker. "Fit" is assured between words and world as the speaker upholds program philosophy; compels accommodative attention; advances the AA message with sincerity, discipline, and enthusiasm; and confirms institutional integrity.

A great deal is accomplished in short compass, then. I will not insist that all of these things happen every time "I'm an alcoholic" is uttered; rote usage by oldtimers and experimentation by the unconvinced are among the possible exceptions to full-bodied sincerity. But there is surely a sufficiency of communicative richness here to challenge reductive synopsis. "Alcoholic"—a problematic designation in any case—becomes a multifaceted token, fusing medical, philosophical, social, and imaginative aspects of a situation whose evolution is not complete, perhaps deliberately confusing them, perhaps aspiring toward an ambiguity so dense that it generates its own independent symbolic authority.

An elusive multidimensionality characterizes the stories, too, and it is inappropriate for us to consider ourselves satisfied with having observed certain kinds of formal pattern and certain recurring intentional structures. These formulaic narratives remain highly susceptible to the subjectivity of the speaker, to unglimpsed actualities of private history and experience, to individual genetic and developmental constraints that may be known, if ever, only by indirection, statistical surmise, intuition, and inference.

The literary theorist Barbara Herrnstein Smith defines narratives as "the verbal acts of particular narrators performed in response to —and thus shaped and constrained by—sets of multiple interacting conditions." With respect to any narrative, she claims,

> these conditions would consist of (1) such circumstantial variables as the particular context and material setting (cultural and social, as well as strictly "physical") in which the tale is told, the particular listeners or readers addressed, and the nature of the narrator's relationship to them, and (2) such psychological variables as the narrator's motives for telling the tale and all the particular interests, desires, expectations, memories, knowledge, and prior experiences (including his knowledge of various events, of course, but also of other narratives and of various conventions and traditions of storytelling) that elicited the telling of it on that occasion, to that audience, and that shaped the particular way he told it. (Smith, 1981, p. 222)

We have charted some of these conditions; others must remain unknown; for some we are offered only the most fragile clues— allusions to, but not specifications of, the fuller life beyond the delimited purposes of AA. Mark says, of story preparation, "I can be thinking about it for a week and something can happen to me on the last day that will slant the way I'm going to approach it." Mutability—or undecidability—may be tracked to the merest coloration inhering in separate words, the echoes and resonances heard perhaps only distantly by the speaker but informing interior significance nonetheless. It is difficult to imagine a truly complete analysis of any of these stories, dismantled lexeme-by-lexeme, supplemented with associations by the speaker and full ethnographic contextualization. We must make do, in large measure, with a communicative equivalent of trust. Our texts here bleed into insoluble dilemmas in the domain of otherness.

Folklorist Jeff Todd Titon (1980) has proposed that the life story must be sharply distinguished from "its historical kin: biography, oral history, and the personal history (or 'life history,' as it is called in anthropology)" (p. 276). The life story, for Titon, is a "self-sufficient and self-contained fiction" (p. 291), and as such it is exempt from evaluation by standards of utility or conformity to institutional preconceptions. By calling it a "fiction," Titon does not mean that the life story is necessarily inconsistent with historical truth, but that it is shaped, crafted, invested with symbolic values, managed by the speaker in compliance with an intricate interior agenda.[3]

A similar point is made by the philosopher George Gusdorf in "Conditions and Limits of Autobiography." Gusdorf's essay concerns literary autobiography, but is applicable with little modification in the present context. "The significance of autobiography should . . . be sought beyond truth and falsity, as those are conceived by simple common sense. It is unquestionably a document about a life, and the historian has the perfect right to check out its testimony and verify its accuracy. But it is also a work of art, and the literary devotee, for his part, will be aware of its stylistic harmony and the beauty of its images" (Gusdorf, 1980, p. 43).

Life stories in AA are, of course, inseparable from well-defined collective ends; but they are, simultaneously, fictions in Titon's sense, designs by which the speaker represents himself to himself and to others by means of symbolic manipulations and value selections. As Gusdorf—using "confession" in a non-religious aspect—puts it:

> Confession of the past realizes itself as a work in the present: it effects a true creation of self by the self. Under guise of presenting myself as I was, I exercise a sort of right to recover possession of my existence now and later. "To create and in creating to be created," the fine formula of Lequier, ought to be the motto of autobiography. It cannot recall the past in the past and for the past . . . it calls up the past for the present and in the present, and it brings back from earlier times that which preserves a meaning and value today; it asserts a kind of tradition between myself and me that establishes an ancient and new fidelity, for the past drawn up into the present is also a pledge and a prophecy of the future. (P. 44)

The data of historical truth are susceptible to shaping, to modification, by both the AA helping injunction and the special, private necessities of the speaker's personal evolving fiction of self.

The "actual" history—the factual chronology—of the speaker is first submitted to normal narrativizing devices: the selection—from fallible memory—of representative scenes and relations, temporal compression and dislocation, and the always perilous linguistic encoding itself. Superimposed upon this already purposeful natural narrative is the generalized propositional structure of AA, by means of which the kernels of narrative may then be further modified or interpreted. Since speakers aspire to exemplify recovery, to validate program principles and emblematize "success" to the audience, idiosyncrasies that could interfere with identification may be flattened; incidents may be screened against a potentially damaging effect. Extension and universalization are weighed against the particularities of that which is entirely private. The program "message" of hope is superior in value to historical truth—but this notion co-exists with the ideal of honesty, so that representations must be carefully, deliberately mediated. These conflicting values serve further to undermine simplistic distinctions between truth-telling and mendacity. Truth and value are linked in ways undreamed of by positivist self-assurance.

The narrative is further conditioned by the manner of its delivery. Even if there were some sort of ideal, perfected narrative in suspension at the start of a speaking event, it would not be transmitted by a neutral medium, but by the speaker who persists in a state of responsiveness, amending and altering "text" up to the instant of utterance and even beyond. The age and sex of the speaker, nationality and race, the markers of class and taste, grooming and dress, the apparent degree of ease or tension, the quality of the voice, posture, the cast of the face—all of these determine the sense of the story. The very channel of communication becomes an interpretive mechanism, keying textual understanding with visual cues, tics and fidgets and quirks, with laughter and smiles, with ironic superciliousness or sarcasm or mimicry, with hesitations and false starts, catches in the throat and the inability to speak, agonizing pauses, and, especially, with tears. The audience plays back to the speaker, as well, and corrections are exchanged: the audience laughs and the speaker finds more wit in the arsenal; the speaker sobs and the audience falls reverently silent, muted and aroused with compassionate identification; the speaker grows tediously homiletic, and the audience becomes restive, shuffling feet and creaking chairs; the audience is nervous, rapt, overwrought, and the speaker, with a self-deprecatory quip, graciously authorizes the momentary dissolution of the mood's intensity.

There are dominant modes of discourse, styles that, while they may range widely in the course of a talk, are governed in the main by the single tone of lamentation, rejoicing, beseechment, admonition, or invective.[4] The dominant discursive mode combines with the dominant of the ensemble of textual strategies, roughly the equivalent of conventional literary types, to produce the final, formed, narrative event, irretrievable but able to supersede itself in future redactions. My tentative list of the recurring textual types includes the following: didactic, epic/romantic, realistic, comic, therapeutic/exploratory, celebratory, and cathartic. There are, of course, hybrids and malformations, too.

It must be supposed that the same speaker, on different occasions, may produce different narrative types and deliver them under different dominant discursive modes—although we might safely speculate that individuals tend toward repetition and predictability in this as in other aspects of their lives. We should, I suspect, count inertia among the combining elements in narrative production.

Typologies within typologies, elegant balances and analogs, may give aesthetic delight and bring the textual object inside a range of limits for comparative applications; but what, then, do we know further of alcoholism and storytelling? Perhaps objectifying AA narrative may serve, paradoxically, a humanizing purpose; bringing AA narratives into familiar taxonomic straits may provoke the reflection that their creators are also entitled to a measure of respectful attention.

These narratives resist abbreviation and labeling; they are not arrays of data, but attempts to externalize and display experience, belief, and symbolic values, perhaps representing these in a fluid near-simultaneity, apparently with no need for rigid categorical demarcation felt by speakers or listeners. And, as quantitative analyses, distributional accounts, lists of formulas and functions, repertoire studies, and exegeses based in poetics and form are inadequate to reckon with the affective and experiential dimensions of other storytelling conventions, so it is with AA. The techniques of fiction seem to be better suited to comprehending—taking all together—the qualities of such situations and the complexities with which they are interlocked.[5]

An anonymous recovering alcoholic writer who identifies himself as "Elpenor"—after a minor figure in the Odyssey who dies of drink and is memorialized on that account—compares the AA narrative to a whole range of folk stories. "At an AA meeting, good listeners become as little children listening to fairy tales. And a fairy tale of sorts is what, typically, we hear" (Elpenor, 1986, p. 44).

The skeletal AA story is perceived here as a retelling of the ordeal of confrontation between the solitary child—the fairy tale hero and now the recollecting alcoholic—and an unspeaking, ambiguous, sometimes malevolent world. Alcohol is like the donor's magical gift, given to facilitate the child-hero's quest, but it is a duplicitous gift: its power resists control, and it finally imperils the very life of the seeker. In the AA resolution of this tale, correction of the initial deficiency occurs not as the successful outcome of the quest, nor in a renunciation of the quest and the repression of its memory, but in a reappraisal of the quest's initial terms, and a recursive reintegration of all subsequent experience. In alcoholism, Elpenor tells us, a key to the problem is the faulty definition of the originating privation.

> What quest were we on when we set forth? What was it we wanted, really wanted? It wasn't anything in particular. That was the trouble. All we had was neediness and vision, bottomless neediness and wondrous vision. Out of these we conjured a god—the god, in fact, whose servant is the Demon. W. H. Auden called him Possibility, and said that his idolaters were legion in modern societies. . . .
> . . . Possibility, after all, is simultaneously the one great true thing (anything *can* happen), the great half-truth (I can do anything I want to), and the great lie (I can *be* anyone I want to). . . . In a drunk's story, Possibility appears as it is to the true idolater: the achingly elusive element in which we live and move and have our dreams; the pool, the drowning pool, of the self. (P. 45)

Redemption inheres, at least partially, in the storytelling. The compelling dramatic power of the narrative is intensified by the speaking presence which testifies to one successful outcome at the same time that it opens itself to a second unsuccessful one, that is, relapse. "After the meeting," Elpenor writes, the speaker "must go out again into the fluid world of Possibility. And out there, as he and every member of the gathering know, waits the certainty of death" (p. 46).

In the psychoanalytic dialogue, "the patient undergoes a kind of conversion, or rather a series of conversions, in the course of which he works out a new, illuminating, and presumably helpful version of his life story." Elpenor compares this process to the AA experience. "So, too, at an AA meeting: there, the newcomer learns to channel the maelstrom of his experience along the lines of a quest story. And there are parallels, as well, between the dramas played out in each kind of session. In AA there is the drunk's mortal struggle to compose his life in words and the counterinsurgent denial of his need to stop drinking, as well as of the proffered way to stop. In analysis the drama is the patient's painful ordeal to become a maker of sense and his fierce resistance to the analyst who can help him" (p. 46).

But analysis is without a tonic social dimension, and consequently of limited use to alcoholics. The dramatic element is inadequate; embodied theater, sacrifice, and primal communality are wanting in analysis, but provided by AA. "The AA drama seems as simple and straightforward a container of meaning as the mind could devise. It has to be, for containing is precisely what it must do for us. We are the incontinent, those whom Dante found wallowing in putrid slop, and what we crave is integrity, coherence, simplicity. AA drama is oral, preliterate. In fact, the whole culture of AA is oral, a tribal culture which gets passed on by means of stories and maxims" (p.47).

Within this tribal culture, as Elpenor sees it, certain individuals, compared to bards, come forward with especially powerful messages. Their aptitudes make them particularly well-suited to AA, and their recited experiences, intrinsically or by virtue of craft and application, seem to harmonize with the needs of their auditors at a higher level of generality than most. Elpenor's "Ted" is such a character. "A myth is constitutive: it makes for a collective identification. That's what Ted's stories do. They weave a magic circle of words around our meetings, making a tribe out of a group of lonely quest-heroes. In his own story, Ted is Odysseus; but in his manner of telling it, he is our Homer. He offers himself up, a creature as wretched and glorious as the powers of speech, for us to identify with, to be at one with, to die with or to live with, if he can only go on telling his story" (p. 47).

Fairy tale, epic, quest-story, myth: the terms are employed some-what capriciously, but again the point must be taken that historical truth is not the principal issue in AA. Historical truth is not evaded in the construction of these stories, but "integrity, coherence, and simplicity" inhere only rarely in strict chronicle, and must be elicited from other modes of telling.

Attempts to classify the oral personal narrative precisely, to locate for it a stable position along the continuum of folk stories, have been made by folklorists, but unexceptionable definition is wanting. Narrative theorist Sandra K. Dolby-Stahl has devoted considerable labor to the problem of the taxonomy of personal narratives, and offered this definition: "The personal narrative is a prose narrative relating a personal experience; it is usually told in first person and its content is nontraditional" (Dolby-Stahl, 1977, p. 20). Dolby-Stahl's definition may seem unexceptionable at first blush, but it fails to define for us all and only personal narratives, as folklorist Linda Dégh has persuasively demonstrated (1985).

Dégh's point is not so much that Dolby-Stahl's definition is incorrect, but rather that the personal narrative is an unsuitable candidate for definition at this degree of rigidity. Dégh states, "There is no justification for separating personal experience stories from other forms of narration to which they are symbiotically re-lated" (1985, p. 108). It should, in fairness, be noted that Dolby-Stahl is fully aware of the problems of taxonomy, and has even attempted to document border disputes in an article that finds per-sonal narrative unexpectedly sharing characteristics with better cir-cumscribed genres. In later work on personal narrative, Dolby-Stahl moved into the arena of heroic confrontation with the twin bêtes noires of intertextuality and undecidability.[6]

The question of classifying the oral narrative of recovery in AA is of little interest here as such. We have noted that these narratives tend to be patterned after a minimal state-event-state story form, but that predictable regularity of adherence to this form in everyday realizations is problematic. We have also observed an interplay of multiple functions in the narratives that must necessarily be ap-praised on a case-by-case basis. Furthermore, individual poetics and rhetoric, improvisation, and variables in response and setting are key determinants in the shaping narrative act and—again—these features interact unpredictably and uniquely, arraying themselves anew in each situated storytelling event. Therefore, it is neither an attempt to propose an incontestable definition nor an effort to supplement already metastasized folkloristic taxonomies to submit that these AA stories are usefully understood as *autobiographical legends;* this term is a condensation, a mnemonic or a glyph, of certain essential but not always quantifiable elements.

We have already confronted the idea of the fictitious in autobiography: chronicle, fantasy, and prophecy are intertwined in the name of a narrative that will not only react to the past but serve in the future, uniting the two with a strong, seamless weld. "Every autobiography is a work of art and at the same time a work of enlightenment. . . . What is in question is a sort of revaluation of individual destiny; the author, who is at the same time the hero of the tale, wants to elucidate his past in order to draw out the structure of his being in time. And this secret structure is for him the implicit condition of all possible knowledge in every order whatsoever—hence the central place of autobiography, especially in the literary sphere" (Gusdorf, 1980, p. 45).

The "secret structures" of the AA narrative are teased out by and for the speaker; but even more than in literary autobiography, these structures must be fully communicable if the speaker is to maintain adherence to AA's helping imperative. "In the final analysis, then, the prerogative of autobiography consists in this: that it shows us not the objective stages of a career—to discern these is the task of the historian—but that it reveals instead the effort of a creator to give the meaning of his own mythic tale. Every man is the first witness of himself; yet the testimony that he thus produces constitutes no ultimate, conclusive authority—not only because objective scrutiny will always discover inaccuracies but much more because there is never an end to this dialogue of a life with itself in search of its own absolute" (p. 48).

Again, the "mythic" is introduced, this time to carry us toward ontological imponderables, but useful nevertheless, because "mythic" always means formal, or formally familiar—and that is the meaning of the paradigm story in AA. The master story—"Bill's Story" converted to a set of faceless generalizations, an armature— is the familiar structure against which individual variants are matched and then coded: once contrastingly for the speaker, once comparatively for the listener. AA stories aspire equally toward generality and particularity, toward communicative utility and the secret structuring of inner consonance. With the passage of time and the labors of introspection and craft, these goals will converge.

Again, the correspondence between the psychoanalytic dialogue and the AA process may be adduced. In recent theoretical discussions of the contested issue of truth in psychoanalysis, historical truth has lost ground to consonance, coherence, narrative truth— truth construed as a mutable, operative construct and not a verifiable absolute. The psychotherapist Wolfgang Loch writes: "Psychoanalytic procedure is based on sincerity, but psychoanalysis does not discover truth understood as a correspondence between facts of the past and propositions in the form of interpretations concerning this past. Rather, it *constructs truth* in the service of self-coherence for the present and the future, on the basis of mutual agreement" (Loch, 1977, p. 238).

According to Loch, the subject's goals in developing a felicitous life narrative in psychoanalysis are similar to those in Alcoholics Anonymous: the achievement of self-determination, a sense of participation, the ability to realize potentialities, to attain "the full and harmonious synthesis of one's feelings, conations and cognitions" (pp. 242–243). The narrative developed out of the continuing interaction of analyst and patient in psychoanalysis is governed by credibility and use-value within the framework of these goals: the standard of evaluation is not verifiability but utility, health, immunity from enslavement to the unreal. The watchful analyst will, from time to time, venture an explanatory remark for the consideration of the patient: "If—and only if—this proffered reason is acceptable to him and has the strength to *convince* him that it is 'true,' it will possibly set him free to behave differently from then on—for example, in respect to strikingly submissive behavior. What I should like to stress is this introduction of reasons that make sense and are thus true—all of which takes places in the *symbolic order of language* —and appeal to the patient's wish to lead a life of his own, to be self-reliant and to actualize potentialities he is only dimly aware of, powers that if handled effectively would change his life" (p. 230).

"Reasons that make sense and are thus true" might be taken as an exact description of much of the disputed rhetoric of AA. The truth is in the comfort of the fit, the responsive conformity of a proposition to the contours of the disorder; truth is not a commodity to be judged by means of appeal to outside authority.

As we have indicated earlier, the attainment of usable truths in psychoanalysis, as in AA, is not the shedding of some superannuated "identity" in preference for another newer, brighter one, but an act of purposeful conservation and cultivation, employing native materials: the formed precipitate of character, the patterns of irrevocable past actions, the transformations of guilt, shame, and error, not repudiated but reconstrued. Loch returns again and again to the need for building a sense of coherence, not only to bridge the past and present, but to bring integrity to the whole continuing structure of an individual life. "What seems to be of even more decisive importance is the individual's need to assure the continuity of his inner life: this makes it imperative for him to meld present conditions with patterns already in use, in order to create coherence in understanding. If we accept this concern for *coherence* as a guiding principle, then we realize that the truths a person is about to gain are its derivatives; expressed the other way round, the *coherence* that the person cannot escape looking for builds meaning and sense —that is, creates *truth*" (p. 231).

Psychoanalysis strives to engender in the patient the feeling of participation and the capacity to communicate, and to mediate, in the process of speaking, the coincidence of experience and thought. The language and ideas of the anthropologist Carl Thune's phenomenological account of AA, "Alcoholism and the Archetypal Past," bear a striking similarity to those of Loch and other philosophical psychoanalytic theorists.[7] The alcoholic's "reinterpretation" of his or her life according to AA strategies leads to a "resolution of . . . paradoxes," or to the recognition that paradoxes were only apparent, chimerical entities made up out of false presuppositions and linguistic misconstruction. "This reinterpretation involves a process of labeling and analysis (better, relabeling and reanalysis) of segments of the past which gives them a new meaning and defines new problems, thereby suggesting different strategies for living. Probably the most important result of revising the past to fit the model is that it acquires a formerly lacking pattern and coherence. The terminology used, as it has been re-created and redefined, is one positing particular relations and structures which the old language was unable to label or easily demarcate" (Thune, 1977, p. 81).

Along with the technology, AA provides a milieu: a social environment in which the new meanings and new problems may be revealed, compared, analyzed, interpreted, perhaps resolved; in many instances, apparently, the mere "sharing," disclosure within the sympathetic collectivity, *is* resolution. The "old language" may have been inadequate because, in effect, it did not exist, having neither vocabulary, channel, nor receptive field. A mere flux of ambiguous feeling-states, of course, has limited worth as a tool for fine discriminations in moral development.

The social dimension of AA must not be underestimated, and is probably the single most consequential point of differentiation between AA and other therapies. The social component in AA is expanded so greatly beyond the analytic dyad or small group as to become a qualitatively distinct order of experience, capable of the production of an altogether different kind of communicative collusion, parallel to the powerful collective self-validations of those theatrical and religious ceremonies in which the certainty of accord is so strong that a temporary relaxation of the bonds of isolation is felt to occur among the participants. And it is specifically in the social dimension that the conception of the AA story as a species of legend attains its vitality.

Legend itself is based in social contingency, or, more exactly, is a primary expressive field for the negotiation of personal responses to social contingency. Indeed, the central and definitive point in the remarkable work done on legend by folklorists Linda Dégh and Andrew Vázsonyi is that social issues permeate legend at all levels, from pragmatics to abstractable content: "Legends are seldom limited to the mere relation of the plot. In most cases the narrative itself cannot be separated from the circumstances of telling, the introductory remarks of the teller, interjected comments, and reflections of both teller and participants that parallel the performance to the end. Furthermore, the closing remarks, explanatory, supplementary or contrasting stories, analogous cases, and modifications or straight refutation of the story in question are also inseparable parts of the legend" (Dégh and Vázsonyi, 1976, p. 101).

We have noted the necessity for understanding AA stories in the framework of the program as a whole, including recurring linguistic formulas, patterns of personal interactions, printed supplements to oral behavior, and continuing verbal exchange inside and outside formal framed meeting time and space. We have devoted considerable attention to the importance of audience receptivity and the reciprocal responsiveness of audience and speaker. Dégh and Vázsonyi make the same point in discussing the general characteristics of legend production:

> In the act of legend creation cooperation between the speaker and his audience is much closer than in the composition of any other prose-narrative genre. One might say that the intimate participation and involvement of the listeners is one of the inherent features of the legend. The teller is not a self-conscious artist who is recognized and admired for his creative fantasy, like the storyteller. He is just one of the group, whose other members share the same knowledge and act as audience or often as associate contributors to his story. At best the teller might differ from the others in one particular area of knowledge in which he possesses extra information and expertise the others do not have, so that he is considered more competent. (P. 101)

Participants in legend sessions take their turns at center stage, then rejoin the audience. Credibility is evaluated, documentation proffered and weighed, and the "data contribution and support of all who are present" are solicited in a drive toward consensus or felicitous suspension. The structure of an AA meeting is contrived to produce a sense of internal unanimity, at least with respect to the general validity of the project and the sincerity of the participants. The performance at the podium is a show within the larger show that is the meeting itself. Participants in the larger show are avid to exhibit commitment and unity to outsiders and newcomers at the same time that they experience it privately. Within this regulative superstructure, the master story is endlessly produced and reproduced, but each time from a somewhat different position, each time reflective of a different degree or quality of belief, adherence, recognition, commitment. "The interaction of the participants brings the legends to life, and the nature of each telling-event acts upon the actual quality of belief. The actual belief manifest at the time of the telling is always the result of the dichotomous relationship between the communal belief system, inherited in tradition and sanctioned by enculturation, and the personal belief of the individual performers" (pp. 102–103).

At the AA podium, the speaker perpetuates the legend of recovery regardless of the degree of his or her own belief in it. The meeting itself is theater, the enactment of a performance that affirms the effective force of the collective, but the show at the podium, the idiosyncratic restatement of the main theme, while likewise a drama in its own right, is also the speaker's provisional but autonomous statement of position, a claim for privileged occupancy of an ever-expanding field. If no claim is ever denied, neither is any accepted until the risk of assertion is taken.

The story of recovery, in more or less the form we have identified, is the master story, the legend field on which the right of membership is claimed, and where belief is negotiated. Dégh and Vázsonyi write: "The legend, in its true essence, is a *question*. Moreover, it is not so much a question as a *provocation* and even not so much a provocation as *dispute*. It is a dispute about the proposition of the legend and about the belief expressed by the proposition. Consequently, this provocative question, this belief under debate is what has to differ from the norms" (Dégh and Vázsonyi, 1973, p. 48).

In the last analysis, the norms in question are those established by institutional authority and sanctioned by orthodoxies precipitated out of movement and counter-movement in centuries of conflict over epistemological supremacy:

> We believe the answer to the question of who determines the norms from which the legend deviates and challenges is: authoritative persons, institutions, corporations, those who are considered as competent by virtue of their occupation, position or acquired reputation and are the only ones who can express their opinion *ex cathedra*. The authority on religious matters is the Church, on medical problems the doctors, on the weather the meteorologists, on earthquakes the geologists and on strange things, shocking events, confusing problems generally the down-to-earth rationalists who hold that any problem can be resolved and that principally there are no mysteries. These are the persons with whom the legend-teller takes issue. No matter what the legend contains, it questions one and the same thing by asserting and provoking contradictions not in favor of certainty but of uncertainty. (P. 49)

In AA, the legend of recovery is provocation to dispute with the normative standards governing at least *three* important orientations: first, the AA story questions the validity of received definitions and stereotypes of alcoholism, which include conceptions of the hopelessness of alcoholism, the immorality of alcoholism, and the futility of alcoholism; second, the AA story questions institutional responses to alcoholism, including marginalization, ostracism, discipline, punishment, incarceration, indifference, neglect, and long-term cause-oriented therapies; third, and at its most expansive, the AA story questions the underpinnings of the very structure of conventional ways of knowing.

Hopelessness is, of course, contravened by the achieved, visible well-being of much of the AA membership. The availability of the disease concept of alcoholism offers an option for reconceiving the scope and limits of personal responsibility, providing the subject with the possibility of remission of paralyzing guilt and opportunities for reconstructive action. The sense of futility is inverted, and squandered time past reconstrued as a vital, even necessary, preparation for the amplitude, enlightenment, and service that characterize the present. The influx of hope, purpose, and value should enable the rehabilitation of personal and work relationships.

The disease concept, along with the helping imperative in AA, may contribute to a devaluation of institutional authority and act as an incentive to question hitherto unexamined affiliations or patterns of dependency. The visible apparatus of social control—hospitals, asylums, prisons, even clinics and other conventional therapeutic sites—is repudiated, and the experience of alcoholism, valorized as knowledge, is accorded primacy. The new utopian formation takes no political position, makes no move to interfere with the institutional structure, but simply stands outside it, alternative but not contrary. Still, the communality of AA is antihierarchic, antistructural, and compels the reflection that normative institutional values are, at the very least, arbitrary. Paradoxes, thought provoking and perhaps—carried to a sufficient extreme—tendentious, permeate the program's fabric: defeat is triumph, failure is success, submission is autonomy, and neurotic misery is . . . happiness—or, at least, the possibility of equanimity despite the hazards of the vicious ontological snares that beset consciousness.

And, as we have noted, these paradoxes and inversions serve to undercut the stability of received categories of thought, and especially the inevitability of binary opposition. Language play (introduced by means of stories and formulas and ultimately the expansive styles of independent thinking that these stimulate) and exemplary alternative conduct (observed as institutional non-compliance, intensive open-ended self-examination, rigorous adherence to the helping imperative, and demonstrated respect for the integrity of others) conjoin to instruct the AA newcomer in a productive elaboration of the insight that begins with the recognition of defeat. The defeat of the subject's symmetrical epistemological premise leaves an open space; creative aspiration toward the new premise of integration in complementarity is invited. The ground of legend is a place of inquiry, and so a wide variety of opinions and a great range of aptitudes and learning must co-exist; the void left by the decomposition of the dominance of the binary is not replaced with another totalitarian scheme, but with an open structure into which the subject may insert himself with humility, receptivity, and a will to be useful. The speaking subject at the podium is a momentary intersection of possibilities; each kernel of narrative becomes the signifier for the whole range of contingencies along which it lies. Specific narratives simultaneously express the whole along with clusters of particulars that may even appear contradictory.

The legend of recovery, with its ever-changing protagonist—the individual over time, or different speakers from one meeting to the next—is the field of belief against which cognitive principles are examined. The legend itself causes no decisions to be made; it is not a standard of truth or excellence or virtue, but only a depiction of a range of possibilities. "The legend," Dégh and Vázsonyi tell us, "is not only able to defy reason but can also extricate itself of its unwanted support. In general, it remains unaffected by friendly or hostile encounters with reality. The legend is neither always untrue nor always true; it is always right" (1973, p. 16).

The autobiographical fiction and the legend of recovery will, ideally, fuse at key points, particularly as the art of the self-life-"writer" and the deliberations of the legend speaker converge in commitment to a productive future. Art and belief reinforce one another, and come to enjoy a rapport with other signatories to the agreement of respect for the legend paradigm. As life and belief alter over time, so, too, will the autobiography in its symbiosis with the legend of recovery. These pliant structures are endlessly accommodating of one another; and AA narratives of recovery are therefore capable of rich, supple, and almost infinite variation.

Appendix:
Five Stories

Appendix: Five Stories

The majority of AA speakers, possibly contrary to out-siders' expectations, are fluent, controlled, and effective. The five speakers here are competent if not consummate, apparently com-fortable in the speaking situation, serious though not without humor. These are "ordinary" AA speakers: taken together they seem a not unfair representation of the AA spectrum. Except for their self-determined inability to drink safely, they probably have little in common; and in their observable behavior they display no special distinctions. The stories are delivered in a relaxed, conversa-tional manner, with little deliberate rhetorical embellishment or showmanship. The real melodramas of AA, in any event, are not normally enacted from the podium at open meetings.

The three men are between forty and fifty-five. Ross holds a fairly well-paid job in medical administration; Spike and Phil are skilled laborers. Spike is African American; the others are of various assimi-lated European backgrounds. Susie, a nurse in her mid-forties, seems tired and somewhat remote, perhaps due to the health prob-lems she mentions in her story. Cindy, in her middle thirties, is younger than the others and more ebullient.

Ross
July 2, 1986

I'm Ross, I'm an alcoholic.

My story is largely a bottle story, so if you're offended by those, I suggest you just sit back and take some inventory, indulge your fantasies, or whatever. I . . . I need to hear about the, uh, the blood, the vomit, and the broken glass. And I presume that others do too.

For lack of something else I'll start at the beginning. I'm the only son of a, uh, Irish Catholic immigrant and a Quaker WASP. I was an only child, and a late child. In the rooms especially lately, I hear a lot of adult children of alcoholics, alcoholics who're from broken homes, that received a lot of abuse—emotional, physical, sexual; who had a lot of rough times that contributed to their, uh, to their alcoholism. Uh, I can't hang it on that. I snatched defeat from victory time after time. I had, essentially, a Norman Rockwell childhood. I was raised over in Jersey, on a lake—which was, at the time, the . . . Pine Barrens; I had a very idyllic childhood. The only thing that was missing was other children. Uh, that caused a couple of misapprehensions; I thought, I always thought that I was a grown-up. I still suffer from that illusion.

Since I was an only child my parents were conscious of not spoiling me; I, uh, didn't get everything I wanted; I did get everything that was good for me, like, uh, private schools and orthopedic shoes. I, uh . . . but in spite of all that I still knew that I was the center of the universe. And, to this day that's the trouble, an idea I have trouble shedding.

I don't remember my first drink. Uh . . . there was always alcohol in the house, and I could have it; if I wanted to have a sip out of my father's beer, or wanted a whole can, I could have it. And . . . it was always there. I do remember my first drunk. I was in a wedding, and I was thirteen. And . . . I don't remember what I drank but it really, it did the job. I was, uh, loud and mouthy, and . . . I put my best moves on my twenty-six-year-old cousin. I had to be taken out to a diner and fed coffee. I guess everybody at the wedding forgot about it—you know, they thought it was either cute or disgusting, depending on your frame of reference. Uh . . . but I didn't forget about it. That marked the beginning of a very special relationship with alcohol. One that endures to this day. A lot of my life has been spent drinking it; and the balance has been spent not drinking it.

There and after throughout my teens I drank whenever I could. I don't know if I always drank to get drunk, but I drank for effect. I drank for the rush. You know when it, uh, when it hit bottom, that's what I was looking for.

I had a relatively uneventful adolescence. I, uh, like everybody else my age, when I was eighteen I started college. And it lasted, uh, six weeks. They bounced my ass out even before the grades came out. I had been to an all-male boarding school, and went to a college that, where females outnumbered males five to one. And, uh, without getting into the war stories, the conclusion is almost inevitable.

After that, I joined the Army. They were ready for me. Higher education wasn't, but the U.S. Army was. I think, in retrospect, that somewhere in my, my military service is where I, I became an alcoholic. Clinically, you know, uh. . . . I am sure that it's where I, uh, began daily drinking, and where I sharpened my, uh, lying and stealing skills that alcoholics need to survive. Again, you know, I hear the, the horror stories about people's military service, getting all shot-up in Vietnam or Korea or whatever war you were old enough for—I spent all my entire enlistment in provincial France. And I had a great job; it was one of the best times of my life. It probably would have been a great deal better if I hadn't been drunk all the time.

I got out of the service and, uh, decided to give higher education another try. This, this time they were a little more ready for me: I lasted for about a year and a half. And then, at the end of that part, in my early twenties, the booze began to turn on me and I knew it. There and after, for it seems like the rest of my life, my, uh, my whole life story revolved on critical drunks.

The first was, uh, when I was twenty-three years old, was my first experience with, uh, withdrawal, that I knew of; uh, incarceration; and Alcoholics Anonymous. I was at—school was over but I was, I was still, still there because I'd smacked up my car behind a whole bunch of Margaritas one night and I was waiting for the parts to come in, and somehow, I got hold of a whole bunch of money. I forget whether it was my VA check came in or money from home or one of my little scams worked or something, but I got a whole bunch of money. Of course I went to the neighborhood bar to drink it up. And, I awoke the next day, in the county jail in Lawrenceberg, New Mexico. I don't know how I got there, but I didn't walk a hundred and fifty miles through the Sonora desert. The sheriff took one look at me and he, he knew what my story was gonna be. He took all my clothes away and put me in this teeny little cell and let me shake it out for a few days. And I really, I had been drunk for a while and it was rough; it was really rough. A few days later, he came to me with a deal: he said he'd give me my clothes back if I'd go to an AA meeting. I said, "Well that, that sounds all right to me, that's, that's a deal." I said, "yeah."

I got my clothes back, I went to an AA meeting, and, uh, it didn't take. This was twenty-some years ago, a very small meeting, in the Southwest. It was a very spiritual meeting—not spiritual, it was a very *religious* meeting. A lot of "Amens." Uh, and I said, "Oh, this, this is probably very good for these people, but it's certainly not for me." The fact that I was sitting there in handcuffs eluded me at the time. But that, that incident, did give me cause to stop and think and assess my drinking. I knew, uh, that I had to do something about my drinking. Stopping—it never entered my mind. But I knew that I had to do something—with my drinking or with my life.

So I came back to this area. I, uh, got a real job. I'd been into these job-a-week phases, you know, where you get your paycheck, drink it up, and, uh, and forget about it. Get another one when the money runs out. A lot of, uh, this was, you know, when you're in your early twenties—I was into a lot of, you know, fast cars and loaded firearms. Really, I wasn't shit. I decided it was time to make a stab at being a grown-up. So I came back, got a real job, finished college at night, got married, had two kids. And, uh, I deluded myself into thinking that I had a handle on my drinking. But what I had done is change my drinking pattern. I, when I had been very, very good, I would reward myself with binges. And of course, it's predictable enough that, uh, the binges came closer together, and they increased in intensity and duration, until I was, uh, past daily drinking and into round, round-the-clock drinking.

About this time, my marriage broke up. I couldn't say that it was due to my alcoholism, although my alcoholism certainly affected it. My ex-wife had had two alcoholic parents and thought that next to them I was a day at the beach. At any rate, my marriage broke up, I moved into the city, and I thought I had it made. I was free to drink unencumbered, uh, all the time. I was dating the barmaid at the Lardner Hotel; I thought that I was in heaven there. And somebody did me a very great favor. This was eight or nine months before I had [left]. Uh, I was at work, and I was all dressed up, and clean and shaven in my three-piece suit looking like death warmed over, and one of the chief residents came up to me—he knew my story, I . . . he was a drinker, too. I know he could . . . whether he was an alcoholic I don't know, but he could hit the long balls, and he said, "Here, take one of these, it'll fix you right up." So he gave me a handful of ten-milligram Valium. As I say, he did me a great favor: in addition to getting me through the day, uh, it sped my bottom immeasurably. I took the Valium, and it cleared me right up; it . . . I, almost instantly, I discovered how good they really worked if you washed 'em down with a couple of twelve-ounce beers.

Then starts the period of, uh—oh, I gave up work entirely, at the time. I had a little piece of money and, uh, decided that work was, was futile. I hadn't any idea what I was going to do when the money ran out; I presumed, *almost* correctly, that I'd be dead by that time. Uh—round-the-clock drinking: the most horrible and vicious cycle I've ever been in. Every two-and-a-half hours, almost to the minute, I would *have* to drink. I could not go more than two and a half hours without drinking. Uh, hallucinations. When, whenever I walked into my apartment, I'd look in the corner and a lot of times I would see the pope in a Coca-Cola tee shirt, sitting right in the corner. Uh, paranoia. I was afraid of newspapers. I was afraid of the doorman in my apartment building. I would wait, I'd sit there across the street and wait till he got called to the phone or went to the bathroom or something and run in then. I don't know why he was after me but I certainly wished he would stop it.

Finally I knew, I knew the end was near when—and I knew that it was probably going to be death. Uh, my family knew the end was near too. There was no alcoholism in my immediate family, but it was all through the extended family. So they had already made arrangements for . . . for a bed at a rehab. And finally one day I made the phone call to one of my family members. And she came and got me. She picked me up, I think, on the corner of, uh, Hamilton and Proby, somewhere in that area. I was wearing a bathing suit and flip-flops. She wrestled me into the car, 'cause I changed my mind constantly. She's four foot eleven and was sixty-seven years old at the time. She brought along a six-pack so that we, uh, she could get me—the rehab was sixty miles away—so she could get me there.

And that's how I came here: drunk, broke, sick, and damn near nude. And that was almost ten years ago. And things have been steadily uphill. Not, ladies and gentlemen, that I didn't do my research.

Several years, uh, in sobriety, I guess I was suffering from an excess of, uh, success—uh, it's a classic story. I stopped going to meetings and, uh, declared myself cured. And, uh, that worked for a few months, and then I got in a situation and took a drink, took another one, and . . . the worst possible thing the next day: nothing. There was no hangover, no remorse, none of that terrible cold feeling that you get. So, shit, I knew I was cured then. And six weeks later I was in detox.

I don't recommend slips as part of any treatment modality because they can kill you. But for me, it tuned my ragged ass right up. There'd been things that, uh, I neglected to do, like, uh, get a sponsor. I had a sponsor appoint himself. I've tried to fire him, over the years. I once literally fired him—he used to work for me. But he got transferred back. I paid some attention to spirituality. Mine is not a heavily spiritual program. I know there's a God; I know he has a very strange sense of humor. Beyond that, my spirituality is rather ephemeral.

What I try to do in working the program is put in a word for simplicity. I once in a while, if I'm beat for something else to do, I'll hit the books. But mainly, I come to the meetings. It took me a long time, and the erosion of a lot of stubbornness to discover that, for me, all I have to do is come here. Every day—or, almost every day, or more than once a day. And somehow—and I don't care how —it works, as they say. I also try to talk to another alcoholic every day, to remind me of who I am. And I try and make a genuine all-out effort to help people. Because it's alien to my nature. I am not a giver. I'm a taker. Those things help me to stay sober. And things, again, have gotten increasingly good for me. I wouldn't go so far as to say they're beyond my wildest dreams, because my dreams are very wild. But very, very good. I catch glimpses of serenity—what I think is serenity. I've never had serenity adequately defined for me. I have the respect of my, uh, my family and children and professional community. I don't owe anybody any money. I've even begun to accumulate things, which I did not set out to do. But I've found that I like them. And it's just made life very easy for me. If I can keep on internalizing the fact that I don't drink—for, the way, the same reason I drank: I want to feel good. It's as simple as that. And hopefully I will have learned the fact that drinking does not make me feel good. It makes me feel bad, to the point of suicide, or implicit suicide. But *this* makes me feel good. It's so simple it's hard to understand.

And I would like to put in, uh, a pitch for simplicity. My sponsor once told me, he said, "Kid, you just have to remember two things: a) don't sweat the small shit; and b) it's *all* small shit."

With that, I'd like to thank you.

Cindy

November 11, 1986

Hi, I'm Cindy, I'm an alcoholic.

I grew up in upstate New York and, um, my sister was eleven years older than I was so I guess I was sort of an only child. And, uh, we moved ten times by the time I was ten so it was, you know, at least once a year. And, uh, that affected my socialization a lot; every time I would start to make friends, the rug would get pulled out from under me and it became much easier to stop trying to make friends, because it hurt a lot when I had to go. So I stayed pretty isolated the whole time I was growing up. We moved to one town and, I guess I was eleven, about to turn twelve, something like that, and, uh, I remember—I just remembered this a couple of weeks ago; it's funny, I'd completely forgotten it—but I remember when I was about ten, my parents, who are not drinkers—they may or may not have the "-ism," but, uh—they had this bottle of Scotch that they'd always keep from Christmas, and I remember taking a slug of that before I had to walk to the bus stop in the mornings, to stay warm, and it tasted good and I liked the feeling. But I don't think I was getting drunk, but it was just interesting that I had forgotten all about that.

When I was about to turn twelve we moved to this one town and I started babysitting. And I babysat for this one man down the block and he, he used to have a lot of teenagers around the house —everybody could drink over there and smoke pot, et cetera—and I really wasn't into that yet, but he made advances to me, and I thought that was great because, uh, that was a new source of affection, and I was pretty hungry for affection at that time. My father sort of—he was around, but he didn't interact with me hardly at all: he went on a lot of business trips, he was into a lot of avoidance behaviors; my mother was having a lot of nervous breakdowns, in and out of the hospital, and when she was around she wasn't really coherent, she sat around and stared a lot, and she was very paranoid. So I was very lonely and I didn't have the awareness then but I was also very, very angry. I didn't understand why I couldn't have anybody in my life too to count on, and, um, so it felt really good when this guy gave me so much attention. So I kind of ate that up, but it turned on me, because he ended up raping me. And, I never told anybody about that because I felt, uh, too guilty, because I had led him on.

And a couple of days after it happened, we moved. So I went into another school and, uh, felt pretty bad, but I, I couldn't really tell anybody, so I began acting out in a lot of other ways. I got involved with all the worst kids and started doing drugs immediately. The first substance I put in my body was LSD—uh, I loved it, except it made me paranoid and it altered the way I felt, but I was still angry, and could still be isolated, and it made me pretty paranoid, but I didn't care. And it gave me people to hang out with, and that was important; I had a peer group for the first time.

So I continued doing drugs for the next, I guess, three years, and acting out a lot in school—um, I had been suspended three times. I finally told the vice-principal in no uncertain terms where he could go and they tried to kick me out of school. So, uh, they insisted that I go see a psychologist—they decided that I wasn't just some little monster like I thought I was but that I was an emotionally disturbed child. So, uh, they sent me into counseling. And, um, I was careful not to tell the counselor any of my secrets, 'cause she insisted on seeing my mother part of the time too, and, uh, that . . . helped me a lot, because I think I probably would have been institutionalized by the time I was seventeen if I hadn't seen her; she helped me get in touch a little bit with some of my feelings and at least I was, uh, able to let my big secret out of the bag and, uh, it was going pretty well, then we moved, again, so I started in another school, and I was told at that time—my mother had been getting better too, and, uh, she was taken off Thorazine and she wasn't in hospitals anymore, and I was told at that time that I couldn't act out when we moved, and I couldn't be upset about this because my mother couldn't handle it, and if I got in all kinds of trouble like I had before, I was going to make her very sick. So I was very careful not to do that, and I acted like everything was okay and just decided that I was going to accept this and, uh, pretty much stuck to that.

Um, I started drinking right around then, too, and, uh, I loved to drink. That was what I had been looking for all along. Alcohol relaxed me and it made me feel friendlier, prettier, smarter, uh, everything that I wanted to be. That, it—the paranoia wasn't there, it was legal, I could go into bars, this was grown up, it was, you know, a lot more acceptable to me. I still did plenty of drugs, but I really liked alcohol; I just couldn't wait for Friday and I would party all the time on weekends. And I never did socialize with anybody—by that time I was in high school—and I never hung out with anybody in high school except the kids that went around the back and smoked joints. I would stay in class for as long as I had to and then I would get out and go get high and drive off with somebody in a car and go and get drunk.

And when I graduated I started working in hotels, and was drinking every day. And that was a lot of fun—it was all young people and everybody liked to party and they had sort of a little family of hotel because we'd all work these crazy hours and get everybody else drunk and then we got out we'd have our own party. And there was real camaraderie in that. Um—I worked in hotel, I had a, a good job on the front desk and, uh, I was making pretty decent money, for at least a high-school grad at that time, in that town—there really wasn't a lot of opportunity—and, uh, I felt good about the job and I was pretty good at it; I had a reputation for remembering people's names and, and stuff like that, and, needless to say, that didn't really last very long. By the last year in that job, um, I had started doing speed on a regular basis along with the alcohol, so then I could get up in the morning, which was hard to do because I was always hungover. But then I would have to drink twice as much to bring myself down from the speed buzz, and, um, so . . . that went on for a long time and my performance just went downhill really fast.

And . . . I, uh . . . the boss that I was working for kept wanting to go out with me. I didn't think that was such a good idea and I, finally, I did start going out with him. That also afforded me a little leeway as far as coming in late, things like that, and the general manager was just disgusted by this and told me to straighten up my act. Not only was I doing this, but I was coming in in rumpled-up clothes and I was snapping at customers and I didn't remember anybody's name anymore and just generally didn't care. Everybody was bothering me. So, he promptly fired me, and, uh, this guy that I was seeing that was my boss told them that if he—that I'd been a good employee for three years and he should give me a chance to quit, and if he didn't then he was going to lose his assistant manager too. So the general manager promptly fired him, too. I . . . I felt pretty guilty about that because this had been a nine-year job for this man and I assumed full guilt and responsibility for losing him his job. So, uh, I married him, and. . . . [Laughter]

He, uh . . . after about eight months of gruesome unemployment and spending every single penny on alcohol and drugs, I finally decided that somebody had to make some money, so I finally got back into hotel on the graveyard shift doing the night audit—that was not really a lot of fun. But I lasted in that for a while and I finally got a couple of bartending jobs and that was terrific. I'm sure I drank as much as I served and, um. . . . But that went along pretty well, I, I tended bar at two different jobs, a day job and a night job, and just stayed loaded the entire time, except when I was asleep.

And I did that for another year—but that wasn't really going anywhere, I wasn't making enough money, I wasn't saving any money, and I thought I should be making a lot more money and I heard that out in Houston, Texas, that, uh, there was a lot of job opportunities and people were making real good money, rents were low, et cetera. And my husband had some family out there, so we went out there. And we did get good jobs, in an oil field, and, uh, started making better money. Never saw any of it, for some strange reason. Um, I didn't do any more speed. I also knew that I had to get away from speed addiction because my body just couldn't take it anymore. And I was real willing to give that up, then I'd be okay. I also gave up vodka and hard liquor, and switched to wine. So I knew my life was going to be wonderful—and it wasn't. Um, I continued to drink, every day; I smoked pot at least three times a day—you know, get up in the morning, to start with. And, uh, I had a thing about drinking in the morning—I wasn't going to drink in the morning, people might smell it on my breath, so I'd smoke a joint instead. But I couldn't wait to get out of work to go home and drink.

We stayed in Texas. I guess about the third year we were there—

um, my husband was about eight years older than I was, and he drank; his progression had gone a little farther. He was more into the isolation. I was still in my early twenties and I still wanted to party and go out and have a good time when I drank. And he wanted to come home from work and down his half a bottle of vodka and be asleep by seven thirty, eight o'clock. So I felt, uh, very angry; he was boring me to death, and I was abandoned, and he obviously had a drinking problem, and he was ruining my life. And I was very unhappy, and I thought I should be good and stay married and all that kind of stuff, but, uh, I finally decided that, that this drunk just didn't want to get better, and so I left him.

He went into treatment, immediately. He had a nervous break-down, losing his spouse in a strange town, and confronting his alcoholism. And, uh, he went into a rehab and started going to AA meetings. And he would write me letters and he called me, and I was avoiding him like the plague, and he finally ran into me one day —I had to see him because of a lawyer's letter—and he said to me, uh, you know, "Look how scared you are, you don't want to talk to me because you don't want to look at yourself. You look at the world through your haze of wine and you're terrified right now to talk to me because you know you have a problem too." And I didn't think too much about what he said, but I remember noticing that I was shaking. He was absolutely right about that, but I thought it was just emotional trauma from having to speak to this man, so . . . I never talked to him again.

Then I proceeded to go after what I thought I wanted all along. Now I could be single, and I could date, and I could go to all these singles bars and go out and party and have a good time. And, uh, I did that for a little less than a year. And I forgot to mention at the end of this marriage also that I had, uh, developed anorexia, and I was down to a size three trying to get down to a size one; and, uh, didn't see anything wrong with that. People told me I looked great. I had lost all this weight, I thought I looked great and, uh, I just didn't want to eat anymore; drinking was enough for me, and I'd, you know, eat a few bites here and there and that would keep me alive and, and that was good.

After I left my husband, I had hopes for all these people being in my life, and there was nobody. The people I worked with were pretty nice but most of them were married and had families and I really didn't have anything in common with them, they didn't drink like I did. And, when I went out to bars, um, I couldn't seem to control what I was doing. I would go out and have a few drinks with people at cocktail hour and everybody would leave and I'd still be there at two o'clock and, uh, I was getting sloppy too. Always before I had been a fun drunk and I had enjoyed it and it wasn't that way anymore; by the end of the night I felt sorry for myself, and I was either maudlin or, you know, just bitchy, um, most of the time I don't remember how I was. And it got to the point where I'd be, you know, go out for cocktail hour, well, I'll go out for a blackout, and. . . . And I, uh, just did not like being embarrassed and having to face people again, and these people would come up to me in, you know, these corporations and stuff and talk to me like I'd talked to them all night or something, and I would have no idea who they were. And, uh, this just became unacceptable, so I quit drinking with anybody at all, and then it was just me and my bottle.

I also became bulimic, and I, uh, couldn't keep up with starving myself anymore—I had such a hole in me, and there were no people in my life, and the alcohol wasn't working anymore and I had a lot of pain and I was not in touch with that at all, but, uh, I started eating, and then of course I had too much guilt to keep it, so that developed into a good case of bulimia. And, uh, I kept getting more and more and more miserable. I would get high as soon as I got up. I was starting to put, uh, vanilla in my coffee, that was just kind of a quirk, I didn't get drunk, and, um, I couldn't wait for lunch to go out and get high again, and then I would go home and I would drink my magnum of wine. And, uh, somebody came over for some reason one day and noticed that I drank a whole magnum of wine and thought that was kind of unusual—I just kind of looked at him, I didn't really think too much of that, either. I had a little denial.

So I, uh, really was getting pretty suicidal; I thought about killing myself a lot. I knew I didn't want to continue living the way I was. I didn't think there was any option so I figured I didn't want to continue living anymore at all. And I remembered back to the time, uh, after I had been raped and I had gone to see this shrink. So I got out the phone book and I went to see a shrink; and figured, you know, I was crazy and maybe they could fix me now, like they did before, and, uh, I walked into this woman's office and—I forgot to mention that with the bulimia I had no idea what it was—and I walked into this woman's office and there was this big sign about bulimics and I started reading it and I was identifying; it was kind of like a, a first AA meeting, I just started crying.

And it turned out she was a food-addictions shrink. So I got into that therapy, and in some ways it was helpful, she helped me get in touch with my feelings, I really had no idea how I felt about my— and she taught me to, to just go happy-mad-sad-glad over and over till I could try to identify which one I was underneath, uh, whatever I had, uh, on the surface—which was usually just numbness. I tried to talk to her about alcohol, because by then I was starting to be willing to think that maybe that was a problem, but she told me that my problem was food and, um, so, I seemed to be feeling a little bit better, so I decided to stay with her.

Then, because I was drinking all the money I had, I, uh, was running out of money, I took a second job in a restaurant, and I met this waiter. And, uh, he liked me right away and I liked him right away, he was real cute, and, uh, he—as soon as I started dating him, I think it was about a week into dating him, I was a little bit late for a date, and he was furious. Just furious. He was not accepting any reasons and where was I and all this kind of stuff; and I thought, wow, if he was that jealous he must really like me. And, uh, so I latched onto him, and, presto-change-o, my bulimia disappeared. I had just substituted one addiction for another. And he was quite enough to obsess on. He wanted to know where I was every single minute of the day. He, uh, never believed where I said I was when I wasn't with him; all kinds of wacky stuff, and I was just as wacky, and that was great.

This progressed, uh, to the point where he didn't believe where I was, and I would start to get really angry because I was telling the truth; and so I would start to fight with him, and, uh, he became violent. And the first time that he hit me, I swore I would never see him; I said, you know, "Get out of my life, I don't ever want to see you again," and when he went out the door, I realized there was nothing else in my life. You know, he was the only person in my life at that time. Because he helped me to isolate—I was not allowed to have any kind of friends, or anything that would . . . not that I did before I started seeing him anyway, but, um, he was a good excuse for that. And, uh, he also—I think by the end, I stayed with him through a lot more of this than I would ever have thought I would, um, I took him back many times and I would swear that I would never see him again and he would get thrown in jail on a D.W.I. or something and I would be right back there. And, uh, I, I knew at that point that I was really totally out of my mind and that there was no hope, because, I had always thought of—you know, women that stuck around for that kind of stuff, battered women and . . . that's, that's really sick, how could you do that and they must want it, and I just thought that was, you know, just disgusting, that these women would allow themselves to be treated in this manner, and I would never do that. And here I was, doing exactly that, and I was completely powerless; and whenever he left, whenever I'd kick him out, I had this same feeling that I was dying, and . . . I was dying.

Finally I called, uh, my sister in New York, who has been in the program for about nine years and, all this time that I was in Texas I had a, a great façade with my family, I was really okay with them because I had this job, I still, I'd managed to keep this job for four years and, uh . . . I was making good money and I had my own apartment and my car ran and I always took good care of the externals, and, therefore, they thought that I was, you know, the, the good sister, because I kept my life together. My sister, who was much saner, kept a messy house, and she was overweight, and, you know, she was . . . not held in the same regard by my mother. And my sister, when I made this call, heard that I was at my alcoholic bottom, and, um, it was kind of an expensive Twelfth Step, she flew all the way to Houston and stayed with me for a week. And I had not called her about alcohol, I'd called her about this man, and I explained to her that I just couldn't stay away from him and I didn't understand what was wrong with me. And I thought I was insane, and I wanted to die.

So she talked to me a little bit about the program, and the program life, and how hard it was to get away from an addiction, always, you know, implying that she meant him. And I remember she made some comment like well, when I came back—she wanted me to go home with her for a leave of absence for a month—and she said when I came back, straight and sober, I probably wouldn't have this problem with him. And I go, "Huh? Sober?" But, uh, slowly it sank in. And by that point, you know, I, I really, I wanted to be dead; enough that, even though I thought the only thing keeping me alive was alcohol, I was willing to put it down. Because she said that if I put it down and I started into this program I would meet other people like me and that, uh, I would find some hope here; and, it wasn't really that I was crazy, that I could probably get back on my feet, I'd been away from my family and I was kind of strung out from drugs and alcohol and if I just got a rest, then I would be okay. And she made me get all the liquor out of my house before we left, even the vanilla—I looked at her really strange, "Who would drink vanilla?" And so I flew back with her and came into a meeting and—I remember my first meeting, I was sitting here thinking, if these people make me say "I'm an alcoholic" I'm just going to scream you-know-what at them and run out the door, but nobody ever did that, thank God. And, uh, by the second meeting I knew I was home. And I knew that that was the problem. And I haven't had a drink since.

And, you know, it, it still amazes me that putting that substance in my body made that kind of a difference in my mind—that I really was, you know, clinically insane, I was not capable of predicting what I was going to do, and that just, even in the very beginning, just putting down the substance and not drinking or drugging any- more, I was accountable for my actions. And that was, you know, my first miracle.

Um, I . . . have gotten so much out of this program; I mean, so much more. Not just being able to live without drugs and alcohol, which is no small thing, but I can be a responsible person today, I can show up for life. I'm learning how to deal with all these emo- tions that, uh, I stuffed, denied, ignored, and it really, I really feel like a newborn just, uh, growing up; and I, I am. I, uh, had always medicated pain, fear, all this kind of stuff and stuffed it down as much as I could. I did have, when I first got sober, I had a little more trouble with the food and I had to go to another Twelve Step program, and there was hope and help there, too, for that. The answer is in these Twelve Steps—I had to get my other Step One, but, uh, the faith in a higher power and, uh, working the Steps in this program has really just turned my entire life around. I made a lot of mistakes when I first came into this program—I don't know if they were mistakes or just how it worked out.

I went back to Texas and I stayed there for a couple months after being up here for a month and getting sober, and I just felt so alone. And I mean there was nobody left there, um, nobody I could see and, uh, all I had was a job and my family was up here and people I had gotten sober with and, I guess that's what it's like to get out of a rehab. And I just—I tried to stick it out, and I knew if I had AA it should work, and I had a sponsor and everybody told me not to move back to New York, that it was another geographical [cure]. And I did it anyway and, uh, I don't know how I knew that that was okay to do but I'm really glad that I did. And now I'm in closer proximity to my family, I'm able to, to be there as a member of the family. Most of my sins with them were just not being there for anything. Today I take my nephew to karate, and take him to school when he misses the bus. I felt so grown up the first time I wrote his tardy slip and signed my name. And you know, just being a member of a family and showing up for work and not having my job gauge who I am, or, you know, my weight gauge who I am. Today it's what kind of person I am and if I'm taking the right action; and if I'm really trying as best I can to practice the principles of the program in my life. And if I'm really doing that and am connected to my higher power, and I'm doing a prayer and meditation, and I talk to my sponsor, I really feel okay about myself and that's a miracle. The isolation that I went through for so many years —I don't ever remember not being isolated before I came into this program. And, to learn to share . . . and I . . . was in the rooms six months before I could ever open my mouth at a meeting, and, um, it feels so good, and, you know, it felt so good just to hear other people share with me, that was all I could do for a long time was sit and listen. And now it's to be able to talk to people and really share how I'm really feeling and, you know, I don't know what I thought; I thought they were going to, you know, just really reject me from the face of the earth and tell me that I had to go find another planet or something if I ever told anybody how I really felt, and I came here and found out that that's just not the case.

This program has really given me a lot; and I have a, a sense of self back. Um, still have a lot of trouble with self-esteem but it's gotten so much better. And, uh, I have a lot of trouble with a lot of defects but I'm, I'm on a road now, and I have a direction now, and things are steadily getting better, and it's all from this program.

Thanks a lot.

Spike

August 31, 1986

Thank you. My name is Spike, I'm alcoholic—a very grateful, recovering alcoholic.

And, uh, I been, I been sober—and I want to mention this because I remember my, my worst days drinking—and I been sober eleven years. And my worst day, that I, that, one of my worst days that, that, that I can remember in my addiction . . . is, is, is . . . there was a lot of . . . involved. I lived in a, I think it was, eight dollar, eight-dollar-a-day room—and a couple of weeks back in rent on that. And, uh, I lived, I lived in Humbert all my life.

And I remember being in, in high school—you know, I thought I was one of the cool, one of the cool gang—you know, you, you get involved with the gang, and you had to, you had to drink, and you had to fight, and you had to learn to swim. And that was the type of life that I, that I lived. I was expelled from high school— sixteen years old. Took my education away from me. Because, due to my drinking, I used to get up in the morning and I used to go out the front door to Sixth Street and to the right was the high school, and to the left was the corner boys. You know, the guys with the rags around their heads and the cap to the side, you know how we looked back in 1965—some of you all come out of that, some of you all. And, uh, I made the left, and went to the corner. So naturally the school got tired and I was expelled.

So, I'm saying that because that was the first thing that alcohol took from me, was, was any chance for me to have any education, just took it right away. And I was . . . involved on this corner for . . . forever, I thought. And this began a, a daily drinking habit for me, you know. And, and not only did I drink, I stayed, at seventeen, eighteen years old, extremely, extremely dirty. You know, I was, you know—I need a haircut now, so link that up, you know. . . . And, my head used to look worse than this. And, I would stay involved in everything that went on on the corner. You know. You know, when the fights started, I was the first one in there. As a matter of fact, they made me out as a "war lord," where I came from. Anytime they wanted to get a fight started they would come get me, and get me a couple of drinks and they know how [I act]. "Give,

give him a couple of drinks and we can get the fight." So, this, this was my reputation for the. . . .

Now, I figured—my mind, my mind was washed, at that age, eighteen, nineteen years old, cause the group of guys that I was with, we believed that we were all black, we were poor, in the ghetto, and this was where we belonged at, and we had to act like it: we had to fight, and drink every day, and have our own [feeling] about white people. That, that was the way my dream was, that, that's the way I was built. And, I remember as the years went on, and the drinking got worse, it went on every day, and I realized that, that you had to, you had to have a little money to drink. So: yeah. So, you know my education was taken away, so, I had to start finding a different type of job. I worked them all: trash truck, washed dishes, everything. I did everything. But I would never keep no job a hundred years; I'd keep it long enough to get a few dollars together, go back to the corner, and—that's how it end, that's how that job would end, I would eventually get fired 'cause I didn't show.

But I had one thing going for me in my addiction that I didn't, I don't see it till now: that I never mind going to work. It was always for the wrong reasons, but I never mind going, and I had that, that was the, that was the good part of me. And we—I constantly stayed involved, in, in my [cycle], and I never tried to step out of it. I never tried to step out and take a look over, in, to see how I was living, because I thought the way I was living was the way it was supposed to be.

But: I got married. I was . . . the same little dirty drunk, you know. But I got, I got married and . . . the fighting never stopped. She was, she was. . . . See, I started losing a few of them fights in the street anyhow, I was getting a little tired of that anyway, my record started getting lopsided, [I wasn't] winning a lot out there. So, I'm twenty-two, twenty-three years old, and the marriage came along. So, I didn't have to go to the street no more, I could beat her up. So, so, if you beat her up, then, she's going to call the police. This is another merry-go-round I got on. I beat her up, and beat her up; ran my kids out the house, you know. You know how we do. Don't pay the rent, you know. Don't bother with groceries. I was married, still walking down to the corner. I never gave up drinking. Never gave it up, not for one second. People start saying,

"Hey, man." No, I'm, I'm not talking about people in the street, I'm talking about people in my family start saying, "Hey, maybe, maybe, *maybe* . . . you drink too much." But if I went down to the corner they say, "Well, you ought to mix that vodka with orange juice, instead of drinking it straight." So I believe them more than I believe the people in my family. So the drinking never, ever stopped.

Now, that marriage that I just mentioned—that's all it was, mentioned, too, cause it was over, it was over; that's all it was. Beat her right, beat her right all away, never come back, ain't never showed up. So, that's the second: that's—education, wife, kids, everything gone. Because, because, I was very, very violent, when I got—I, I could really think I could fight. Pfuh. Weigh about ninety pounds, dirty, half-pint of whiskey in my pocket, I could whip everybody. And that's the way I felt, you know?

Now, I went along, later—after the marriage was gone, people, people started hating me. My mother, she wasn't speaking too regular to me. You know what mom used to do, she used to come down to the corner, and I used to feel embarrassed. . . . "Come on, you ain't took no bath in a couple of days, get in the car." I'm *twenty-three years old,* here's my mother. "Come on, now get in the car." "You want me to get in the car, I'll get in the car." Take a bath. Maybe feed me. . . . She feed me, give me a few bucks. "You better try to find a job." And, you know, out of all these jobs that I had, I had—uh, trash jobs, this type of job, washing cars, everything. And, I was working at, uh, Dortmunder Steel in Trimble, and I was making . . . I think it was five an hour. I said, "Shh, I don't need no education for five bucks a hour. . . ." And I got laid off, and I went into about a three-month drunk, I was depressed by losing that five-dollar an hour job. But my mother-in-law came one day to the house say "Man, I'm going, I'm going down to Delaware, down to General Motors, see, see—put an application in, get a job." I said, "Oh, man, you know you got to be white and you got to have an education, now you know that." "Come on, we're going to try it anyhow." And we went down and damn if they didn't hire me on the spot. . . .

I worked a double first night I worked there. And then I didn't realize they was paying ten-something an hour, I could die when they told me that. *Ten dollars!* I said, "Oh, man!" . . . Alcoholic, couple kids . . . I'm just about free, making three-hundred dollars a week, and all I do is give mom a little something, two-fifty. . . . So this goes on like this, and this money started coming, and I just started spending money, buying old ragged cars. So you buy a car and you drink and you tear them up and the police is involved. So I started getting locked up, for drunken driving, speeding, you know, all these kind of things start happening. I got fired from this job. Twice. *Twice.* They fired me the first time they said, uh, uh—you see, they violated my rights because they didn't give me a union man, and my union had a case, and they brought me back and paid me for the three weeks they had me on the street. They *paid* me for that. Second time they fired me, they set me up. They outsmarted me on this one. They say, "He'll get drunk, he'll get drunk. Friday night get here he'll be drunk." Friday night I staggered in drunk. So they sat back and waited till I ran into the wall with the car. Man took me right up front and they fired me. But I had the general foreman, believe it or not, that this here little white man, he just couldn't *believe* that nobody acting like this normal. He said, "I don't *believe* you like that!" And the day that, uh, I went back to see about getting a job back—but let me go back about a minute.

When I got fired at, that second time, this was one of the worst days of my, my addiction. I was out of a job, I had a little money in the credit union—I ran and nibbled all that up, some of you know the checks ain't come . . . about five, six weeks, and all of a sudden it dawned on me: dummy, you ain't got nothing now. So my stepfather, he get a little mad at me. The rent money ain't come. You know. Mom trying to hold on. So, I jumped on a bus one day. And I came up to Philadelphia. And I ended up on Fifteenth and Market, I was drinking in them Italian clubs there, you know, up and down the street there, and they was giving me them big double shots like that for a buck; I went crazy.

And I ended up on South Street. And I stayed on South Street —I lived on South Street, for a week, with a little Mexican guy. I had a few dollars, and every morning that I woke up somewhere he was about twenty feet from me; and me and him go get a bottle of whiskey, bottle of wine, and I was, it was starting to show. I was a street person. For about three, four days—it started to scare me. You know. And, I think, the fifth or sixth day, I had a few bucks left, man, and, and for the grace of God, man, I walked off South Street. I might still been in there if I hadn't. I walked off South Street, walked back up toward Market Street, and you, you know what I looked like? Drinking five days, sleeping? You know. I said, *"Damn."* So I caught the bus; I caught the, the el; I got to Sixty-ninth Street and caught the bus and went home. And seem like my mother must of saw me coming three blocks off, shaking her head. She stepped out of my way, pointed right to the bathroom. And that was one of my, one of my worst days, that was, that was coming to the end. And—back to that job.

This, this general foreman, Tony Ricci, he sat down, we was—there was a table, it was, I was in the middle, one union man and five guys from race relations. They didn't care if I worked there or not. And he just looked his head in the door and he said, "Now you can't work in my department drunk no more." And he walked out, he never got involved in it; and what he did was gave me my job back right there. So, the guy turned around, say, "He just gave you your job back." So—and I ducked him. I didn't stop drinking, but I ducked him. I—'cause I knew he could fire me, I ducked him. And, as the years went on, the last couple years—I don't know if anybody else felt this, but, but I felt, I felt the end coming. I *knew* it was coming. I didn't know whether to go back down to the bar and ask the guy that was drinking alongside of me, "Is this the end?" Or go ask my mother, "Is this the end coming?" You know . . . was I going to die? But I knew something was coming. And every time I'd drink, I start not liking it. And I got, I looked at myself. And I said, "Man, you do making thirty thousand dollars a year and can't pay ten, ten dollars a week to stay in this dirty-ass room." And I, I sat in the Blue Hotel the last night of my—no, uh, the last night I *thought* of my drinking—and I had a fifth of Sea-gram's gin and I was drinking it and the *end* was, was, was really swarming over me. You know, the end was there but I just, just didn't give up. I kept pouring that drink wondering what was wrong. I said, *"Damn,* what's wrong now? Maybe I ain't got no ice in the glass, maybe that's it." But when the bottle was gone, man, the tears came.

And I, I went to Gibbon. Gibbon—and they sent me upstairs to some counselor, and he said, he said, "What's wrong?" And, and I remember sitting there talking to him a whole hour and not one time till the end I said, *"Maybe* . . . I got to stop drinking." And that's when he reacted. He said, "Well maybe this, this, we can help you with that." But he said, "All that stuff about your wife and your job, and your car wrecks and your fights and being . . . I can't help that." He said, "I can't help none of that." So I told him, I said, uh, I said, "All right, all right, who could I go see?" He shoots me right over to detox; I get to detox, man, and I look around the walls, and "Easy does it," and . . . I said, "Damn, what the hell is all this?"

But, about four days had went by, and I'm still mumbling. So, uh, Zora called me, she said, "Hey, Spike, I thought you couldn't stop drinking." I said, "I can't." She said, "But you ain't drinking four days, what you mean you can't?" That's when *I* realized. I said, "Yeah, I sure didn't." I said, "How many more days I got in here?" She said, "You got another three or four." So I stayed there seven days. I felt like I'd graduated from Yale University. Seven days without a drink. And I went right to the AA meetings. And do you know what I did? I went down to those meetings, stayed there one, two—went to work every day, took a bath every day, got a haircut. I said, "God *damn*." Money in my bank book.

All them changes—I didn't recognize none of them. Do you know I went back out there and drank *again?* And I figured I'm all right; I'm cured; I can handle it. I ain't heard nothing nobody told me. And I went back out and drank. And then when I fell, that time, that first time was just the bottom; the second time was the bottom with the cover up. It was time for me to surrender.

When I surrendered and came back to the program, I was grateful. And . . . I been here since. Now, I been sober ten, eleven years and . . . it's due to this program that . . . I'm very grateful today. You know . . . because I remember the time that, when things were going wrong, then you always lean toward your only, only crutch was alcohol. Whatever goes wrong now, I bring it right here; and it works. You know, I was wondering if I'd ever, ever stop drinking, you know? And I sat in the rooms about a year, still had a little, like, *maybe, maybe.* But my sponsor say, "Yeah, *maybe;* maybe you'll be drunk again." So that kept me coming. And I used to come up here a lot, and I heard a lot of people up here say it: same thing. I said, *"Man,* I get tired of hearing this everywhere I go. Jesus Christ, over and over: *'easy does it,' 'keep coming back,'* what the hell's going on?" But by that time I had two goddamn years. Had a new car outside. Bank book was like that. See, I was a little slow, you know, slow to pick up on that. But I knew, I knew, I knew that . . . I didn't want to hurt no more. I knew that pain was real. And, see, when I came into this program, and I *did* hear, for those first five, six months; and I went back out there, and what I heard in those few months was starting to outweigh that alcohol. Starting to lift up over it. I said, "Man, all of them damn people, all of them can't be wrong." And I'm back in my, back in the bottle again, and I started thinking about AA. You know, when you, when you been in this program, it's kind of hard to go out and taste anyhow, you know; this program [is] hey, hey, hey, *easy*. You know, gets you every time. And it got me.

Now . . . I found that I'm here, I'm here in this program . . . forever. You know. I heard a few people say, "Man, you been going to meetings a long time." You know? If, if they don't make me mad, then I'm going to try to sell them about, "You need to be going, too." You know: some people you got to tell that to. You know. But I, But I found that this program is . . . you know, you know, I remember when me and my sister used to be in the bedroom, we used to all be piled in the same bed, my mom going to work. And we always talked about what we wanted to do, and what we going to be doing when we forty years old. You know I'm doing exactly what we talked about?

You know—now I will talk, for this next minute, about the best, one of the best times in my life, since I was sober. Me and Ruth, she back there somewhere—my girlfriend—program gave me . . . gave me perfect love. She's back there somewhere. And, I found that this one particular time—I had a lot of good times—just one particular time, we went to Canada. Now we always talked about having credit cards, and [you know], having credit cards, and, and flying here and there; and we packed up, took the luggage to the airport, little dudes come running out, snatched the luggage . . . throw a couple dollars on them. Lady took us to the airport, took us right to the seats. Airplane cranked up and shot on off. And the whole time I'm . . . I'm complaining: "Jesus Christ. . . ." Because . . . I never thought about . . . the dreams that I had. They kind of left me for a minute. So, we get up . . . I'm getting airsick. . . . So, we get down, and land, come up the little guy, put the luggage up for us, take it right to the airport, go right to the hotel—the hotel was mixed up but we got another one—right to the hotel. And do you know, when all that was over, all I had to do was *sign* things? And, you know, that's what the program comes around to give you sooner or later; you know, and, and, I'm [at this best] in my life, right today. I'm at the best that I've ever been. And that's due to this program, Ruth, and Nellie, and I'm glad to be here. Thank you.

Susie

April 14, 1985

Hi, everybody. I'm Susie, I'm an alcoholic.

I was born and raised in South Jersey. I came from an alcoholic family, and a, a very abusive family. My childhood was very painful, and I don't like speaking about that . . . uh . . . because it brings back all that pain.

I went to Catholic elementary school—did fairly well. I went to grade school—did fairly well. Didn't make any friends because of the place I, where I lived. I had a small brother and, of course, a mother and father. My father was a very active alcoholic until the day he died . . . he didn't think he had a problem. I always said I wasn't going to be like him when I grew up. I didn't know what I wanted to be, uh, I felt like I didn't belong anywhere. I used to go around, I said, "I can't find myself," whatever that's supposed to mean.

I . . . went to . . . Catholic high school—did fairly well in school. Graduated like everybody else. But then I went out one day a week during the—on Saturday, and I liked dancing, dances, and they had a dance at the YMCA, so I used to go there, to these dances. And I met a man, at the age of fifteen, and fell madly in love with him.

We got engaged. I went to my parents and asked them for consent to get married and they told me no. So—to spite them—I ran off with this man and we got married. We ran off down south to Maryland and—I thought he was going to be my knight in shining armor and he was going to sweep me away from where I lived and we were going to live happily ever after.

I married this man and after I married him I realized the only reason I married him wasn't because I loved him, uh, because I didn't know what love was till I came to these rooms. I was very naive at this time, you know, I didn't know anything about being a mother, a wife, because I didn't even know what, what I wanted out of my life.

We got married and, uh, we went to Connecticut and I like it up there. I was away from the environment I lived in at Humbert, uh. . . .

Picked up my first drink that night. And I liked what it done for me right away: made me feel pretty and I was able to, to mingle in with the other people that were in the room. But my husband told me the next day, said that I had made a complete fool out of myself. Apparently I had a blackout and I did . . . some . . . thing, that I don't remember doing. And I called him a liar.

Out of this marriage I conceived a little boy, uh, I can remember carrying him and wondering, what was I, how am I going to raise a baby. In many ways I was one myself. I didn't want the, uh . . . I didn't know how to be a mother. I didn't know how to give this baby any love, but then I never received any.

I had my baby. But in the meantime I was drinking quite a lot. I got introduced to going out to a bar one night a week and right away I liked it because there was the dark lights and the loud music and I was able to drink.

I used to drink and, uh, my baby used to lay in the crib crying to be fed and changed. And a lot of times I was unable to get out . . . of my own bed to feed him. My neighbor used to have to come down and do this for me; and she used to scream to me that my drinking was abnormal. And I used to tell her what to do, and it wasn't any of her business what I did. She wasn't my mother.

I continued drinking and, uh, our marriage finally wound up in the battle in court. I divorced him.

I brought my baby back home to this house that I detested—I needed; but there was, uh, I was abused as a kid, a child growing up and I got . . . physically and mentally. . . . So before I ever picked up a drink I was sick.

I arrived home and I thought my whole life was going to change, uh, if I had gotten a job and straightened out my life in some degree and become a mother and become a, a, a responsible person. I, uh, I came home. I did straighten out, for a little while.

Got a job; uh, had a babysitter to watch my little boy while I worked. *When* I worked. Huh. When I worked I was a good worker.

I was taking bottles into work. I was a nurse. I was at Cornelia Hospital. And then I would take these bottles into work and then every five minutes I was running into the ladies' lounge and my supervisor saw that I was always taking my pocketbook.

And, of course, anybody who lives in Humbert knows that right across the street from Cornelia Hospital is the Handel Bar. And I used to hang out in there, uniform and all. I would go over at lunch time and think I was going to go over and get one quick drink and go back to work. But that quick drink lasted all day long and I wouldn't go back to work. I would stay in that bar. And the monkey got on my back, and I said, "I don't need this job, um, this is what I want to do, I want to drink myself to death." I called up my supervisor one time and I told her that I was home, sick in bed, with the juke box blasting from where I was in the bar and the guys in the back playing shuffleboard. She knew exactly where I was. And, uh . . . my job finally ended because of my drinking.

But that didn't stop me. No.

I started having blackouts, quite rapidly and a lot. I never knew what a blackout was but I had, I had a lot of times that I lost, because, uh, I drank all the time in the bar. I used to drink in this bar north of . . . called Armstrong's. And at this time all the Mad Dogs would drive in with their motorcycles. And I thought this was really neat—this was really exciting. I liked this. You know, anything, uh, different I liked. I was waking up in, uh. . . . My blackouts were taking me to . . . strange places. Waking up in places I didn't know how I got there, much less care. I did a lot of things that I'm ashamed of—a lot of things that, uh, at that time I couldn't forgive myself for.

I came in the program in 1973. And from 1973 to 1974 I went out three times. Uh, I remember the first time I decided I needed some help I went to Cornelia-Humbert—Dank Hall at this time, and, uh, talked to a lady, and she asked me was I drinking that day and I told her yes. And she asked me could I come in and talk to somebody and I said yeah. I went in and I talked to a man, uh, he talked to me for quite a long time. And that man, later on, he became my sponsor. He talked to me and he—the only thing I remember him saying was I never had to hurt from alcohol again. Talked about a rehab center. He talked about a program that was housed in building ten—a ninety-day program. So I decided I would try it and I would go. I went in. He took, he took time off and he went and took me.

I arrived at Abigail State. I didn't know what to, what I expected. I guess I expected to be locked up in . . . having prison guards or whatever. I was, I didn't know. But I went. They had meetings there three days a week. I hated the meetings. I hated you people. But I hated myself.

People would come out and try to extend their hand and I used to run away from them. They had the Twelve Steps of the program there. I thought they were something you walked up. I didn't understand the Steps. They mentioned God and at the time I didn't want no part of him. Because I thought he was a very just God—unforgiving God; he was never going to forgive me for all the things that I had done. It was always said to me when I was willing to have . . . to have forgiven myself . . . God forgave me a long time ago, but I had to learn to forgive myself.

They mentioned people, places, and things in this program. I didn't understand that. I didn't understand what they were even talking about.

They talked about you didn't pick up the first drink you won't get drunk. Well, I didn't understand that either. I never thought it was the first. What does it matter if it's your first drink?

My sponsor used to come up and pick me up and take me out to outside meetings, and I would see his car coming, because he was always on time, and I used to run when I saw his car coming, because I didn't want to go. I was, I was afraid of walking in, into these rooms. I'd start getting, uh. . . .

I made the ninety-day program and I left. I didn't put nothing into the program at all. I came out and I went back home. They didn't want me to go back home but I went back home anyhow. Here I am, had ninety days under my belt, and I feel good, I was getting three meals a day and, uh, I had all the meetings I was going to attend, or so I thought. Uh. . . . I came home.

I wasn't home not more than a month. I was still being picked up for meetings and taken out. I used to get in quite a lot of battles with my father about these meetings—"You don't need 'em," he went on and on and on. . . . I decided one day that I didn't want to live anymore. I wanted to die. I went to a doctor and I asked, I told him, I conned him, really; I told him I couldn't sleep at night. Then he gave me some Librium and Valium. And, uh, this day I decided I was going to end my . . . I wanted . . . to, to do away with myself and I took quite a bit of pills knowing fully well I was being picked up . . . and taken to a women's meeting in Sinclair. And I took all these pills. And I went to that meeting and, uh, I don't remember what happened. They said that I jumped out of their car and I went into a bar and I ordered a drink, and I came to forty days later in Craven-Humbert medical in intensive care where I OD'd and almost died. And when I came to the only thing that I did was I cussed God for letting me live, because I really wanted to die.

And the first person I saw when I awoke, my eyes opened, was my sponsor. And I went back to Abigail State, building four, behind locked doors because I was suicidal. I went there and, uh, they asked me if I knew where I was and I told them yes. I thought, I thought, here I am, I'm in your crazy ward and this is where I belong. They were doing the shuffle. They walked like zombies. I decided to walk like them. I wanted to fit in somewhere. I did not believe I was an alcoholic. I was crazy. Um, they . . . would walk into walls. I just followed. Whatever they did . . . I did whatever they did.

A man came up and told me I didn't belong there and sent me back down to building ten. Back down to building ten I went. The administrator of the building—he was Nick Pope, uh, I can say his name today because he passed away—he welcomed me back to building ten, and he pleaded with me to stay for ninety days again. I told Nick Pope what to do with himself and the building, that I was only staying a month.

I did not, again, put any effort into the program at all. You people were still there with your, your smart clothes and your shining eyes. I wanted what you had, but I didn't want to go to any lengths to get it.

So I went out again in 1974. I barricaded myself in my house and I drank. And I came to. And I looked in the mirror. . . . For as, as long as I can remember as a child and even, even in my drinking I will not look at, in the mirror a lot at myself. Because I didn't even like myself. I didn't like what I had seen, or what I had become. I saw a woman [dead]. That's the stuff that my low self-esteem that I had in myself at that time.

I came to and I called my sponsor and I told him that I was

drinking and I needed help. He said, "Be ready in fifteen minutes. You're going to a meeting." I went to that meeting, at Humbert Options, it's called. I don't remember the meeting. I don't remember who spoke, or even who was there. But I was there. Like they said, bring the body and the mind'll follow.

Sometimes I wonder about that.

I went that night . . . I stood up and I told who I was and I was an alcoholic. I think that's when I completely surrendered to the fact that I was powerless over alcohol. So I started making meetings there pretty regular. But I wasn't making their step meetings. I was going to meeting meetings, and I started making New Humbert. I was down there for around three months and I wanted to belong to a group—so I asked whoever it was [that had the meeting], uh, how much dues did I have to pay to be a member. And they told me you paid your dues way before you came here. I said, "Well, what does that mean?" So they explained to me what it means and I started going down to New Humbert and I got to know quite a lot of people and I grew to love very much. Uh, they were always there for me, when I needed help, I always could call there, call one of them and they were always there to help me.

I thank God. . . . I was . . . in every area, not only spiritually but physically. I didn't believe in God until my sponsor told me fake it. Fake it till you make it. So he told me, "When you're down on one knee, get down on the other and say your little prayer to whoever." So I start doing that. And I slowly start getting better, my mind started clearing up . . . to some degree. I still say to him when I'm talking to him [what I think]. It says "restores sanity" but they don't say when. So I'm . . . still a little crazy but that's okay since, um. . . .

So I started making meetings down in Humbert, I was making meetings up here, a little bit. I start. . . . When I first walked into Serenity House I was scared to death of [those few people]. I wanted to please everybody. I was a people-pleaser. I wanted to please everybody and everybody to like me. But today I don't care if anybody likes me. *I* like me. You know, I'm not here for a popularity contest. I'm not here because I tripped over a, my foot. [Drinking] —that's what got me here.

I moved up here because of a . . . physical problem. And my health is very bad today. But I'm able to deal with it because I have this program and I did find God in here, uh, I started believing. I knew I didn't come in here because I wanted to. I came in here because God pushed me in here [and said "you're staying"]. I started making meetings because I had to change.

I still have a lot of work to do on myself. I still have some character defects, but some of them are slowly getting better.

I've had a lot of tragedy in my sobriety, too. I buried my whole family. But I have the biggest family I could ever want in here. I got all, all over that. I picked up the pieces and continued to start living. Today I have my self back. I have people that I can call any time of the day or night—and they never hang up on you. They've held me when I'm not able to hold myself up. They've give—uh, this program has given me back everything. You people are my strength and my hope.

Thank you very much.

Phil

November 22, 1986

Hello everybody. I'm an alcoholic, my name is Phil.

I got to go back to the beginning. I, I should say that I'm a, I'm a BIC . . . that's Brooklyn-Irish-Catholic. And I was raised very religiously. I do not come from a drinking family. My mother was not a drinker. I didn't like the taste of alcohol. I was a very fearful person before alcohol. I was afraid of heights; I was claustrophobic. Yes, I was born and raised and lived in Brooklyn—I was part of a gang. I was very brave, when I was with my friends; I was very pacifist when I was by myself.

I got into drinking at the age of fifteen. I came into AA and found out about an invisible line. I don't ever remember an invisible line. I can sit here and tell you I went into a bar one day and had a ball and a beer, and I liked the reaction, because I was very introvert, and after I had the ball and a beer, I would talk to some people; and after I had the second ball and beer, I even became a little jovial; and after the third ball and a beer, I didn't remember anything anymore. And that was to be the pattern of my drinking for the next fifteen years. I can never—I cannot sit here and tell anybody in this room about social drinking, 'cause I don't know what a social drink is. I came into AA in 1969, and I didn't even know what an alcoholic was. I did not think I had a problem with alcohol.

Chronologically, between the ages of fifteen and sixteen, I used to wake up from drunks in alleyways, somebody's car, hospitals, and, most of the time, in jail. When I was sixteen, the principal called my mother up to school and told her she'd save the taxpayers a lot of money if she'd sign me out of school. I was truant 180, 180 days. And my, you know, it was just me and my mom, so she worked and I was drunk somewhere. When I left school, I was supposed to go to continuation school once a week, and I did that the first two weeks. But I was getting very [fond of] bars. I used to go to a bar, and drink, and get drunk, I guess, I *guess* have a good time. And around two o'clock in the morning I guess I looked in the mirror and didn't like what I saw, so I took a barstool and threw it through the mirror. I got a lot of scars on my face and parts of my body from how brave I used to be when I was in bars. But in order to keep me out of jail, my mother would pay these bar bills. Now, believe me, I do not come from a rich family. My mother would first started borrowing from her credit union, then the banks, finance companies, started hitting the Shylocks.

In 1955, I woke up in a jail cell, which I did many, many mornings—but when I'd wake up in these jail cells the cell was always open; I was—it was a regular habitat for me. They knew me. But this one morning it was closed. And, uh, to make a long story short I was being booked for homicide. And in 1955, the death penalty was still in effect in New York. And I didn't remember if I did it, if I didn't do it. I knew I was capable. I knew when I drank I got very violent. But I had no alibi. And I remember praying; and I sat down, knelt, knelt down in that jail cell praying, making one more promise to God.

[And after that, I tell you, was the first job I lost: I was very religious, I tell you, I was an altar boy and I got thrown off that because I was stealing the wine. But, you know, when I started drinking I left the church, too.]

And four hours later the bartender was the one who saved my ass, got me out of it. And all those praying deals I made in jail with God—the deals, I won't drink, anyone get me out of this mess—

and I walked out of the jail, we went down half a block to the bar, and we started the whole rat-race again. And I yet did not still feel that I had a problem, of any kind, with alcohol.

September 12 was my birthday. On September 12, 1956, I was seventeen. And that very same day my mother took me down to the recruiting station. Made me sign myself into the United States Army. I really believe my mother thought she . . . she couldn't take any more of it. And I guess she was under the impression that the army was going to change me. I'll tell you right now, the army did not change me.

I went in the army, and I went to Fort Dix. And I, when I first found out, at that time, that New York was one of the, one of three states you could drink at eighteen. And I knew I had no problem passing for eighteen; but I found out you had to be twenty-one in other states and I knew that I, no way I could get away with twenty-one. And of course, being introvert—I didn't make friends that easy —there was no way I was going to get proof. But I figured as long as we were at Fort Dix there was no problem, because I'm only a hop, skip, and a jump from New York. My mother's gone now, but I don't know to this day if she ever told them that I had a, she thinks, a problem drinking. But they sent me to Fort Jackson, South Carolina. And I hated the South. And I went down to Fort Jackson, South Carolina, and I even managed to get an ID that said I was twenty-one. It was funny: they never gave me any passes at Fort Jackson, South Carolina; and I couldn't take that three-point-two beer.

And I remember this guy coming around said if you joined the paratroopers you get thirty days leave. I'm afraid of height. But I wanted to go to town. So I signed. And the army was very nice, they kept their word. They gave me a pass for thirty days. And, what I was supposed to do was I was supposed to go to this airbase in Columbia and catch an air, a plane from that air force base, which is called a hop, to Floyd Bennett field, and you pay a dollar for the chute. So I figured before I go on the plane I better go have a few drinks. So, and Columbia, South Carolina . . . I can remember is a church-going town, very quiet, nice, all white [southern] houses. But I went to a bar there to have a few, a few balls and a few beers before I went on the plane, and twenty-eight days later I come out of the blackout and I was still in Columbia, South Carolina.

I had to keep my word to the army, so I had to go to jump school. I went to Fort Bragg, North Carolina, to take training with the Eighty-second Airborne. And I was there one day, when they sent me to Fort Campbell, Kentucky, to take the training with the Hundred-and-first. And I figured I'd play their silly game, but I won't go jump out of no plane, matter of fact I wasn't even going to get in the plane. I was never in a plane in my life.

I even went to Fort Benning, Georgia, to jump off their two-hundred-fifty-foot tower, drunk. When I came back it was one day before I was supposed to go out on one of our first five, first of five practice jumps. And I decided this is the time to quit. So I went in the back where you go to quit and I found out what they do to quitters. You see, when you, in the paratroopers, and you decide you're going to quit, for eight hours you double-time round the compound yelling out, "I'm a quitter." And I figure there's no way in hell they're going to get a kid from Brooklyn to run around the compound yelling, "I'm a quitter." So I asked the jump-master, I says, you know, "Are you allowed to go to town the night before you make your first jump?" And he says, "Oh, sure, you're allowed, you're entitled to your last meal." I—he says, "One other thing: when you get on that plane and you chicken out, don't worry about it, you can come back." Any young kids here, don't believe that.

I went to town that night, and I got drunk, and I brought back two pints of Seagram for when I go on the plane in the morning. And by the time I got on that plane at four-thirty in the morning, I was pretty well lit. It's, uh, it's not a good thing, believe me, because, you know, I always say, when I drink, if I want to kill myself, that's one thing; but, you see, when you're jumping out of a plane, it's what you call twenty men on a stick. It's forty men go on a plane, twenty men on each side. And I was number fifteen. And what you're supposed to do is, I was supposed to check the guy's in front of me's chute, while the guy behind me checks mine. I never checked nobody's nothing.

When it came to my turn to jump, I, I did what they tell you not to do in jump school, they say never look down, but you know, I had to go, "What's going on down there?"—and I told the guy I wasn't going out. And he told me he wears a size twelve boot and I told him to use it, and I made seventeen jumps and never jumped out myself. I was always kicked out of a plane.

I bring up the seventeen jumps because you're only required to make one jump every three months to get your hazardous duty pay, which was fifty-five dollars. But, see, when I jump, it was an excuse to drink. And, even to this point in time I never thought I had a problem with alcohol.

My company went to Germany. We were going to, going to go to Germany to do maneuvers with the Eleventh Airborne, and we were going by boat, and I wasn't going to go on no boat. So, I was sober, and I went to the company commander and I told him that I thought I had . . . I was one of twelve children, I thought they were all in the navy. That's what I told him. I says, "You know, if I wanted to go on boats I would have joined the navy." And I said I would, I would very seriously consider going AWOL and spending the remaining two-and-a-half years in the stockade before I'd go on a boat. And they sent me on a plane to Germany. They sent me on a cargo plane, so I should have taken the boat.

And when I got to the place, it was called Augsburg, Germany, it's twenty miles outside of Munich, I always thought I was going to see all these *frauleins,* and this nice bock beer, I was going to have a real ball. I never seen Munich; I never seen a *fraulein;* and I never tasted the bock beer. I got to Germany, and made one jump. It was a night jump, and I was drunk, and I was fooling around—because, you know, you become an expert with a chute, you can make it go to the left or to the right, forward, backwards, like a car, you know, and you get real cocky, and you jump on a guy's chute and dance, you can do a lot of things with a chute. Because you're drunk, you don't give a damn, and I was seventeen. And I got caught in a tree. And, you know, all you have to do is just hit your thing over here, you come out of your chute, but not me—I'm banging against the tree [with the left side] and I'm banging against the tree; and I told my buddy to cut me down and he's drunk, he cuts me down. I broke my leg in three places. So I figured, at least, at least I'll get a medical discharge and get out of the army. But I didn't get a medical discharge.

And they sent me back stateside, and they sent me back south. They sent me to Fort Gordon, Georgia, that's Augusta, Georgia, that's where the president plays golf. And I was in, they put me in a transportation outfit, and they let *me* drive tractors and trailers. I was supposed to take tractors and refrigerator trailers from Fort

Gordon, Georgia, to Fort Polk, Louisiana. I made three tries; I never got out of the state of Georgia. I put two of them off cliffs. And I, I, I got to say in all fairness to the army they were very . . . they tried. They gave me . . . and I drove it to a mess hall; they made me a general's aide and I lost his car. Needless to say I, I got in quite a little trouble in the army. But I never got court-martialed. I was—I should play the number fifteen because I had more Article Fifteens, I did more KP—I still do the potatoes at home—I did more KP, I spent more guard duty—I think that's what I did in the army.

But on one night in September, this fine southern lieutenant come over to me and told me that "Ah should GI the whole barracks bah mahself." And that's Friday night; and I knew that was unfair. I knew that wasn't right. I knew I was supposed to GI my own area, bunk, footlocker, blah-blah-blah. And he didn't like boys from Brooklyn. So I did that: I did my own footlocker, wall locker, and bunk, and then I went to town. With no pass. And I decided I was going to get drunk and take care of this . . . southern gentleman when I came back. And I got back to camp at two, three o'clock in the morning, and I was too drunk to bother nobody—but he wasn't. He was there waiting for me. And he put his hands on my shoulder, and I picked up a footlocker and bashed him over the head with it. Sent him to the hospital. They court-martialed me and I beat the court-martial, because someone eyewitnessed that he put his hands on me first. But I was only winning a little battle. They rode me. Until they got me to . . . a bad conduct discharge out of the army.

So, uh, when I came back home I went back to my old profession, and that's lifting the elbow in the bar. And, uh, I got a job, through hanging out in the bars, driving tractors and trailers. Guess where I had to go. South. Down to Florida, Tennessee, Alabama. But I made good money.

And I remember, I wanted to always be a police officer. And I remember buying a brand new Ford with no chrome, whip antenna. And one Saturday afternoon I went into a Crawford's men's store and I bought a trench coat and a fedora; and I went to F. W. Woolworth's, and I bought a sheriff's badge. Toy pistol. Had a flashlight. And I got drunk that night, and I went down the Coney Island section of Brooklyn, and I hustled people in lovers' lane.

When I woke up the next morning in the West Eighth Street police station, because this detective I hustled didn't care for it. . . .

I used to become other people when I drank. I used to—I remember I went to see *Elmer Gantry*. When I came out I went to the Red Hook section of Brooklyn, which is a very tough section of Brooklyn, and I was trying to save souls in a bar. I went to see *Al Capone* and I used to go in the bar with my hand in like I got a gun in my pocket—you know, it's a wonder how I'm alive.

When I, when I got in that trouble in Coney Island they took my license away. I, I believe today—my uncle was a cop for twenty-some-odd years in the neighboring precinct, and I think they knew the name, and what they got me for was drunk and reckless driving. They took my license away so I, you know, I had to lose that job. And, and, I spent a lot of time, with the money I had, getting drunk and not working. And when the money wore out, I had to get a job. I had to get a job in a factory—I was a silk-screener for radio receptors. And the job was in a section of Brooklyn where you had to, had to take a train to New York, to Fourteenth Street, and then get another train back to Brooklyn. It's the craziest way to go to work—it's an hour and twenty minutes by train, about a twenty-five-minute ride by car. But I couldn't drive. To make a long story short they . . . I used to work from seven in the morning till four, and right outside the factory there was a bar. I used to go to that bar and I used to give the bartender my check on Thursdays. See, what I used to do, I used to drink there and the porter would get me up at six o'clock so I could go to work.

Sometimes there was this girl that would ride the same train with me. . . . And she would take me home, or, you know, you got to take a shower sometime, so we got married. Everything was nice for the first two weeks. Then I decided that I was entitled to have a night out with friends. And, and I should tell you, I had no friends. The only friends I had was Rheingold and Seagram's Seven. And the only time I cheated on my wife was with Rheingold and Seagram's Seven. And I would go out and get drunk, and she would have a miscarriage, and I'd get drunk and she'd have another miscarriage, and I'd get drunk and I said, you know, she couldn't even give me children.

And I remember when my first daughter was born, and I was a butcher at the time, a kosher butcher—uh, making good money, and had put all—you know, it was—I was up on . . . she had no necessity to go to city hospital to have the baby. But that's where she wound up. And I guess I played the role when my first daughter was born, I went to Coney Island hospital, drunk, and I looked through that little window where they show the babies, and I seen a big mark on my daughter's eye and I wanted to know what that was and they said an "instrument baby" and I didn't know what the hell that was. I played the role, so I, I attacked the doctor. Who . . . I really didn't care, to be very honest.

But I found out, when you take a new baby, I used to take them into the bar, you get a lot of free drinks. So my, when Joanne was a little baby, she met . . . a lot of bars in Brooklyn. When she was only about, I don't know, four or five months old, I know it was a cold, blistery morning, and I came home. Evidently, I was drunk, and, evidently, my wife gave me a hard time. So I took her daughter out of the crib, in diapers, and threw her on the street. When I came back in she gave me a hard time so I threw her out. And I locked the door and went to sleep. I lived in the housing projects—and I always tell this story because I never want to forget what alcohol has done to me. And she took the baby under her nightgown, I guess, and went to the manager's office to get a key to get back in. Uh. Why she didn't call the cops I don't know. Oh, and I got up next morning and wanted to give my wife a kiss and I don't want to tell you what she gave me. But, see, I didn't remember.

I used to fight with my wife, hit her a few times, I thought she had stolen, steal money out of my wallet. Because all I remember having is a few balls and a few beers, but you don't spend thirty or forty dollars on a few balls and a few beers.

I got a letter, I got a letter one morning from the Motor Vehicle Department saying I owed for a traffic ticket I didn't pay. And I guess I got a bit of honesty and decided I wanted to straighten my life out; so I'm going to go there and tell them I have about four or five other [with them], get my life straightened out. When I got there, One Hundred Centre Street, and I got there a little early, so I figured, before I see the judge [I'd have] a few balls and a few beers. And I went and had a few balls and a few beers and now I, I feel no pain, I feel good; and, I went to the judge and he said fifteen dollars and told him I have other tickets and he said a hundred dollars bail. Now I knew, as drunk as I was, that no bail bondsman would take a hundred dollars, so—I thought I was lying—I said I had a pregnant wife at home. He told me either a hundred dollars or go to jail. There's a lot of women here, I can't tell you what I told the judge I'd do if he wasn't wearing his black robe. And the language I used. But he was very polite. He told me to spend the next thirty days on Hart's Island. And that's what I did. I spent the next thirty days over there playing basketball, [going to] driving lessons, and digging graves. And talking about how I was going to get this judge when I got out.

I spent my whole life planning to get people. You know, I'm still, I, I say today, I'm like an elephant, I don't forget. And, uh, that's one of the things I'm working on.

When I came out, he got promoted to chief magistrate, and to make a long story short I got fined $350. And he was giving me time payments. And I told the judge, "Don't do no favors. Just give me a date and I'll pay it." And he did. When the time come I couldn't raise the money, I had to borrow it from my aunt. She gave me the $350. And that night I went—went out to party, I woke up I didn't have three dollars and fifty cents on me. Also when I came out of jail I found out my wife was pregnant. And I couldn't understand for the life of me how she was pregnant and I'd just spent thirty days on Hart's Island. So I accused her of all kinds of infidelity. When my second daughter was born I refused to go to the hospital and take her home—I disowned the kid.

I went to see a priest. I said I'm having a little trouble with my marriage. This Jewish girl I married is now keeping me from my religion, she keeps me from going to church. You know, I, I tried to put all these things on her. And he told me that, you know, what I, what I had to do was, we were young and, you know, we should separate a little bit and get our head together. Next to the bartender he was God. So, I thought I had a legal separation. So now I went back to my bachelor life. And it was very nice. I would go meet a girl, we'd have a beautiful dinner, we'd go to a nice movie, everything's nice, then we'd go to the bar. And I'd never see the girl again. Because I get *very nasty*. And, even to this point in my life I never thought I had a problem drinking; [I knew, but, if I take a drink I get nasty, so I, I learned].

And by this time I was driving an ambulance and I can sit here [and tell you a long] story about that so I won't get into that. But

I, I, I met this girl in the ambulance, I took her to the hospital. And we, we got acquainted, and she liked to drink. By this time, uh, I already had had hepatitis; I, I was laid up six months with it, and they told me I'd live a normal life if I didn't drink. So, at—that was in 1962. In 1962 I became periodic. Every time I wanted to commit suicide, or felt like I wanted to die I would drink.

But anyhow I met this girl and I . . . told her I had hepatitis, I can't drink. And, she says okay and she'd sit in the bar and she'd drink and I'd drink orange juice and I'd sweat. And the biggest fights that me and this girl had was to leave the bar before four o'clock. Because I never drank at home, you know, I would take her home and then run back to the bar and, and do my thing. I went out with this girl three years, I don't think she ever knew I drank.

Anyhow, we, we did this for a while, all right? It was a good set-up. I'd be on ambulance call and I'd call up from the bar drunk [and tell her I'd got another ambulance call]. She was drunk when I called her so neither one of us remembered in the morning. So we had a very good relationship.

One Fourth of July I, I, I was sober, and my mother wanted me to take her to Long Island to see her brother. I think she regretted that after that, too, but that's. . . . And I guess when I was drinking, my girlfriend, I'd promised to go away with her for the weekend. But I didn't remember that, I remembered that I was supposed to take my mother to Long Island and I did. When I came back I went over to see my girlfriend that following Tuesday, whatever it was, and she says to me, "I'm going to an AA meeting Friday, would you take me?" I says, "I work for an ambulance company, they sell crutches . . ." But I took her. And I sat at that meeting, and there was two women speaking, and all I heard them say was, something to the effect of, if you can go to a bar and have *a* drink and leave then chances are you're not an alcoholic. And I couldn't wait for that meeting to end. And when my girlfriend . . . I took her home. And I went to the bar, I ordered a ball and a beer, and I left the bar, I felt good: I ain't no alcoholic. I did this in eight bars.

I would go to these meetings—open meetings, I didn't go to closed meetings, I won't . . . I remember taking this girl to a closed meeting, with an ambulance, and I had to go out, and the guy says to me, "Uh, are you an alcoholic?" I says, "Hell no, she is." So they told me I couldn't stay there; so I left and went and got drunk.

I got to say that I did this for twelve days. I would go to these meetings and I did not want to say that I was an alcoholic. But, *I never knew I had a problem*, until I was introduced to AA. See, I guess I always thought that I could stop drinking anytime I wanted to. Anyhow, I would go to these meetings and I'd figure I'm not going to drink because the girl's doing so good. And I'm just, I'm not going to drink to help her out. And one day I asked them, "Can I, you know, can I stop smoking one day at a time?" And they said, "Sure, Phil, come to the meetings." And I'd go in the bathroom sneaking cigarettes. I asked if I could go on a diet. They say, "Just keep on coming to the meetings." And I'd be sneaking the cheesecake. See, I wasn't drinking. I didn't drink. I'd go to these silly meetings, look at these silly Steps, and give you answers to every one of them, but I didn't drink. And after eight months of doing this, on a Friday night I went to somebody's first anniversary, and, uh, after that we went to this twelve o'clock meeting at this clubhouse, and me and my girlfriend we went up there . . . and, uh, the speaker didn't show up and he asked her to speak. And that peed the hell out of me. I kept that broad sober eight months and they ask her to speak. So I walked out of the meeting, and I went down the road to a bar, and I ordered a ball and a beer. And I think, [being very sincere], that's when I had my spiritual awakening. And I sat there with a drink in my hand and I said, you know, "What the hell am I doing here?" And I went back to the meeting. You want to talk about humility? I had to ask *that girl* to help me. And, that's when the program started for me. And after her three years of sobriety she decided she'd marry me—'cause that's my wife Peggy I'm talking about.

But I don't regret any time I've spent in this program. They told me it wasn't—when I came in—they told me it was no rose garden. And I, I never had car accidents when I was drinking, I've had plenty of them when I'm sober. But I don't drink and I go to meetings. And I try to put these Steps in my life.

Thank you so much.

Notes

Introduction

1. Confusions, contradictions, and inconsistencies of the kinds that occur in mental life are impermissible in a "sound" expository literature and hence, perhaps, the adoption by commentators of misleading, one-dimensional positions. In *Understanding the Alcoholic's Mind* (1988), Ludwig suggests a reconciliation of apparently mutually exclusive positions in the notion that the peculiar alcoholic subjectivity can comprehend them all simultaneously.

First-person accounts of alcoholism may be found in Hall (1974), McConville (1995), Meryman (1984), Sandmaier (1980), Stromsten (1982), Wholey (1984), and in the central AA text, *Alcoholics Anonymous* (Alcoholics Anonymous World Services, 1976a). The monthly AA *Grapevine* is also a good source of primary narratives, commentary, and information, relying almost exclusively as it does upon unsolicited contributions from its predominantly AA-affiliated readership.

The novel is ideally suited to describing situated alcoholism over time—and many of the books listed above make good use of the techniques of fiction. Charles Jackson's novel *The Lost Weekend* (1944) is necessary reading for anyone who cares about alcoholism in fiction. Novels by Arnold (1982) and Moore (1955) deal sensitively with alcoholism in women protagonists. Suggestions for further reading in both primary and secondary literature may be found in Crowley (1994) and Gilmore (1987) along with their first-rate essays on significant artists and trends. Crowley touches briefly on the vast subject of chemical dependency in film.

My attitude toward AA is sympathetic—as will become clear—though not without reservations. Recent skeptical and hostile critics include Fingarette (1988), Peele (1989), Kaminer (1993), and Trimpey (1992). Jack Trimpey is the founder of Rational Recovery, a self-help program based largely on Albert Ellis's Rational-Emotive Therapy techniques. RR borrows some strategies from AA, but deemphasizes AA's cornerstone "spirituality" in favor of reason and a program of deliberately restructured individual self-determination. The RR approach is laid out in Trimpey's *The Small Book* (the title parodies the name by which AA's *Alcoholics Anonymous* is often referred to among affiliates, the "Big Book"). RR seems to have had some success, and Trimpey's arguments

213

warrant a fair hearing. The venom that he lavishes on AA, however, seems somewhat at variance with the very rationality he advocates.

The *Utne Reader* (No. 30, 1988 November/December) carried a special twenty-five-page "skeptical look at AA and other twelve-step programs."

In *Trinities,* Nick Tosches's recent novel of the organized drug trade, the protagonist, Johnny DiPietro, recalls his experience with "the fellowship." His reflections could represent those of any skeptic.

> The doctors had persuaded him to go to AA when they released him. And he had gone. But after a while, he had begun to see it as a racket. Most of those who attended, by his standards of reckoning, had never really drunk all that much to begin with. They came to meetings, he suspected, as others went to bars or did church work: to socialize. For some, AA seemed to be a substitute for life, a microcosm with its own mythology, hierarchy, and language, a refuge where those who failed to find elsewhere the attention, love, and sense of importance they craved could preen and thrive. For others, it seemed to be a counteraddiction that built not strength but weakness. Elevating themselves from drunkards to alcoholics, from fuck-ups to suffering souls, the not-so-anonymous followers of AA seemed to enjoy the self-importance and self-sympathy of pretending to be in the throes of a disease. They were snobs that way, skid-row elitists who bestowed delusory dignity on drunkenness by calling it alcoholism. Johnny had watched his mother rot slowly and painfully from cancer. To him, that was a disease. What kind of disease could be controlled by volition? he asked. But then again, AA had not much use for free will. Its credo of powerlessness and blind submission to a lackluster deity of drunkards insured the stunting of souls, the snuffing of willpower, the dousing of what ancient wisdom called the heroic spark. Surely more people put down the bottle in the centuries before AA than in the decades of its existence. With its dictatorial insistence on endless meetings, indoctrination, and conversion, it denied that there are men, and women, whose powers are diminished, not enhanced, by the strictures and influences of conformity, who find no comfort in gathering, who are lessened, not greatened, by remanding their destinies to others. Like every religion and cult, its ultimate message was: there is no other way. And that message, as always, was anathema to Johnny. It was bad enough coming from the Church, whose sword of authority had been drawing blood for nearly two millennia, but coming from a cult whose history went back only sixty years to some schmuck named Bill, it was preposterous. (Tosches, 1994, pp. 325–326)

See also Chapter 6 for some further remarks on AA's hostile critics.

2. Readers unfamiliar with AA should consider attending some open meetings—so called because they are not restricted to alcoholics or people who are concerned about their own drinking. Open meetings last about an hour and

usually feature one or two speakers, sometimes followed by remarks volunteered from the floor. Regional AA offices may be contacted by telephone for information about the times and locations of meetings.

3. *Constructive Drinking: Perspectives on Drink from Anthropology,* edited by Mary Douglas (1987), is a good compendium of recent thinking on nonpathological alcohol use from constructivist perspectives. *Beliefs, Behaviors, and Alcoholic Beverages: A Cross-Cultural Survey,* edited by Mac Marshall (1979), approaches many of the same issues, as does Marshall's monograph (1979), *Weekend Warriors: Alcohol in a Micronesian Culture.* Earlier standard anthologies which contain substantial qualitative and cross-cultural material include McCarthy (1959) and Pittman and Snyder (1962). The *Journal of Studies on Alcohol,* Supplement No. 9, "Cultural Factors in Alcohol Research and Treatment of Drinking Problems," edited by Dwight B. Heath, Jack O. Waddell, and Martin D. Topper (1981), is also of interest.

4. The polarities of the discussion in its political dimension are embodied in two works: E. M. Jellinek's important *The Disease Concept of Alcoholism* (1960) and Herbert Fingarette's *Heavy Drinking: The Myth of Alcoholism as a Disease* (1988). The titles tell the stories. A high-pitched, overstated polemic, *Heavy Drinking* nevertheless represents a point of view that must be taken seriously. (Fingarette is briefly discussed further in Chapter 6, below.)

Responsible commentators entertain multiplex explanations.

"Discoveries are coming out in such rapid-fire succession that many experts see the dawn of a new age of enlightenment, wherein alcoholism will be proven to have a tapestry of subtle biological causes. Though the disease may be set in motion by environmental and/or psychological factors, alcoholics fall prey to their illness because their metabolisms, due either to genetic predisposition or to the effects of heavy drinking, differ distinctly from those of nonalcoholics" (Franks, 1985, p. 48).

Vaillant suggests that perhaps the "best one-sentence definition of alcoholism available to us" is one provided by the National Council on Alcoholism: "The person with alcoholism cannot consistently predict on any drinking occasion the duration of the episode or the quantity that will be consumed" (Vaillant, 1983, p. 44). One of the virtues of this "definition" is that it bypasses etiological and nosological questions altogether.

It is worth remembering Ernest Kurtz's remarks on the disease concept at the beginning of his discussion of "The Meaning and Significance of Alcoholics Anonymous" in *Not-God:*

As Dr. E. M. Jellinek observed in discussing the cliche that "alcoholism is a disease," acceptance of this truism was fine, and just about everyone agreed with it. The difficulty arose, Jellinek pointed out, because there existed no agreement about just what "alcoholism" was, nor any real consensus even among doctors about just what constituted "disease." Given such confusion, it was fortunate for the serenity of Alcoholics Anonymous that it treated the problem of alcoholism as disease as an "outside issue." AA thus on principle escaped direct confrontation with the problem as the fellowship itself lived out its Tenth Tradition [See note 5, below, for the Twelve Traditions].

[*Not-God*] is not bound by that Tradition, but entering the controversial discussion over alcoholism as disease would be at least as unhelpful to its purpose as public controversy over the question would be to AA's mission. For one thing, Jellinek's acute observation is, if anything, even truer today. Two decades of continuing, sophisticated medical research and psychological investigation have revealed complexities rather than produced any agreed-upon understanding. Further, neither disease as entity nor "dis-ease" as concept furnishes the most helpful category for the task of historical analysis at hand. Rather, one clear intuition arises from the historical narration and contextual analysis that have been presented: especially as religious in its inspiration, the Alcoholics Anonymous understanding of alcoholism begs for exploration within the insight that disease can also be a metaphor. (Kurtz, 1979, pp. 199–200)

Not-God is the most substantial work on Alcoholics Anonymous that I know, with themes and ambitions that range well beyond its nominal subject. The book is indispensable for anyone who might wish to locate AA, the alcoholism movement, and cognate enterprises in the framework of American cultural and religious history.

5. A short version of the Twelve Traditions of AA: (1) Our common welfare should come first; personal recovery depends upon AA unity. (2) For our group purpose there is but one ultimate authority—a loving God as He may express Himself in our group conscience. Our leaders are but trusted servants; they do not govern. (3) The only requirement for AA membership is a desire to stop drinking. (4) Each group should be autonomous except in matters affecting other groups or AA as a whole. (5) Each group has but one primary purpose —to carry its message to the alcoholic who still suffers. (6) An AA group ought never endorse, finance, or lend the AA name to any related facility or outside enterprise, lest problems of money, property, and prestige divert us from our primary purpose. (7) Every AA group ought to be fully self-supporting, declining outside contributions. (8) Alcoholics Anonymous should remain forever nonprofessional, but our service centers may employ special workers. (9) AA, as such, ought never be organized; but we may create service boards or committees directly responsible to those they serve. (10) Alcoholics Anonymous has no opinion on outside issues; hence the AA name ought never be drawn into public controversy. (11) Our public relations policy is based on attraction rather than promotion; we need always maintain personal anonymity at the level of press, radio, and films. (12) Anonymity is the spiritual foundation of all our traditions, ever reminding us to place principles before personalities.

6. This is the questionnaire I used: (1) Recall the first time you told your story in a meeting. Consider preparation, goals, intentions, attitudes, audience responses, and your own reactions to the experience. (2) What kinds of changes did you make in subsequent tellings, either sooner or later in your speaking

career? (3) What do you consider it most important to convey in speaking? What points do you always try to make? What impressions do you like to manage? Do your intentions change from one speaking situation to another? (4) How do particular audiences or situations alter your attitudes, style, preparation, expectations, etc.? (5) How would you instruct others to tell their story? What advice would you give with respect to effectiveness, sincerity, clarity, organization, or any other important points? (6) How do you think about what kinds of information to include and what to omit? What about the question of honesty versus privacy? Are certain issues or historical facts of no interest or concern to an audience? Are some matters not even for a sponsor's ear? How do you judge what's relevant? (7) How do you listen to someone else's story? How do you go about identifying? What kinds of stories do you like or dislike? What makes a story powerful or instructive? Can you remember particular stories that have affected you profoundly? What might make a speaker seem insincere or incompetent? Can someone speak too early in his/her experience with the fellowship? Could you ever consider a speaking occasion bad, stupid, or worthless, or would you insist on finding some value in it? (8) How do these stories help in maintaining sobriety—from the speaker's or the audience's side? (9) What other benefits—besides maintaining sobriety—might be gained from speaking? What other kinds of values might be derived or expressed from the storytelling situation?

The full texts of nine interviews and seventeen stories may be found in my original dissertation, *Toward Rhetorical Immunity: Narratives of Alcoholism and Recovery,* University of Pennsylvania, 1988.

7. Nan Robertson has interviewed people who agree with me. She writes: "There has been criticism that AA headquarters are overly sensitive to pressure from the most rigid and narrow-minded members, particularly old-timers, who regard the Big Book and other authorized AA literature almost as Holy Writ. 'If anything is going to destroy AA,' said Dr. John Norris, for years an AA trustee, 'it will be what I call the "Tradition lawyers." They find it easier to live with black and white than they do with gray. These "bleeding deacons"—these Fundamentalists—are afraid of and fight any change' " (Robertson, 1988, p. 105).

8. Books by Crowley (1994), Dardis (1989), Gilmore (1987), and Goodwin (1988) are indispensable among recent work on literary alcoholism. Crowley's *The White Logic* marks a qualitative leap forward in its provocative linkage of alcoholism and literary modernism.

1. The Ecology of *The Bacchae*

1. In addition to *Steps* (1972), see Bateson's *Mind and Nature: A Necessary Unity* (1979), David Lipset's fine intellectual biography of Bateson (1980), and Mary Catherine Bateson's fascinating memoir of her father and Margaret Mead (1984), *passim.*

2. Bateson's account of mental events in the modulations from drunkenness to sobriety points beyond the mere transcoding of which I think symbolic

interactionists are sometimes guilty when they discuss conversion experiences and "identity" change. Bateson seems to understand something of a subject's inner experience of alcoholism and the actual quality of its erasure or supplanting in recovery.

Anthropologist Paul Antze dismisses Bateson's article as "much more an application of cybernetic theory than an exercise in the analysis of symbols" (1987, p. 177, n.1). But that theoretical application in fact provides not just an analysis—a transcoding—of characteristic symbolic structures in alcoholic thinking, but also a basis for understanding the principles of symbol formation and exchange in alcoholism and in AA. Bateson gives us an interpretive key to the process of transformation (and hence, perhaps, a therapeutic opportunity) in an alcoholic's mind when critical levels of dissonance are reached—that recognition of the need for change on which AA is predicated—and to the subsequent quality of the altered subjectivity.

3. The Twelve Steps of AA are as follows:

1. We admitted we were powerless over alcohol—that our lives had become unmanageable.

2. Came to believe that a Power greater than ourselves could restore us to sanity.

3. Made a decision to turn our will and our lives over to the care of God *as we understood Him.*

4. Made a searching and fearless moral inventory of ourselves.

5. Admitted to God, to ourselves, and to another human being the exact nature of our wrongs.

6. Were entirely ready to have God remove all these defects of character.

7. Humbly asked Him to remove our shortcomings.

8. Made a list of all persons we had harmed, and became willing to make amends to them all.

9. Made direct amends to such people wherever possible, except when to do so would injure them or others.

10. Continued to take personal inventory and when we were wrong promptly admitted it.

11. Sought through prayer and meditation to improve our conscious contact with God *as we understood Him,* praying only for knowledge of His will for us and the power to carry that out.

12. Having had a spiritual awakening as the result of these steps, we tried to carry this message to alcoholics, and to practice these principles in all our affairs.

The Preamble, in full, reads:

Alcoholics Anonymous is a fellowship of men and women who share their experience, strength, and hope with each other that they may solve their common problem and help others to recover from alcoholism.

The only requirement for membership is a desire to stop drinking.

There are no dues or fees for AA membership; we are self-supporting through our own contributions. AA is not allied with any sect, denomination, politics, organization, or institution; does not wish to engage in any controversy; neither endorses nor opposes any causes. Our primary purpose is to stay sober and help other alcoholics to achieve sobriety.

See Introduction, note 5 for the Twelve Traditions.

4. For the Serenity Prayer, see p. 114. The popularity of this prayer is by no means limited to AA and similar programs.

5. Hyde's (1975) important essay on the poet John Berryman is noted in Chapter 3. Hyde worked as an alcoholism counselor and used the knowledge he gained in practice to cut to the quick of Berryman's elaborate edifice of denial.

6. I am not satisfied with the term "theology" as used by David Lipset and many other writers to identify a very loose body of AA doctrine, lore, and opinion; the term carries misleading authoritarian implications and seems to make no space for non-believers, skeptics, and revisionists. "Philosophy," on the other hand, is too grand a word, with its promise of an organized system backed by a powerful analytic arsenal. "Program" seems to me happily secular and vague enough to be useful in most instances, though there is a disquieting echo of thought-reform, Manchurian-Candidate style, which might provide comfort to some of AA's more exuberant enemies.

7. The Manchester quip turns up in Berton Roueché's *Alcohol: Its History, Folklore and Its Effect on the Human Body* (1960). This short book began life in the *New Yorker*'s "Annals of Medicine" series and was first published under the title *The Neutral Spirit;* it may be, ounce for ounce, the best buy on the subject. Other useful primers include Kessel and Walton (1965), Maxwell (1984), and Milam and Ketcham (1981).

2. Some Americana

1. On April 20, 1988, the United States Supreme Court in effect declined to intercede in public debate over whether alcoholism should be defined as a "disease" or "willful misconduct," noting that authoritative opinion on the matter is divided. The hapless veterans who initiated the lawsuit—the vets wanted statutory time limits for education benefits claims waived, maintaining that their failure to file for benefits within the prescribed limits had been caused by alcoholism understood as an involuntary disease entity—are contemporary cousins of the protagonists of temperance fiction. Both, in states of initial innocence, are thrust into bewilderingly adverse situations well beyond their control and both, blindly susceptible, develop addictions that go unrecognized until so deeply engraved that help is problematic. Legislated responses to alcohol problems seem not to get to the heart of the matter; narrative responses sometimes produce useful interpretive maps, if not solutions.

For biographical information on Whitman, see Allen (1955) and Kaplan (1980).

2. See Trachtenberg (1982) and Lasch (1977) for sources and discussion of the development of the modern urban family. Brooks (1947) and, especially, Reynolds (1988) provide overviews of the literary culture in which Whitman navigated. Although not specific to Whitman or temperance literature, Douglas (1977) is probably essential for students of the period. Halttunen (1982) and Tompkins (1985) are also of interest.

3. Leslie Fiedler remarks that the saloon was long felt to be the "anti-type of the home, at least in Protestant America" (Fiedler, 1960, p. 260). See Blocker (1989), Lender and Martin (1982), and Rorabaugh (1979).

4. For interpretations of reform and especially temperance activism in nineteenth-century America, see Asbury (1950), Blocker (1989), Clark (1976), Daniels (1878), Furnas (1965), Gusfield (1986), Kobler (1973), Krout (1925), Lender and Martin (1982), Rorabaugh (1979), Tyler (1962), Tyrrell (1979), Walters (1978), and Wilentz (1984).

For temperance literature, see Lender and Karnchanapee (1977) and Reynolds (1988). Arthur's (1966) *Ten Nights in a Bar-Room*, first published in 1854, is standard and classic; Roe's (1909) much later *Rum and Ruin*, read in conjunction with Whitman and Arthur, might lead a reader to suppose that the form peaked early and became developmentally inert.

5. During its early, exploratory period in the late 1930s, AA debated the inclusion of women in its operations. First only the interested wives of the originally all-male membership were considered, but soon female alcoholics became candidates for AA's recognition and support. See Alcoholics Anonymous World Services (1980 and 1984).

6. Popular "guidebooks" written in the immoral reform mode purported to advise upwardly mobile rustics on how to cope with urban iniquity. One of those guidebooks, *Secrets of the Great City: A Work Descriptive of the Virtues and the Vices, the Mysteries, Miseries and Crimes of New York City*, by Edward Winslow Martin (1868), is of ethnographic interest to students of alcohol, crime, vice, social diseases, and even one or two of the less unsavory aspects of nineteenth-century city life. In the chapter, "The Morgue," Martin recites a cautionary anecdote which ends on this note:

> He had heard much in his country home of the dangers to which unsophisticated strangers were apt to fall in the Metropolis, but he had laughed at the idea of his being so silly as to allow himself to be treated so. He would take just one glance at the shady side of city life, to satisfy his curiosity, and have something to talk about at home, and would then start on his return. . . .
>
> Weary with waiting and watching, the friends of the young man will come hurriedly to the city, and the police authorities, who know well where to look for such missing ones, will take them to the Morgue, where their lost darling lies waiting for them.
>
> Young man, if curiosity tempts you to seek to penetrate the secrets of the great city, remember that you may learn them only to your cost. (Martin, 1868, pp. 480–483)

7. The metaphor of the theater is explored in detail in Jean-Christophe Agnew, *Worlds Apart: The Market and the Theater in Anglo-American Thought, 1550–1750* (1986).

8. Whitman draws extensively on Charles Lamb's remarkable essay of 1822, "Confessions of a Drunkard" (Lamb 1985), to the extent of quoting long passages without precise attribution. Lamb's candid plea for understanding is an important early position paper in the disease/misconduct debate.

9. The epigraphs are loaded with none-too-subtle thematic pointers. Extracted from Washingtonian and other temperance songbooks and poetry collections, they are rhetorically typical. This one—attributed to "Willis"—is a veritable *piñata* of interesting psychosexual morsels (Whitman, 1963, p. 204):

> They say 'tis pleasant on the lip,
>   And merry on the brain—
> They say it stirs the sluggish blood
>   And dulls the tooth of pain.
> Ay—but within its glowing deeps,
> A stinging serpent, unseen, sleeps.
>
> Its rosy lights will turn to fire,
>   Its coolness change to thirst;
> And by its mirth, within the brain
>   A sleepless worm is nursed,
> There's not a bubble at the brim
> That does not carry food for him.

10. The behavior of Margaret is both conceptually and formally symmetrical with that of the murderous Indian in the story of Wind-Foot. The problematic qualities of these dark-skinned minor figures could bear further attention.

11. Best known in an enhanced version by Robert Burns, the ballad "John Barleycorn" is distributed throughout the English-speaking world. It seems simple enough at first that a mood-changing substance should be personified, named, honored, and thereby made tractable, or placable, or otherwise user-friendly through linguistic shorthand. Bateson can help us here: the "force" of the grain now turned into strong brown ale is construed not as systemic but as external, having some sort of life independent of consumption and metabolization. Inherent in the grain, the beverage, or the transformation process, the force is then imposed upon the drinker from without, perhaps by invitation, perhaps not. Once named, the grain's natural history is compared allegorically with the human life-cycle, and perhaps a sort of consolation drawn from the persistence, even enhancement, of its "force" after death: if the harvested, fermented plant has the power to animate men, may not men abide in unrevealed forms after their death? Allegorical expansion allows the beverage to speak, to assert itself, to joke, and—in an Irish version of "John Barleycorn" —even to affirm the virtue of moderation.

The name, once granted autonomy under its own recognizance, goes free to assimilate qualities, behaviors, and historical characteristics not self-evidently connected by conventional logic to the originating motives. John Barleycorn becomes a sort of linguistic golem, able to incorporate any figural refuse at hand at the instigation of a mere moment's whimsy.

The problem in Burns arises with the overlay of signs of profound psychosexual disturbance that link alcohol with a primitively apprehended, prepotent, murderous father. The little story of John Barleycorn, emerging from someplace midway between origin myth and ethnoscience, is made to take on a burdensome supplement of brutal, primitive sexuality.

There is a complex association in the poem between values ascribed to alcohol and an incompletely controlled image-vocabulary that, minimally, invokes ambivalent internalized infantile notions about parents and conveys some uncertainty with respect to sexual identity. Two discrete bundles of images, initially only distantly related, have begun to interact, to share features and characteristics, and finally to merge under the unifying sign of a proper name.

For the poems and variants, see Burns (n.d., p. 73), Kennedy (1975, pp. 608, 627–628), Lomax (1934, p. 173), O Lochlainn (1960, p. 177), and Williams and Lloyd (1959, p. 56).

Freud's 1908 paper, "On the Sexual Theories of Children" (1963, p. 35) is a key text; the so-called sadistic conception of coitus may also be tracked in Fenichel (1945, p. 92).

12. A contemporary instance of the trope recurs in *Table Money,* Jimmy Breslin's powerful novel of alcoholism among present-day working-class Irish-Americans in Queens. The alcoholic protagonist, Owney, struggles to keep promises of varying sincerity to stop drinking. Each failure is heralded by the appearance of a phantom prizefighter:

> In front of Brendan's, a man appeared with a broom. He had the suggestion of gray hair covering an old red scalp. He began sweeping the sidewalk. Now he changed. He became younger, and uglier, and he was standing on the sidewalk in boxing trunks, with his bare chest heaving with effort. His face was smeared with Vaseline and his eight-ounce gloves were dark and old from sweat over many rounds. Now the gloves came up and they beckoned to Owney. He looked clearly at the opponent, alcohol, and he parked the car and got out to mix it up. (Breslin, 1986, p. 144)

Here is a chilling description of an alcoholic's "decision" to resume drinking in earnest despite a commitment to moderation. It is not unusual for speakers in AA to describe their relapses—"slips"—as occurring in similar autistic or fugue-like states.

> Owney finished his drink and he was reaching out to put the glass down so he could go up to the Golden Gloves fight when at this moment his own fight began. The opponent was there, all right. A lot older than these Golden Gloves kids upstairs; a nose broken and bent, the front teeth long missing, the scar tissue over the eyes turning pasty in the

fluorescent lights. Old soggy gloves beckoned. Owney was alone at the bar, with customers and bartenders gone up to the fight, and nobody saw or heard the punch that Owney took. He stumbled behind the bar and got a hand on a bottle of Fleischmann's and he was about to pour it into a glass and then he simply began to drink from the bottle, as if it were a soft drink. (P. 308)

13. The therapeutic concept of denial is discussed in virtually everything written on alcoholism. See, for example, Vaillant (1983) and Ludwig (1988).

14. A perspective of considerable poignance is gained on these passages by comparing them with Upton Sinclair's memories of London's antics during this period. See Sinclair's interesting pro-temperance screed, *The Cup of Fury* (1956).

He had purchased some trick drinking glasses, which had tiny holes around the rim; when a guest tilted the glass to drink, the liquid would run down his neck. His swimming pool was constructed with a secret passage under the water. Jack would dive in and swim through that passage and come up in another place, leaving his guests terrified, sure that he had drowned. A book bearing the title *A Loud Noise* was left around; when the cover was opened, a fire-cracker inside exploded. Rope arrangements permitted guests' beds to be rocked from another room; hapless visitors, thus shaken from their beds in the dark of the night, would dash out of their rooms, shouting "Earthquake! Earthquake!" And Jack would laugh: this was humor, this was fun, this was wit. (Sinclair, 1956, pp. 165–166)

15. Job, Ecclesiastes, Marcus Aurelius, *King Lear*, Beckett, Cioran, and Thomas Bernhard spring to mind.

16. The "pasteboard masks" passage is uttered by Ahab on "The Quarter Deck," p. 262 of the Penguin *Moby Dick* (1972). "The Whiteness of the Whale" is on pp. 287–296. Here is more: "Is it that by its indefiniteness it shadows forth the heartless voids and immensities of the universe, and thus stabs us from behind with the thought of annihilation, when beholding the white depths of the milky way? Or is it, that as in essence whiteness is not so much a color as the visible absence of color, and at the same time the concrete of all colors; is it for these reasons that there is such a dumb blankness, full of meaning, in a wide landscape of snows—a colorless, all-color of atheism from which we shrink?" (pp. 295–296).

One may also wish to reflect on the hyperborean final scenes of Edgar Allan Poe's *The Narrative of Arthur Gordon Pym*.

3. Rehabelletration

1. These "reasons" apparently stood Exley in good stead through the production of two further memoir-like novels, *Pages from a Cold Island* and *Last Notes from Home*. Neither of the later works displayed anything like the unity

or power of *A Fan's Notes;* and each, despite occasional passages of considerable presence, was marred by self-pity, resentment, and mawkishness. Exley's death in the early 1990s was almost certainly drink related.

2. See Lewis Hyde, "Alcohol and Poetry: John Berryman and the Booze Talking" (1975), and Thomas B. Gilmore, *Equivocal Spirits: Alcoholism and Drinking in Twentieth-Century Literature* (1987). In Chapter 7, "John Berryman and Drinking: From Jest to Sober Earnest," Gilmore argues, *contra* Hyde, that, rather than the reflections of a bipolar contest between sobriety and craving, Berryman's poetic manipulations of drinking, sobriety, and a range of intermediate states are symbolic constructions—complex, sometimes unclear, and ambiguously motivated. The apparent conflict with Hyde may be no more than a matter of question-framing, the difference between an aesthetic and a therapeutic line of approach. Gilmore's interdisciplinary study is sensible and literate, and many of his concerns are parallel with my own.

3. We are speaking only of the poetry here: in his expository prose Berryman was exemplary in his precision. *Recovery* falls somewhere between the two—but its appearance of analytic scrupulousness is exactly the issue: is that scrupulousness to be understood as a function of the fictitious narrator, of the author, or of an untestable exchange between the two through an upspringing defensive grid?

4. Dilemmas about intention and sincerity are of course the common coin of literary study, but our purpose here reaches beyond straight textual analysis and toward questions of value in use. In an antic postmodern frame of mind, I might urge the adoption of a term that brings in a connotation of the health- or life-giving properties we are in search of, particularly in the AA stories. Consumption eudaemonics?

5. See Haffenden, *The Life of John Berryman* (1982), especially Chapter 16, "The Sick and Brilliant Public Man," pp. 340–359. Dylan Thomas's public drinking exploits have been well documented by John Malcolm Brinnin and Constantine Fitzgibbon, and blisteringly satirized by Peter De Vries in the novel *Reuben, Reuben.* See Fitzgibbon's *Drink* (1979) for the interesting story of the biographer's own alcoholism and recovery—and, incidentally, a good quick survey of the field from a British perspective.

6. This bothered Lewis Hyde, too, as he explains in "Alcohol & Poetry: John Berryman and the Booze Talking": "Bellow is right, there was a relationship between this poet's drinking and inspiration, but he has the structure of it wrong. For an alcoholic, imbibing itself is fatal to inspiration. The poems weren't killing Berryman. Drink was not the 'stabilizer' that 'reduced the fatal intensity.' Alcohol was itself the 'death threat' " (Hyde, 1975, p. 9). Although not connecting Bellow directly with public and collegial facilitation of Berryman's drinking, Hyde is cogent on the problems of media exploitation, pandering, and the persistence of stereotyping. It is not true, Hyde claims, that Berryman's "delusion" that his art depended on his drinking was " 'too far down' " to be " 'attacked directly.' " The attack, however, would have required considerable renunciation.

He would have had to leave behind a lot of his own work. He would have had to leave his friends who had helped him live off his pain for twenty years. And the civilization itself, which supported all of that, weighs a great deal. *Life* magazine unerringly made the connection between our civilization and disease and went straight to Berryman as their example of the poet from the sixties. They called the piece "Whiskey and Ink, Whiskey and Ink," and there are the typical photographs of the poet with the wind in his beard and a glass in his hand. Berryman bought into the whole thing. Like Hemingway, they got him to play the fool and the salesman the last ten years of his life. (P. 12)

From the specifics of Berryman's case, Hyde generalizes about the "enabling" atmosphere of university English departments and other literary enclaves, pleading not for repression and intolerance but for the very lives of addicted artists:

I am not saying the critics could have cured Berryman of his disease. But we could have provided a less sickening atmosphere. In the future it would be nice if it were a little harder for the poet to come to town drunk and have everyone think that it's great fun. You can't control an alcoholic's drinking any more than he can, but the fewer parasites he has to support the better. (P. 12)

7. John Mack, a "wise urban psychoanalyst," is quoted in Vaillant (1983) on the dynamics of drinking, denial, rationalization, and isolation. The words are addressed to "a young patient." Not a few of our themes are echoed in this passage.

The drinking becomes a vicious cycle; hence your feeling of self disgust. . . . But only drink can anesthetize these awful feelings, which in turn bring a further violation of one's sense of self. You fear the boredom, depression and loneliness that will come in the wake of giving up the drinking. Yet . . . I am persuaded that these feelings are the *result* of the drink . . . brought about by drinking itself. Thus, the drink is more the cause of the isolation and the feelings of boredom. . . .
    But once you are addicted to alcohol . . . it is not within your powers to make this decision [when and when not to drink]. The alcohol has an uncanny capacity to stimulate all sorts of rationalizations . . . in the service of not giving it up. It is as if the alcohol had a life of its own and took over the personality and brought about attitudes and reactions which will foster further drinking. (Pp. 180–181)

8. Berryman's late poems are collected in *Henry's Fate & Other Poems, 1967–1972* (1977).
9. The entire long Chapter 6, "Who? Who? Who is Mr. Blue?" is a curious *mise en abyme*, and its manipulations and specifications of themes of selling,

physical culture, sexual obsession, storytelling, competition, and barroom life should be noted.

10. *One Flew Over the Cuckoo's Nest,* the work of R. D. Laing and David Cooper, the Living Theatre, Haight-Ashbury, and so on.

11. It should be noted that the second volume, *The Drunks*—and particularly the last two hundred pages—is a gold mine of AA "lore": the formulaic construction of primary speaking events, audience responses, and speech styles in informal, non-scheduled interactions.

12. There are comparable passages in London, Berryman, and Exley, prompting the speculation that a detached, clinical interest in their own physical decomposition and mental decline is negatively symptomatic in certain cases, providing the raw material for new modes of denial and rejection of sobriety just as powerfully as it may provide motivation to achieve sobriety.

4. Paradigm and Form

1. See Hart (1961), Hofstadter (1963), Nye (1970), and Tompkins (1985).

2. See, Lears (1983) and Susman (1984) for discussions of Barton. Lears's complex and essential argument in "From Salvation to Self-Realization" is continuous with his account of antimodernism in *No Place of Grace* (1981). Alcoholism was recognized and problematized in the context of emergent industrial modernity, and must to some extent be reckoned a disorder specific to the modernist transformations of mechanization, rationalization, dehumanization, overdevelopment, surveillance, and bureaucratic distention. It might be argued that the therapeutic gesture of Alcoholics Anonymous is to offer an authentic experience based in ideals of primitive communalism—care, face-to-face interaction, meaningful reiteration—to replace the spurious comforts of drink-induced self-erasure.

For interesting if tangential reflections on American literary style and sensibility, see Kenner (1975). According to *Dr. Bob and the Good Oldtimers* (Alcoholics Anonymous, 1980), literature influential upon early AA included the Book of James, Henry Drummond's *The Greatest Thing in the World,* and a Methodist periodical, "The Upper Room." Later in his life, Dr. Bob's favorite reading included *The Varieties of Religious Experience,* Augustine's *Confessions,* Lloyd C. Douglas's *The Robe,* and Ouspensky's *Tertium Organum.*

3. For the Adult Children of Alcoholics movement, see Woititz (1983), Seixas and Youcha (1985), and Wilson and Orford (1978).

4. Wilson's felt isolation in childhood and adolescence is explored in Thomsen (1975) and in *'Pass It On'* (Alcoholics Anonymous, 1984).

One of AA's quasi-official "slogans" is "live and let live," a commendable enough position when there are no real problems in the neighborhood. But "live and let live" ceases to be tenable equipment for living when one is confronted with a virulent bigot or an armed psychotic.

5. This passage may be compared interestingly with Fitzgerald's recollections in *The Crack-up* (1945).

6. We must take him at his word; but it is curious to note that the only historical figures named—in fact, the only proper names that occur—in "Bill's Story" are Napoleon and the golf superstar Walter Hagen.

Cawelti's (1965) interpretive history of the concept of success in America is interesting and helpful.

7. Eister (1950) is thorough on the Oxford Group, and Kurtz (1979) discusses its influence upon AA. See also Alcoholics Anonymous World Services (1957, 1980, 1984). The Oxford Group phenomenon seems bizarre today; some of its internal contradictions surfaced dramatically when leader Frank Buchman made flattering remarks about Hitler to the press. See also Edmund Wilson, "Saving the Right People and Their Butlers." Wilson's lacerating 1934 profile of the Buchmanites is, happily, not generally applicable to contemporary AA.

> The whole occasion makes an impression infinitely sad and insipid. I have seen these people before: these people whom their work does not satisfy . . . who are coming to realize that their functions in society are not serious and to seek anxiously for something to hang on to. . . . If they were a little more uncomfortably neurotic, they would be going to psychoanalysts; if they were sillier, they would be nudists; if they were cleverer, Gurdjieff would get them. . . . They have invested [Christ] with the fatuous cheerfulness of the people in the American advertizements and of the salesmen who try to sell you what they advertize. One of the characteristic features of the Oxford Group is the continual chuckling and bubbling, the grinning and twinkling and beaming which goes on among its members, and which makes an outsider feel quite morose. (Wilson, 1958, pp. 525–526)

8. Light here, clarifying and harmonizing, is an image of complementarity and as such must necessarily be distinguished from the whiteness that plagued Jack London and the lightning that heralded the coming of Dionysus. Whiteness, unlike this crystalline transparency, is opaque, signalling a kind of blockage; it is a malignant transform of light—light gone wrong, light that has rotted. Dionysus's birthday lightning implies the violence inherent in opposition.

This shifty signifier puts in a brief appearance in Lewis Hyde's *The Gift*. In his discussion of Ezra Pound, Hyde says, in passing: "Twitted once by Eliot to reveal his religious beliefs, Pound (after sending us to Confucius and Ovid) wrote: 'I believe that a light from Eleusis persisted throughout the middle ages and set beauty in the song of Provence and of Italy.' This 'undivided light' occasions beauty in art, and vice versa—that is, beauty in art sets, or awakens, the knowledge of this light in the mind of man." And, a moment later: "The liquid light, the *nous,* the fecundity of nature, the feeling of the soul in ascent —only the imagination can articulate our apprehension of these things, and the imagination speaks to us in images" (Hyde, 1983, pp. 218–220).

9. In both Thomsen (1975) and Alcoholics Anonymous World Services

(1957), an anecdote from Wilson's childhood involving a boomerang is used to demonstrate that his pride and tenacity were well established even in his tenderest years.

10. An AA joke refers to the "short form" of the Serenity Prayer: "Fuck it." This is more than just a cynical gloss on the principles of acceptance and passivity enjoined in much AA literature; it also underscores the unitary character of the three-part prayer.

11. See Jellinek (1962), and Lender and Karnchanapee (1977).

Jellinek's phase model is similar, skeletally, to the presentation of coding categories Rudy used to quantify his data. Rudy's categories were derived from, then modified by, the stories told by alcoholics in AA—although not in most cases, I gather, in open meetings. Both schemes in turn suggest elaborated versions of the questionnaires that have been evolved for the self-testing of drinkers who wish to decide if they are alcoholic. (See Rudy, 1986; the Baltimore questionnaire is reprinted in, e.g., Vaillant, 1983. Contra Fingarette, 1988, and others who argue for what amounts to case-by-case assessments of drinking problems, there are extensive data from before the creation of AA to support the contention that alcoholism runs a predictable course.)

This is a summary of Jellinek's phase model:

Symptoms or functions of the Prodromal Phase: palimpsests (blackouts); surreptitious drinking; preoccupation with alcohol; avid drinking; guilt feelings about drinking behavior; avoidance of reference to alcohol; increasing frequency of palimpsests.

Symptoms or functions of the Crucial Phase: loss of control; rationalization of drinking behavior; social pressures; grandiose behavior; marked aggressive behavior; persistent remorse; periods of total abstinence; changing the pattern of drinking; dropping friends; quitting jobs; behavior becomes alcohol centered; loss of outside interests; reinterpretation of interpersonal relations; marked self-pity; geographic escapes; change in family habits; unreasonable resentments; protection of supply; neglect of proper nutrition; first hospitalization; decrease of sexual drive; alcoholic jealousy; regular matutinal drinking.

Symptoms or functions of the Chronic Phase: prolonged intoxication; marked ethical deterioration; impairment of thinking; alcoholic psychoses; drinking with persons far below social level; recourse to "technical products" (Sterno, after-shave lotion, vanilla extract); loss of alcohol tolerance; indefinable fears; tremors; psychomotor inhibition; drinking takes on obsessive character; vague religious desires develop; entire rationalization system fails. At this point, there may be susceptibility to rehabilitation, especially in AA, but, failing the appropriate intervention, probable outcomes are insanity and death.

12. To "qualify" or "give a qualification" in East Coast usage means to tell enough of one's story as a lead speaker, meeting chairperson, or floor speaker to establish credibility as a member of AA. Though it is used casually, a whiff of irony seems to hover about the term.

13. The texts are Labov and Waletzky (1967) and Labov (1972), pp. 354–396. See also Robinson (1981) for more on personal narrative. Chatman (1978) provides a thorough and thoughtful general introduction to the sub-

ject of narrative. Mitchell's (1981) anthology *On Narrative* has become a standard text.

5. Intention and Reception

1. A sponsor is an experienced member of AA selected by mutual agreement to assist a newcomer in "working the program," negotiating the Twelve Steps, and confronting personal problems. For the role of the sponsor in AA, see the pamphlet, *Questions and Answers About Sponsorship* (1976b). See Ogborne and Glaser (1981) for a review of the literature surrounding the difficult problem of the "Characteristics of Affiliates."

David Rudy writes: "The data on AA affiliates may be characterized as an illustration in one organization of 'Keller's Law,' that is, 'the investigation of any trait in alcoholics will show that they have either more or less of it' " (1986, p. 20).

2. The measure and quality of perfectionist teleology inherent here is, I suspect, a matter for arbitration solely on the strength of private needs.

One may consult Kurtz (1979), *passim*, but especially pp. 175–199 and pp. 231–249, on the crucial opposition in American theology and in AA doctrine between perfectionism and the acceptance of limitation.

3. Hymes and Cazden (1980), "Narrative Thinking and Story-telling Rights: A Folklorist's Clue to a Critique of Education." This is an important concept in relation to the egalitarian set-up of AA. "In sum, if one considers that narrative may be a mode of thought, and indeed, that narrative may be an inescapable mode of thought, then its differential distribution in a society may be a clue to the distribution of other things as well—rights and privileges, having to do with power and money, to be sure, but also rights and privileges having to do with fundamental functions of language itself, its cognitive and expressive uses in narrative form" (Hymes and Cazden, 1980, p. 131).

4. Compare these remarks with a passage from Lewis Hyde's discussion of Walt Whitman and the gift of poetic speech. Hyde is addressing Whitman's invocation to the soul near the beginning of "Song of Myself":

> The soul acknowledges and accepts what has entered the self by uttering its name. This responsive speech we call "celebratory" or "thanksgiving." In the fairy tales the spoken "thank you" or the act of gratitude accomplishes the transformation and frees the original gift; so in the poetry, for the soul to give speech to the stuff of experience is to accept it and to pass it along. Moreover, by Whitman's model, the self does not come to life until the objects flow *through* it. (The increase does not appear until the gift moves to a third party.) Celebratory speech is the return gift by which what has been received by the self is freed and passed along. (Hyde, 1983, p. 189)

Later, in his chapter on Pound, Hyde speaks again of the gift of speech, this time in terms of resistance or blockage caused by the inappropriate exercise of will: "At times when the will should be suspended, whether it is good or bad is irrelevant. Or to put it more strongly: at such times all will, no matter its direction, is bad will. For when the will dominates, there is no gap through which grace may enter, no break in the ordered stride for error to escape, no way by which a barren prince may receive the *virtù* of his people, and for an artist, no moment of receptiveness when the engendering images may come forward" (p. 228).

Hyde will perhaps forgive me if I note a consonance here with such AA injunctions as "Listen and learn"; "Thy will, not mine"; and "Keep it simple, stupid."

5. One may consult Georges (1969), "Toward An Understanding of Storytelling Events," for an intelligent discussion from a folklorist's standpoint of interactivity in storytelling, complete with diagrams of amoeba-like entities representing the fusion of sender and receiver during narrative occasions.

6. Meaning and Value

1. The alternative or anti-institutional character of AA may conceivably induce anxiety at several levels. Any formation with a powerful communal dimension may prove disturbing to individuals with a significant economic or emotional investment in existing structures of dominance. See Introduction, note 1, for other remarks.

2. One may consult Edmund S. Morgan, *Visible Saints* (1963) and Patricia Caldwell, *The Puritan Conversion Narrative* (1983), for the "morphology of conversion" and attendant interpretations and refinements. See also Zora Neale Hurston, *The Sanctified Church* (1983), for another slant on the subject. William James's *The Varieties of Religious Experience* (1982) remains the central text.

3. Among valuable recent works in the voluminous literature on autobiography are Langness and Frank (1981), Lejeune (1989), Olney (1972 and 1980), Runyan (1982), Spengemann (1980). And Barthes (1974, 1977) is always there for us.

4. The terms are Kenneth Burke's, arrayed thus in the foreword of *Towards a Better Life* (1966). Before recalling Burke's list, which is more stylish, I had listed celebration, lamentation, exploration, instruction or admonition, and amusement. The point to be taken is the range of variety rather than a particular taxonomy.

5. See Gilmore (1987) for bibliography as well as intelligent commentary on, especially, Lowry, Cheever, O'Neill, and Fitzgerald.

6. See Bascom (1965) and Abrahams (1976) for pertinent attempts to arrest the fluid continuum of folk narrative. Stahl's earlier efforts (1977a, 1977b, 1983) warrant attention, and [Dolby-] Stahl (1985) is especially interesting, not only on merit but because of its thorough bibliography.

7. See, especially, Spence (1982) for thoughtful synthesis and useful bibliography.

References

Abrahams, R. D. (1976). The complex relations of simple forms. In D. Ben-Amos (Ed.), *Folklore genres* (pp. 193–214). Austin: University of Texas Press.

Agnew, J.-C. (1986). *Worlds apart: The market and the theater in Anglo-American thought, 1550–1750.* Cambridge: Cambridge University Press.

Alcoholics Anonymous World Services. (1957). *Alcoholics Anonymous comes of age: A brief history of A.A.* New York: Author.

Alcoholics Anonymous World Services. (1973). *Came to believe: The spiritual adventure of A.A. as experienced by individual members.* New York: Author.

Alcoholics Anonymous World Services. (1976a). *Alcoholics Anonymous: The story of how many thousands of men and women have recovered from alcoholism* (3rd ed.). New York: Author.

Alcoholics Anonymous World Services. (1976b). *Questions and answers about sponsorship.* New York: Author.

Alcoholics Anonymous World Services. (1980). *Dr. Bob and the good oldtimers: A biography, with recollections of early Alcoholics Anonymous in the Midwest.* New York: Author.

Alcoholics Anonymous World Services. (1984). *'Pass it on': The story of Bill Wilson and how the Alcoholics Anonymous message reached the world.* New York: Author.

Alcoholics Anonymous World Services. (n.d.). *Three talks to medical societies by Bill W., co-founder of Alcoholics Anonymous.* New York: Author.

Allen, G. W. (1955). *The solitary singer: A critical biography of Walt Whitman.* New York: Grove Press.

Antze, P. (1987). Symbolic action in Alcoholics Anonymous. In M. Douglas (Ed.), *Constructive drinking: Perspectives on drink from anthropology,* (pp. 149–181). Cambridge: Cambridge University Press.

Arnold, E. (1982). *A craving.* New York: Dell Publishing Co.

Arthur, T. S. (1966). *Ten nights in a bar-room.* C. H. Holman (Ed.). New York: Odyssey Press. (Original work published 1854)

Arthur, T. S. (1871). *Six nights with the Washingtonians.* Philadelphia: T. B. Peterson & Brothers.

Asbury, H. (1950). *The great illusion: An informal history of Prohibition.* Garden City, NY: Doubleday & Co.

Barthes, R. (1974). *S/Z*. (R. Miller, Trans.) New York: Hill and Wang.

Barthes, R. (1977). *Barthes on Barthes*. (R. Howard, Trans.) New York: Hill and Wang.

Barton, B. (1952). *The man nobody knows*. Indianapolis: Bobbs-Merrill Co.

Bascom, W. (1965). The forms of folklore: Prose narratives. *Journal of American Folklore, 307,* 3–20.

Bateson, G. (1972). The cybernetics of "self": A theory of alcoholism. In *Steps to an ecology of mind* (pp. 309–337). New York: Ballantine Books.

Bateson, G. (1979). *Mind and nature: A necessary unity*. New York: Bantam Books.

Bateson, M. C. (1984). *With a daughter's eye: A memoir of Margaret Mead and Gregory Bateson*. New York: Washington Square Press.

Berryman, J. (1969). *The dream songs*. New York: Farrar, Straus and Giroux.

Berryman, J. (1973). *Recovery/Delusions, etc.* New York: Dell Publishing Co.

Berryman, J. (1977). *Henry's fate & other poems, 1967–1972*. New York: Farrar, Straus and Giroux.

Blocker, J. S., Jr. (1989). *American temperance movements: Cycles of reform*. Boston: Twayne Publishers.

Breslin, J. (1986). *Table money*. New York: Ticknor & Fields.

Brooks, V. (1947). *The times of Melville and Whitman*. New York: E. P. Dutton & Co.

Burke, K. (1966). *Towards a better life*. Berkeley: University of California Press.

Burns, R. (N.d.). *The Complete Poetical Works*. Boston and New York: Houghton, Mifflin and Co.

Cain, A. H. (1964). *The cured alcoholic: New concepts in alcoholism treatment and research*. New York: John Day Co.

Caldwell, P. (1983). *The Puritan conversion narrative: The beginnings of American expression*. New York: Cambridge University Press.

Campbell, J. (1949). *The hero with a thousand faces*. Cleveland: World Publishing Co., Meridian Books.

Cawelti, J. G. (1965). *Apostles of the self-made man*. Chicago: University of Chicago Press.

Chatman, S. (1978). *Story and discourse: Narrative structure in fiction and film*. Ithaca: Cornell University Press.

Clark, N. H. (1976). *Deliver us from evil: An interpretation of American Prohibition*. New York: W. W. Norton & Co.

Crowley, J. W. (1994). *The white logic: Alcoholism and gender in American modernist fiction*. Amherst: University of Massachusetts Press.

Daniels, W. H. (1878). *The temperance reform and its great reformers: An illustrated history*. New York: Nelson & Phillips.

Dardis, T. (1989). *The thirsty muse: Alcohol and the American writer*. New York: Ticknor & Fields.

Dégh, L. (1985). "When I was six we moved west": The theory of personal experience narrative. *New York Folklore, 11,* 99–108.

Dégh, L., and Vázsonyi, A. (1973). *The dialectics of the legend*. Folklore Preprint Series 1, No. 6. Bloomington: Indiana University.

Dégh, L., and Vázsonyi, A. (1976). Legend and belief. In D. Ben-Amos (Ed.), *Folklore genres* (pp. 93–123). Austin: University of Texas Press.

Dodds, E. R. (1951). *The Greeks and the irrational.* Berkeley: University of California Press.

Dolby-Stahl, see Stahl.

Douglas, A. (1977). *The feminization of American culture.* New York: Avon Books.

Douglas, M. (Ed.). (1987). *Constructive drinking: Perspectives on drink from anthropology.* Cambridge: Cambridge University Press.

Dundes, A. (1980). The number three in American culture. In *Interpreting Folklore* (pp. 134–159). Bloomington: Indiana University Press.

Eister, A. (1950). *Drawing-room conversion: A sociological account of the Oxford Group movement.* Durham, NC: Duke University Press.

"Elpenor." (1986, October). "A drunkard's progress: AA and the sobering strength of myth." *Harper's*, pp. 42–48.

Exley, F. (1968). *A fan's notes.* New York: Vintage Books.

Fenichel, O. (1945). *The psychoanalytic theory of neurosis.* New York: W. W. Norton & Co.

Fiedler, L. A. (1960). *Love and death in the American novel.* Cleveland: World Publishing Co.

Fingarette, H. (1988). *Heavy drinking: The myth of alcoholism as a disease.* Berkeley: University of California Press.

Fitts, D. (Trans.). (1962). *Aristophanes: Four comedies.* New York: Harcourt, Brace & World.

Fitzgerald, F. S. (1945). *The crack-up.* New York: New Directions.

Fitzgibbon, C. (1979). *Drink.* Garden City, NY: Doubleday & Co.

Franks, L. (1985, October 20). A new attack on alcoholism. *New York Times Magazine*, pp. 46–50.

Freud, S. (1963). On the sexual theories of children. In P. Rieff (Ed.), *The sexual enlightenment of children* (pp. 25–40). New York: Collier Books.

Furnas, J. C. (1965). *The life and times of the late demon rum.* New York: Capricorn Books.

Georges, R. A. (1969). Toward an understanding of storytelling events. *Journal of American Folklore, 82*, 313–328.

Gilmore, T. B. (1987). *Equivocal spirits: Alcoholism and drinking in twentieth-century literature.* Chapel Hill: University of North Carolina Press.

Goodwin, D. W. (1988). *Alcohol and the writer.* New York: Penguin Books.

Graves, R. (1955). *The Greek myths.* Baltimore: Penguin Books.

Grene, D., and Lattimore, R. (Eds.). (1959). *Euripides V: Three tragedies.* The Complete Greek Tragedies. Chicago: University of Chicago Press, Phoenix Books. (Includes *The Bacchae*, W. Arrowsmith, trans.; *Electra*, E. T. Vermeule, trans.; and *The Phoenician Women*, E. Wyckoff, trans.)

Gusdorf, G. (1980). Conditions and limits of autobiography. In J. Olney (Ed.), *Autobiography: Essays theoretical and critical* (pp. 28–48). Princeton: Princeton University Press.

Gusfield, J. R. (1986). *Symbolic crusade: Status politics and the American tem-*

perance movement (2nd ed.). Urbana and Chicago: University of Illinois Press.

Haffenden, J. (1982). *The life of John Berryman.* London: Ark.

Hall, N. L. (1974). *A true story of a drunken mother.* Boston: South End Press. (Reissued with a new introduction in 1990)

Halttunen, K. (1982). *Confidence men and painted women.* New Haven: Yale University Press.

Hart, J. D. (1961). *The popular book: A history of America's literary taste.* Berkeley and Los Angeles: University of California Press.

Heath, D. B. (1987). A decade of development in the anthropological study of alcohol use, 1970–1980. In M. Douglas (Ed.), *Constructive drinking: Perspectives on drink from anthropology* (pp. 16–69). Cambridge: Cambridge University Press.

Heath, D. B., Waddell, J. O. and Topper, M. D. (Eds.). (1981, January). Cultural factors in alcohol research and treatment of drinking problems. *Journal of Studies on Alcohol,* Suppl. No. 9.

Heilbrun, C. G. (1988). *Writing a woman's life.* New York: Ballantine Books.

Hofstadter, R. (1963). *Anti-intellectualism in American life.* New York: Vintage Books.

hooks, b. (1993). *Sisters of the yam: Black women and self-recovery.* London: Turnaround.

Hurston, Z. N. (1983). *The sanctified church.* Berkeley: Turtle Island.

Hyde, L. (1975). Alcohol and poetry: John Berryman and the booze talking. *American Poetry Review, 4,* 7–12.

Hyde, L. (1983). *The gift: Imagination and the erotic life of property.* New York: Vintage Books.

Hymes, D., and Cazden, C. (1980). Narrative thinking and story-telling rights: A folklorist's clue to a critique of education. In *Language in education: Ethnolinguistic essays* (pp. 126–138). Language and Ethnography Series. Washington, DC: Center for Applied Linguistics.

Jackson, C. (1944). *The lost weekend.* New York: Farrar & Rinehart.

James, W. (1982). *The varieties of religious experience.* New York: Penguin Books. (Original work published 1902)

Jellinek, E. M. (1960). *The disease concept of alcoholism.* New Haven: Hillhouse Press.

Jellinek, E. M. (1962). Phases of alcohol addiction. In D. J. Pittman and C. R. Snyder (Eds.), *Society, culture, and drinking patterns* (pp. 356–68). Carbondale and Edwardsville, IL: Southern Illinois University Press.

Kaminer, W. (1993). *I'm dysfunctional, you're dysfunctional: The recovery movement and other self-help fashions.* New York: Vintage Books.

Kaplan, J. (1980). *Walt Whitman: A life.* New York: Bantam Books.

Kazin, A. (1970). *On native grounds: An interpretation of modern American prose literature.* New York: Harcourt Brace Jovanovich.

Kennedy, P. (Ed.). (1975). *Folksongs of Britain and Ireland.* New York: Schirmer Books.

Kenner, H. (1975). *A homemade world: The American modernist writers.* New York: William Morrow & Co.

Kessel, N., and Walton, H. (1965). *Alcoholism*. Baltimore: Penguin Books.

Kitto, H. D. F. (1956). *Form and meaning in drama*. New York: Barnes & Noble, University Paperbacks.

Kobler, J. (1973). *Ardent spirits: The rise and fall of Prohibition*. New York: G. P. Putnams's Sons.

Krout, J. A. (1925). *The origins of Prohibition*. New York: Alfred A. Knopf.

Kurtz, E. (1979). *Not-God: A history of Alcoholics Anonymous*. Center City, MN: Hazelden Educational Services.

Labov, W. (1972). *Language in the inner city: Studies in the black English vernacular*. Philadelphia: University of Pennsylvania Press.

Labov, W., and Waletzsky. J. (1967). Narrative analysis: Oral versions of personal experience. In J. Helm (Ed.), *Essays on the verbal and visual arts* (pp. 12–44). Proceedings of the 1966 Annual Spring Meeting of the American Ethnological Society. Seattle: University of Washington Press.

Lamb, C. (1985). Confessions of a drunkard. In A. Phillips (Ed.), *Selected prose*, (pp. 155–161. New York: Penguin Books.

Langness, L. L., and Frank, G. (1981). *Lives: An anthropological approach to biography*. Novato, CA: Chandler & Sharp.

Lasch, C. (1977). *Haven in a heartless world: The family besieged*. New York: Basic Books.

Lears, T. J. J. (1981). *No place of grace: Antimodernism and the transformation of American culture, 1880–1920*. New York: Pantheon Books.

Lears, T. J. J. (1983). From salvation to self-realization: Advertising and the therapeutic roots of the consumer culture, 1880–1930. In R. W. Fox and T. J. J. Lears (Eds.), *The culture of consumption* (pp. 1–38). New York: Pantheon Books.

Lejeune, P. (1989). *On autobiography*. Minneapolis: University of Minnesota Press.

Lender, M. E., and Karnchanapee, K. R. (1977). "Temperance tales": Anti-liquor fiction and American attitudes toward alcoholics in the late 19th and early 20th centuries. *Journal of Studies on Alcohol, 38,* 1347–1370.

Lender, M. E., and Martin, J. K. (1982). *Drinking in America: A history*. New York: Macmillan Publishing Co.

Lipset, D. (1980). *Gregory Bateson: The legacy of a scientist*. Englewood Cliffs, NJ: Prentice-Hall.

Loch, W. (1977). Some comments on the subject of psychoanalysis and truth. In J. H. Smith (Ed.), *Thought, consciousness, and reality: Psychiatry and the humanities* (Vol. 2, pp. 217–255). New Haven: Yale University Press.

Lomax, J. A., and Lomax, A. (1934). *American ballads and folk songs*. New York: Macmillan Co.

London, J. (1981). *John Barleycorn*. Santa Cruz: Western Tanager Press. (Original work published 1902)

Ludwig, A. M. (1988). *Understanding the alcoholic's mind: The nature of craving and how to control it*. New York: Oxford University Press.

McCarthy, R. G. (Ed.). (1959). *Drinking and intoxication: Selected readings in social attitudes and controls*. New Haven: College and University Press.

McConville, B. (1995). *Women under the influence: Alcohol and its impact.* London: Pandora.

McDaniel, J. (1989). *Metamorphosis: Reflections on recovery.* Ithaca: Firebrand Books.

Marshall, M. (1979). *Weekend warriors: Alcohol in a Micronesian culture.* Palo Alto: Mayfield Publishing Co.

Marshall, M. (Ed.). (1979). *Beliefs, behaviors, and alcoholic beverages: A cross-cultural survey.* Ann Arbor: University of Michigan Press.

Martin, E. W. (1868). *The secrets of the great city: A work descriptive of the virtues and the vices, the mysteries, miseries and crimes of New York City.* Philadelphia: Jones, Brothers & Co.

Maxwell, M. (1984). *The Alcoholics Anonymous experience.* New York: McGraw-Hill Book Co.

Melville, H. (1972). *Moby Dick.* New York: Penguin Books. (Original work published 1851)

Meryman, R. (1984). *Broken promises, mended dreams.* New York: Berkley Books.

Milam, J. R., and Ketcham, K. (1981). *Under the influence: A guide to the myths and realities of alcoholism.* New York: Bantam Books.

Mink, L. O. (1970). History and fiction as modes of comprehension. In B. Fay, E. O. Golob, R. T. Vann (Eds.), *Historical understanding* (pp. 42–60). Ithaca: Cornell University Press.

Mitchell, W. J. T. (Ed.). (1981). *On narrative.* Chicago: University of Chicago Press.

Moore, B. (1955). *The lonely passion of Miss Judith Hearne.* Harmondsworth, Middlesex: Penguin Books.

Morgan, E. S. (1963). *Visible saints: The history of a Puritan idea.* Ithaca: Cornell University Press.

Newlove, D. (1978). *Sweet adversity.* New York: Avon Books.

Newlove, D. (1981). *Those drinking days: Myself and other writers.* New York: Horizon Press.

Nietzsche, F. (1967). *The birth of tragedy* and *The case of Wagner* (W. Kaufmann, Trans.) New York: Random House, Vintage Books. (Original work published 1872.)

Nye, R. (1970). *The unembarrassed muse: The popular arts in America.* New York: Dial Press.

Ogborne, A. C., and Glaser, F. B. (1981). Characteristics of affiliates of Alcoholics Anonymous: A review of the literature. *Journal of Studies on Alcohol, 42,* 661–675.

Olney, J. (1972). *Metaphors of self: The meaning of autobiography.* Princeton: Princeton University Press.

Olney, J. (Ed.). (1980). *Autobiography: Essays theoretical and critical.* Princeton: Princeton University Press.

O Lochlainn, C. (1960). *Irish street ballads.* New York: Citadel Press, Corinth Books.

O'Reilly, E. (1988). *Toward rhetorical immunity: Narratives of alcoholism and recovery.* Ph.D. diss., University of Pennsylvania.

Otto, W. F. (1965). *Dionysus: Myth and cult* (R. B. Palmer, Trans.). Dallas: Spring Publications.

Ovid. (1955). *Metamorphoses* (R. Humphries, Trans.). Bloomington: Indiana University Press, Midland Books.

Peele, S. (1989). *Diseasing of America: Addiction treatment out of control.* Boston: Houghton Mifflin Co.

Pittman, D. J., and Snyder, C. R. (Eds.). (1962). *Society, culture, and drinking patterns.* Carbondale, IL: Southern Illinois University Press.

Percy, W. (1975). *The message in the bottle.* New York: Farrar, Straus and Giroux.

Prince, G. (1987). *A dictionary of narratology.* Lincoln: University of Nebraska Press.

Propp, V. (1968). *Morphology of the folktale.* Austin: University of Texas Press.

Reynolds, D. S. (1988). *Beneath the American Renaissance: The subversive imagination in the age of Emerson and Melville.* New York: Alfred A. Knopf.

Robertson, N. (1988). *Getting better: Inside Alcoholics Anonymous.* New York: William Morrow & Co.

Robinson, J. A. (1981). Personal narrative reconsidered. *Journal of American Folklore, 94,* 58–85.

Roe, E. R. (1909). *Rum and ruin: The story of Dr. Caldwell.* Chicago: Laird & Lee.

Rorabaugh, W. J. (1979). *The alcoholic republic: An American tradition.* New York: Oxford University Press.

Roueché, B. (1960). *Alcohol: Its history, folklore and its effect on the human body.* New York: Grove Press.

Rudy, D. R. (1986). *Becoming alcoholic: Alcoholics Anonymous and the reality of alcoholism.* Carbondale and Edwardsville, IL: Southern Illinois University Press.

Runyan, W. M. (1982). *Life histories and psychobiography: Explorations in theory and method.* New York: Oxford University Press.

Sandmaier, M. (1980). *The invisible alcoholics: Women and alcohol abuse in America.* New York: McGraw-Hill Book Co.

Sapir, E. (1956). *Culture, language and personality.* D. G. Mandelbaum(Ed.). Berkeley: University of California Press.

Searle, J. (1969). *Speech acts.* New York: Cambridge University Press.

Searle, J. (1979). A taxonomy of illocutionary acts. In *Expression and meaning: Studies in the theory of speech acts* (pp. 1–29). Cambridge: Cambridge University Press.

Seixas, J. S., and Youcha, G. (1985). *Children of alcoholism: A survivor's manual.* New York: Harper & Row.

Sinclair, U. (1956). *The cup of fury.* Manhasset, NY: Channel Press.

Slater, P. E. (1968). *The glory of Hera: Greek mythology and the Greek family.* Boston: Beacon Press.

Smith, B. H. (1981). Narrative versions, narrative theories. In W. J. T. Mitchell (Ed.), *On narrative* (pp. 209-232). Chicago: University of Chicago Press.

Spence, D. P. (1982). *Narrative truth and historical truth: Meaning and interpretation in psychoanalysis.* New York: W. W. Norton & Co.

Spengemann, W. C. (1980). *The forms of autobiography: Episodes in the history of a literary genre*. New Haven: Yale University Press.

Stahl, S. K. D. (1977a). The oral personal narrative in its generic context. *Fabula, 18,* 18–39.

Stahl, S. K. D. (1977b). The personal narrative as folklore. *Journal of the Folklore Institute, 14,* 9–30.

Stahl, S. K. D. (1983). Personal experience stories. In R. Dorson (Ed.), *Handbook of American folklore* (pp. 268–276). Bloomington: Indiana University Press.

[Dolby-] Stahl. S. K. (1985). A literary folkloristic methodology for the study of meaning in personal narrative. *Journal of Folklore Research, 22,* 45–69.

Stromsten, A. (1982). *Recovery: Stories of alcoholism and survival*. New Brunswick, NJ: Rutgers Center of Alcohol Studies.

Susman, W. I. (1984). *Culture as history*. New York: Pantheon Books.

Thomsen, R. (1975). *Bill W.* New York: Harper & Row.

Thune, C. E. (1977). Alcoholism and the archetypal past: A phenomenological perspective on Alcoholics Anonymous. *Journal of Studies on Alcohol, 38,* 75–88.

Titon, J. T. (1980). The life story. *Journal of American Folklore, 93,* 276–292.

Tompkins, J. (1985). *Sensational designs: The cultural work of American fiction 1790–1860*. New York: Oxford University Press.

Tosches, N. (1994). *Trinities*. New York: St. Martin's Paperback.

Tournier, R. E. (1979). Alcoholics Anonymous as treatment and as ideology. *Journal of Studies on Alcohol, 40,* 230–239.

Trachtenberg, A. (1982). *The incorporation of America: Culture and society in the gilded age*. New York: Hill and Wang.

Trimpey, J. (1992). *The small book: A revolutionary alternative for overcoming alcohol and drug dependence*. New York: Delacorte Press.

Tyler, A. F. (1962). *Freedom's ferment: Phases of American social history from the colonial period to the outbreak of the Civil War*. New York: Harper & Row, Harper Torchbooks. (Original work published in 1944)

Tyrrell, I. R. (1979). *Sobering up: From temperance to Prohibition in antebellum America, 1800–1860*. Contributions in American History, No. 82. Westport, CT: Greenwood Press.

Vaillant, G. E. (1983). *The natural history of alcoholism*. Cambridge: Harvard University Press.

Walters, R. G. (1978). *American reformers, 1815–1860*. New York: Hill and Wang.

Whitman, W. (1963). *The early poems and the fiction*. T. L. Brasher (Ed.). In G. W. Allen and S. Bradley (General Eds.), *The collected works of Walt Whitman*. New York: New York University Press.

Whitman W. (1973). *Leaves of grass*. S. Bradley and H. W. Blodgett (Eds.). New York: W. W. Norton & Co.

Wholey, D. (1984). *The courage to change*. Boston: Houghton Mifflin Co.

Wilden, A. (1980). *System and structure: Essays in communication and exchange* (2nd ed.). London: Tavistock Publications.

Wilentz, S. (1984). *Chants democratic: New York City & the rise of the American working class, 1788–1850.* New York: Oxford University Press.

Williams, R. V., and Lloyd, A. L. (1959). *The Penguin book of English folksongs.* Harmondsworth, Middlesex: Penguin Books.

Wilson, C., and Orford, J. (1978). Children of alcoholics. *Journal of Studies on Alcohol, 39,* 121–142.

Wilson, E. (1958). Saving the right people and their butlers. In *The American earthquake: A documentary of the twenties and thirties* (pp. 518–526). New York: Farrar, Straus and Giroux.

Woititz, J. G. (1983). *Adult children of alcoholics.* Pompano Beach, FL: Health Communications.

Index